224.2
N51   Nicholson, Ernest W.
              Preaching to the exiles.

PREACHING TO THE EXILES

TO
THE PRESIDENT
AND
FELLOWS OF UNIVERSITY COLLEGE
CAMBRIDGE

E. W. NICHOLSON

PREACHING TO THE EXILES

A Study of the Prose Tradition
in the Book of Jeremiah

SCHOCKEN BOOKS · NEW YORK

© Basil Blackwell 1970

Library of Congress Catalog Card No.
74-146021

Published in U.S.A. in 1971
by Schocken Books Inc.
67 Park Avenue, New York, N.Y. 10016

PRINTED IN GREAT BRITAIN

CONTENTS

PREFACE

I wish to record my gratitude to Professor John Emerton, Dr. Ronald Clements and the Reverend John Sturdy for the help they have given me in the preparation of this book. My thanks are due also to Professor George Anderson for many helpful and important suggestions, and to Dr. John McKay who corrected my manuscript and made a number of valuable comments. I cannot be thankful enough to my wife Hazel for her endless patience and constant encouragement.

This study was started when I came as a Visiting Fellow to University College Cambridge in 1967. I am deeply indebted to the President and Fellows of the College for the facilities they placed at my disposal and to the Leverhulme Trust who generously financed my stay in Cambridge at that time.

Pembroke College, Cambridge   E. W. Nicholson
Michaelmas 1969

INTRODUCTION

In Jeremiah xxxvi it is recorded that in the fourth year of the reign of Jehoiakim (605/4 B.C.) Jeremiah dictated to his scribe and companion Baruch a scroll of oracles which he had uttered in Yahweh's name 'concerning[1] Israel[2] and Judah and all the nations' (v. 2) since the beginning of his prophetic ministry in the reign of Josiah until that time. Subsequently, in the winter of 604 B.C., Baruch read this scroll on his master's behalf before a congregation in the Temple (vv. 9f.). Immediately after this it was read before a group of royal and state officials (vv. 14f.) and then before the king himself by whom it was burned and destroyed (vv. 22f.). In spite of this, however, the prophet, at the command of Yahweh, had the oracles rewritten (vv. 27f.) to which were added, we are told, 'many similar words' (v. 32).

---

[1] Following most commentators, על is to be translated 'concerning' rather than 'against'. The translation 'against', as proposed for example by C. H. Cornill, *Das Buch Jeremia*, Leipzig 1905, p. 388 and W. Rudolph, *Jeremia*[3], Tübingen 1968, p. 228, rests on the view that the scroll contained only oracles of woe. But this can by no means be assured and the more neutral translation 'concerning' is to be preferred. Cf. also the remarks of C. Rietzschel, *Das Problem der Urrolle*, Gütersloh 1966, p. 9.

[2] LXX[BN] read 'Jerusalem' for MT 'Israel' and this reading has been adopted by a number of commentators (cf. B. Duhm, *Das Buch Jeremia*, Tübingen and Leipzig 1901, p. 289; C. H. Cornill, *op. cit.*, p. 388; W. Rudolph, *op. cit.*, p. 228). Against such a reading it might be argued that the statement in v. 32 that to this original scroll 'many similar words were added' already presupposes much more of the material in the book of Jeremiah than could have been present in the scroll (cf. P. Volz, *Der Prophet Jeremia*, Leipzig and Erlangen 1922, pp. xliv–xlv), material which contained oracles not only concerning Judah but also Israel. But the phrase can just as plausibly be interpreted as referring to material added at the time of the writing of the second scroll after the destruction of the first by Jehoiakim. Or again, the expression 'all the nations' (v. 2) may also presuppose much more of the present book, including chapters xlv–li, than was contained in the *Urrolle* and thus oracles dealing with Israel, though the possibility that the *Urrolle* did in fact contain sayings concerning foreign nations renders this argument hazardous. Nevertheless, the narrative very probably belongs to a relatively late stage in the development of the Jeremiah tradition and does presuppose much more material than the scroll's contents, including oracles and sayings concerning Israel, and for this reason the reading of the MT is preferable. The LXX[BN] reading 'Jerusalem' may have arisen from a misunderstanding of an abbreviated form of 'Israel'. Cf. Volz, *op. cit.*, p. 325.

The primary purpose of this narrative, as we shall see later, is theological and not, as commentators have so often suggested, merely biographical. At the same time its essential historicity need not be questioned, although the fact that in its present form it probably belongs to a relatively late stage in the formation of the material in the book must be borne in mind when assessing the historical value of some of its details.[1] For our present purposes, however, the important factor is that this narrative has been widely taken by Old Testament scholars to be of key significance in the attempt to understand the origin and composition of the book of Jeremiah. Indeed, with its description, unique in the Old Testament, of how the written collection of Jeremiah's oracles had its beginnings at the instigation of the prophet himself, it has been regarded as shedding light on the manner whereby other prophetic collections in the Bible assumed or began to assume written form.[2]

Three elements in this narrative have been of particular importance in the discussion of the origin and growth of the book of Jeremiah. In the first place it indicates that at a relatively early stage and on the initiative of the prophet himself there came into existence a written collection of the oracles and sayings which he had uttered during the first two decades or so of his ministry.[3] The second factor which has been of some significance is the note that this original collection, having been rewritten after its destruction by Jehoiakim, was supplemented with 'many similar words' (xxxvi. 32).[4] Thirdly, and closely associated

[1] For the nature and purpose of this narrative and its literary form and composition see below pp. 39ff.

[2] For a recent discussion see A. H. J. Gunneweg, *Mündliche und schriftliche Tradition der vorexilischen Prophetenbücher*, FRLANT 73, Göttingen 1959, pp. 34ff., 45ff.

[3] According to Jer. i. 2, xxv. 3 Jeremiah's prophetic ministry began in the thirteenth year of the reign of Josiah (626 B.C.). This date has not gone unchallenged, and a number of scholars have rejected it in favour of later possible dates for the prophet's call. Thus, for example, it has been suggested that the text should be emended to read 'twenty-third' rather than 'thirteenth', thus placing the prophet's call in 617/16 B.C. (cf. for example T. C. Gordon, 'A New Date for Jeremiah', *ExpT* 44, 1932/33, pp. 562–565). More support has been given to the view that the prophet's call took place in 609 B.C. at the beginning of Jehoiakim's reign (recently argued afresh by J. P. Hyatt, 'The Beginning of Jeremiah's Prophecy', *ZAW* 78, 1966, pp. 204–214), whilst a date not earlier than 605 B.C. has recently been advocated (cf. C. F. Whitley, 'The Date of Jeremiah's Call', *VT* 14, 1964, pp. 467–483). The majority of commentators, however, still accept the date recorded in the book of Jeremiah itself. For a discussion of the problem and full bibliography see H. H. Rowley, 'The Early Prophecies of Jeremiah in their Setting', in *Men of God*, London 1963, pp. 133–168 (first published in *BJRL* 45, 1962–63, pp. 198–234).

[4] Most scholars have taken this as representing the standpoint of the later editor of the book of Jeremiah and a broad indication of the literary growth of the book by means of successive stages of literary redaction and editing of the *Urrolle* of 604 B.C.

with the latter, great importance has been attached to the role here played by Baruch and on the basis of this and other texts (cf. esp. xlv. 1) the view has been widely held not only that he was responsible for committing to writing the first collection of Jeremiah's oracles but that he also expanded it with other later sayings and at the same time composed numerous narratives, including that in chapter xxxvi describing the compilation of the scroll, centring on events and incidents in his master's life. Of the material in the present book, therefore, it is widely accepted that the poetic oracles, contained mainly in the first half of the book, represent substantially[1] the original sayings of Jeremiah whilst the historical narratives and biographical passages, found for the most part in the second half of the book, are generally attributed to Baruch.[2] There has been no consensus of opinion, however, on the origin of the many prose sermons and discourses which are found throughout the book interspersed with both poetic and biographical material,[3] some scholars regarding them as authentic Jeremianic speeches, some taking them as having been composed by Baruch or other of the prophet's disciples, and yet others deriving them from the Deuteronomists, or editors influenced by them, on account of the marked degree of Deuteronomistic language and style discernible in them.[4]

Broadly speaking, therefore, the majority of scholars, with much variation in detail, have adopted the view that the present book of Jeremiah had its beginnings in the *Urrolle* compiled in 604 B.C. which was subsequently substantially expanded by Baruch and then eventually given its final dimensions by an editor or series of editors who added further material.[5]

---

[1] The radical view of Duhm according to which only 280 verses (almost all in Qina metre) in the MT are Jeremiah's own words has been rejected by the majority of commentators.

[2] Substantially chapters xxvi–xxix, xxxiv–xxxvi, xxxvii–xlv. But see next footnote.

[3] For example, chapters vii–viii. 3, xi. 1–17, xiii. 1–14, xiv. 11–16, xv. 1–4, etc. The so-called biographical passages such as xxviii, xxix, xxxiv, xxxv also contain prose discourses.

[4] For the various views see below pp. 24ff.

[5] This is substantially the view presented by the main commentators during the past generation: B. Duhm, *op. cit.*; C. H. Cornill, *op. cit.*; P. Volz, *op. cit.*; W. Rudolph, *op. cit.*; A. Weiser, *Das Buch des Propheten Jeremia*, ATD 20–21, Göttingen 1952/55; J. P. Hyatt, *The Book of Jeremiah*, IB 5, New York 1956; J. Bright, *Jeremiah*, The Anchor Bible, New York 1965. In his well-known monograph *Zur Komposition des Buches Jeremia*, Kristiania 1914, Mowinckel presented essentially the same solution to

---

But see above p. 1 footnote 2 and see further the remarks of E. Nielsen, *Oral Tradition*, London 1954, p. 78.

Viewed in this manner, the book as we have it is the result of a purely or predominantly literary activity; it owes its present form as well as much of the material in it to the scribal and literary activity of Baruch and other authors and editors. The question immediately arises, however, whether such an approach with its preoccupation with a literary evolution of the material in the book is valid or adequate. That is to say, it must be asked whether other creative processes in addition to the work of an author or editor have contributed to the growth and formation of the book of Jeremiah. To put it another way, serious consideration must be given to the possibility that the book represents substantially the final literary expression and deposit of a tradition which grew and developed at the hands of a body of people who sought not only to transmit the prophet's sayings but to present an interpretation of his prophetic ministry and preaching on the basis of theological concerns and interests which were of vital importance for them in the age in which they lived. Such a tradition would have emerged and evolved not at the hands of individual authors and editors but within the context of an active preaching and teaching ministry which addressed itself to a listening audience, just as the preaching of Jeremiah himself and the Word of God which he proclaimed were at every stage addressed to an audience. This means that although much of the material in the book can be attributed directly to Jeremiah himself, that is, preserves his *ipsissima verba*, we must also reckon with the probability that much of it owes its origin and composition directly to a circle of traditionists. In addition, we must also allow for the possibility that individual units of material in the book which comprise originally separate sayings and speeches are not simply the product of a process of editing implemented according to purely literary canons but arose directly out of the manner in which such sayings and speeches were transmitted and used by the traditionists in their teaching and preaching.

Considerations such as these raise the possibility of a different approach to the growth and formation of the book of Jeremiah from the widely accepted approach briefly outlined above. Of particular relevance for our present purposes is the possibility that much of the prose material in the book, and especially the sermons and discourses,

---

the problem of the composition of the book but greatly minimized the contribution of Baruch and rejected the view that he was responsible for the narratives. In his later work, however, he revised this opinion of Baruch's role and now lent his support to the more widely held view of the contribution of Baruch to the formation of the book (cf. S. Mowinckel, *Prophecy and Tradition*, Oslo 1946, pp. 61f.).

grew and developed within such a circle of traditionists, for, as we shall see, it is precisely in this material that the evidence for such a circle is at its clearest.[1] If such a possibility can be sustained then the problem of the origin and provenance of this material becomes one of attempting to determine the particular theological tradition upon which it is based and which it seeks to present as well as the identity of the circle in which such a tradition had its home and the historical context and religio-sociological situation in which it emerged. It is with such an approach to the problem of the prose material in the book of Jeremiah and with an investigation of the results which can be achieved on the basis of it that we shall be concerned in this study.

Before turning to an investigation of this, however, something more must be said concerning the approach here adopted and the general presuppositions underlying it. The question that arises is clearly one of method and one which has been of central concern in recent Old Testament research.[2] It is beyond the scope of the present study to enter into a discussion of this problem here. I should like to draw attention, however, to contributions of two English scholars, P. R. Ackroyd and D. R. Jones,[3] which are of particular significance in this connection since they both present important insights into the manner in which the Old Testament prophetic literature took shape and was

[1] This was suggested many years ago by H. Birkeland, *Zum hebräischen Traditionswesen*, Oslo 1938, p. 42. Cf. more recently, I. Engnell, *Svenskt Bibliskt Uppslagsverk²*, I, 1962, cols. 1105–1106.

[2] The literature on this problem is extensive and the following represents only a selection of some of the more noteworthy contributions: S. Mowinckel, *Prophecy and Tradition*, Oslo 1946; G. Widengren, *Literary and Psychological Aspects of the Hebrew Prophets*, Uppsala Universitets Årsskrift, no. 10, 1948; G. W. Anderson, 'Some Aspects of the Uppsala School of Old Testament Study', *HTR* 43, 1950, pp. 239–256. These works offer a critique of the earlier work of the Swedish scholar Ivan Engnell (esp. his *Gamla Testamentet I*, Stockholm 1945) whose views have been very much a storm-centre in the discussion of methodology in Old Testament study; (for a later statement of his views see his 'Methodological Aspects of Old Testament Study', *SVT* 7, Leiden 1960, pp. 13–30). The views of Engnell and other Scandinavian scholars associated with his views (cf. E. Nielsen, *Oral Tradition*, London 1954) have been subjected to strong criticism by A. H. J. Gunneweg, *Mündliche und schriftliche Tradition der vorexilischen Prophetenbücher*, FRLANT 73, Göttingen 1959; G. Widengren, 'Oral Tradition and Written Literature among the Hebrews in the Light of Arabic Evidence, with Special Regard to Prose Narratives', *AcOr* 23, 1959, pp. 201–262. Of more recent works on methodology mention may be made of C. Kaiser, *Einführung in die exegetischen Methoden*, München 1964; H. Ringgren, 'Literarkritik, Formgeschichte, Überlieferungsgeschichte', *TLZ* 91, 1966, pp. 641–650; K. Koch, *The Growth of the Biblical Tradition*, London 1969. For a historical survey see H. Hahn, *The Old Testament and Modern Research*, Philadelphia 1954 and London 1956, pp. 119–156.

[3] P. R. Ackroyd, 'The Vitality of the Word of God in the Old Testament', *ASTI* 1, 1962, pp. 7–23; D. R. Jones, 'The Traditio of the Oracles of Isaiah of Jerusalem', *ZAW* 67, 1955, pp. 226–246.

transmitted as well as the role played by circles of traditionists in this process and, of special relevance for our present purposes, the way in which such a process is evidenced by the book of Jeremiah itself.

In his discussion of the problem Ackroyd directed his attention to a general investigation of the contribution towards the shaping of the Old Testament material by 'the living application of the recognized word of God . . . to the ever new needs of a community sensitive to the vitality of that word'.[1] He defines such a contribution in terms of an exegetical process whereby, for example, oracles and sayings originally delivered by a prophet in the specific religious and historical situation in which he ministered were ever and again interpreted and applied by those who transmitted them to situations which arose in the particular age in which they themselves lived. Ackroyd sees such an exegetical principle to have operated to a marked degree in the work of the Deuteronomists where it is particularly noticeable in the way in which they have handled the great deal of prophetic material at their disposal.[2] One striking example of this which he cites is the threefold occurrence in 1 Kings of one and the same saying pronounced by three different prophets (Ahijah, Jehu ben Hanani, Elijah) against three different kings of northern Israel respectively (Jeroboam, Baasha, Ahab):[3]

> Anyone related to Jeroboam (Baasha, Ahab) who
> dies in the city the dogs will eat;
> and he who dies in the open country the birds
> of the air will eat.
>   (1 Kings xiv. 11; xvi. 4; xxi. 24)

We must agree with Ackroyd in rejecting as highly improbable any suggestion that the second and third occurrences of this saying are quotations by the prophets in question of an original oracle delivered, as in its first occurrence, by Ahijah. He is also surely correct in rejecting the view expressed by some scholars[4] that the Deuteronomists were forced to repeat the oracle in all three texts through sheer lack of the necessary imagination and creative ability to coin suitable alternative oracles for the second and third incidents recorded.[5] Ackroyd himself has advanced an entirely plausible and much more satisfactory solution to the problem in his suggestion that the Deuteronomists employed this oracle in the three passages in question because they saw in it, whatever

[1] P. R. Ackroyd, *op. cit.*, p. 7.

[2] *Ibid.*, pp. 7ff.

[3] *Ibid.* pp. 7ff.

[4] Cf. R. H. Pfeiffer, *Introduction to the Old Testament*, London 1948, pp. 382, 405, 406. Cf. Ackroyd's remarks, *op. cit.*, p. 9.

[5] P. R. Ackroyd, *op. cit.*, p. 9.

its precise origin may have been, a word of divine judgement proclaimed by a prophet which was vital and meaningful in relation to
each of the three events recorded: 'The element of truth in it (the
oracle) cannot but be of enduring value. . . . In each case the divine
oracle has its message, and the application of one word to three
different situations proves not the versatility of the transmitter,
certainly not his threadbare imagination, but rather his sense of its
vitality and meaning as comment on the pattern of history'.[1]

The actual manner in which the Deuteronomists have presented this
oracle is instructive of their exegetical technique, for in all three texts
it appears within the context of and forms the climax to a short sermon
delivered by each of the three prophets in question. It is this use of the
sermonic form of address which characterizes the method of the
Deuteronomic and Deuteronomistic authors through whom it makes
its first appearance in the literature of the Old Testament.[2] The
Deuteronomistic corpus is marked throughout by an oratorical manner
of presentation which renders its style one of the most distinctive in the
whole of the Old Testament. As such it exhibits a verbose and
repetitious nature which points for its origin not to the pen of an
author—as a literary style it would have to be judged amongst the
poorest in the Old Testament—but to the lips of a preacher or teacher
who was vitally concerned with impressing the urgency of his message
upon the minds and consciences of those who listened. It was only after
it had been developed and practised orally that it found expression in
literature, and even then it was still being employed essentially as a
means of instruction and exhortation rather than as a literary style.
Thus we find in the book of Deuteronomy itself the homiletical
presentation and actualization of legal and cultic ordinances of very
varied age and origin,[3] whilst in the Deuteronomistic history we meet
time and time again with the similar presentation of old material, as in
the case of the oracle to which reference has been made, together with
sermons and discourses, such as that contained in 2 Kings xvii. 7ff.,
which have for their purpose a theological interpretation of the events
of Israel's history. In a word, the method of the Deuteronomists
witnesses to an exegetical principle which had for its basis their acknow-
ledgement of the enduring vitality of the Word of God and for its
goal their desire and determination to actualize that Word for the
generation to whom they addressed themselves. At a later stage in

[1] *Ibid.*, p. 10.
[2] Cf. L. Köhler, *Hebrew Man*, London 1956, pp. 167–170.
[3] Cf. G. von Rad, *Studies in Deuteronomy*, London 1953, pp. 11–24.

our investigation some attempt will be made to show how the Word of God spoken by the prophet Jeremiah has been subjected to just such a method.

In addition to the evidence of the operation of such an exegetical principle in the method of the Deuteronomists, Ackroyd, following Jones, finds strong indications of its use in the formation of the book of Jeremiah itself with which we are particularly concerned.[1] This arises from a consideration of the narrative in chapter xxxvi concerning the writing of the scroll in 605/4 B.C. to which we have referred. The question which has occupied the minds of commentators is what motivated the prophet to have a collection of his oracles committed to writing at that particular moment in his career and why, further-more, he wished to have them read before a congregation gathered in the Temple. The answer which immediately springs to mind is that he wished to have them preserved for posterity. But this cannot have been the sole reason since it would leave unexplained why he felt compelled to have them proclaimed anew in the Temple. It has been suggested that his primary reason for having them written down was in order that Baruch could read them in the Temple since he himself was banned, for some reason of which we are not told, from its precincts (Jer. xxxvi. 5).[2] Such a suggestion has the advantage of shifting the emphasis from the writing of the scroll to the reading of it, but it still leaves unanswered the major question why Jeremiah wished to have oracles which he had uttered in the preceding years of his ministry repro-claimed at that time. What was there in the situation that led him to restate his old oracles rather than formulate new ones with which Baruch could have confronted the cultic assembly? The two most important factors here are the particular historical circumstances in which he issued the scroll and had it read and also the general nature of the contents of the scroll. The year 605 B.C. was of momentous significance on the international scene in the Ancient Near East, for in the spring or early summer of that year the Babylonians established their supremacy by their crushing defeat of the Egyptians at Carchemish on the Euphrates.[3] Subsequent to this they began their advance into

---

[1] P. R. Ackroyd, *op. cit.*, pp. 12ff.; D. R. Jones, *op. cit.*, pp. 228ff.

[2] Cf. S. Mowinckel, *Prophecy and Tradition*, p. 61; E. Nielsen, *op. cit.*, p. 66. Against this, Engnell (*Svenskt Bibliskt Uppslagsverk*[2], vol. I, col. 1102) thinks of the written document as the authorization of Baruch as the prophet's envoy, after the analogy of Ancient Near Eastern royal messengers who bore a written copy of a state message as their credentials but delivered the message in question orally.

[3] For the historical background see J. Bright, *A History of Israel*, London 1960, pp. 305f.; *idem, Jeremiah*, pp. 181f.; M. Noth, *The History of Israel*[2], London 1960, pp. 280f.

Syria–Palestine. That there was a connection between these events and the writing of the scroll of Jeremiah's early oracles is very probable, for if we cannot determine the precise contents of this *Urrolle* we know that its general nature was one of divine judgement against Jerusalem and Judah and that it proclaimed that the instrument of Yahweh's judgement would be the Babylonians (Jer. xxxvi. 29). When this is borne in mind then the reason for the writing and reading of the scroll immediately becomes apparent: the Word of Judgement spoken by Yahweh through Jeremiah was on the point of fulfilment; the 'enemy from the north' had now terrifyingly materialized.[1] Thus Jeremiah in these actions was announcing the imminent fulfilment of the Word of God spoken by him in previous years by applying it to the situation brought about by the advance of the Babylonians in 605 B.C. No new oracle, as Jones remarks,[2] could have had such a devastating effect upon those who heard it; it was above all the sudden realization of the power and imminent fulfilment of the divine Word spoken in times past by the prophet to which those who heard the scroll read reacted (Jer. xxxvi. 16). Similarly, the action of the king in destroying it (Jer. xxxvi. 23) is not to be interpreted in terms of mere cynicism or contempt but as his attempt to nullify the power of the prophet's woeful words just as the rewriting of them (Jer. xxxvi. 27f.) was to ensure that they remained in force.[3]

If it can thus be maintained that Jeremiah took up oracles which he had uttered in the early years of his ministry and applied them to or interpreted them in terms of the situation of a later time, so also the possibility immediately arises that those who transmitted his sayings subjected them to a similar process, that is, were sensitive to their vitality as the Word of God which rendered them meaningful for and applicable to situations which confronted them in the age in which they themselves lived. They would thus not only have been heirs of the prophet's sayings but would also have shared with him the same creative method. In this way his oracles and sayings would have continued as a living force by being applied or adapted and developed by the circle who transmitted them to meet the ever changing needs of

---

[1] On the problem of the identification of this enemy and the possibility of an original connection between it and the Scythians see the discussion with full bibliography in H. H. Rowley, *op. cit.*, pp. 140ff.

[2] Cf. D. R. Jones, *op. cit.*, p. 230.

[3] Cf. D. R. Jones, *op. cit.*, p. 230; cf. the remarks of W. McKane, *Prophets and Wise Men*, London 1965, p. 121: 'It may not be extravagant to say that Jehoiakim believed that only by burning the scroll and destroying the prophetic *dābār* could he prevent the prediction from working itself out.'

B

the community in which they lived and worked. There would thus have evolved a tradition centring upon the prophetic ministry and preaching of Jeremiah and the material in the book of Jeremiah would have emerged as the expression of that tradition. In other words, the material in the book of Jeremiah may be plausibly regarded as the deposit of a tradition which embodies the oracles of Jeremiah as they were transmitted and used by a circle of traditionists as well as material which is the direct product of such a circle.

The purpose of the present study is to suggest that the large amount of prose material in the book is best understood not as the literary work of individual authors and editors but as essentially the product of such a tradition. This prose comprises two different types of material, on the one hand numerous sermons and discourses and on the other many narratives of a historical nature centring on events and incidents in the life of the prophet such as the record of the compilation of the *Urrolle* in chapter xxxvi to which we have referred. Of particular significance in this connection are the sermons and discourses, for a number of them show clear signs of having been composed on the basis of original Jeremianic sayings which they incorporate, to some extent at least, or presuppose. It is precisely here that our brief examination of the method and technique of the Deuteronomists becomes relevant once more, for the sermons and discourses in Jeremiah look very much as though they took shape as the result of the application of a similar method and technique. Furthermore, it is not only in their form that they resemble the manner in which traditional material has been presented in the Deuteronomistic corpus; the fundamental purpose for which they were composed is identical, viz. the desire on the part of a circle to actualize for the generation to which they belonged the prophetic word spoken in times past, in this instance by Jeremiah. When we add to these parallels the striking parallels in both language and style which, as we shall see presently, have long been observed between these sermons and discourses and the Deuteronomistic literature, then the possibility immediately suggests itself that they also took shape at the hands of the Deuteronomists. It is with such a possibility that we shall be concerned in this study.

In order to clarify further the approach here proposed we may examine briefly the manner in which scholars have generally dealt with the question of the origin and composition of these prose sermons and discourses in Jeremiah. As we shall see at a later stage in our investigation, widely differing solutions have been offered to this problem.[1]

[1] See below pp. 21ff.

With few exceptions, however, the basic concept of the actual manner in which these sermons and discourses evolved and assumed their present form is in each case the same, viz. that they are the result of a predominantly or entirely literary activity on the part of an author or editor. For the purpose of our examination of this approach we may centre our discussion on John Bright's recent commentary, since it represents the latest large scale investigation of the problem along these lines.[1]

For Bright the prose sermons in the book of Jeremiah represent a separate Jeremianic tradition which does not preserve the prophet's own words but rather a record of his preaching 'as it was remembered, understood, and repeated in the circle of his followers'.[2] He expresses his basic point of view as follows:[3]

> 'We may suppose that, when Jeremiah preached, his hearers—and these may well have included, and almost certainly did include, men who were in sympathy with the Deuteronomic reform and the theology which under-girded it—often recalled the gist of what he had said without remembering his exact words, and that, as they passed on what they had heard, there grew up a tradition of Jeremiah's preaching based on his words, but not preserving them exactly.'

Bright believes that some of this material was reduced to writing at an early stage since some of it is already present in the biographical passages in the book (e.g. in chapters xxvii, xxix. 16–20, xxxii. 17–44, xxxiv. 12–22, xxxv. 12–17), but asserts that in general it assumed fixed form later than the poetry and even after this may have been further expanded in the course of its transmission. The differences in the length of the prose sermons and discourses in the LXX and MT is taken as evidence of such expansion.[4] Furthermore, Bright argues that this expansion was not merely verbal but possibly also included some development of Jeremiah's thought and the adaptation of it to new situations. It is also suggested that in some instances the prophet's ideas may have been misunderstood by the circle responsible for this prose tradition of his preaching.[5]

This view advanced by Bright may be questioned on a number of grounds. Reduced to its simplest terms, his position, as I understand it, is basically this: the prose sermons in Jeremiah represent the written deposit of a series of the prophet's sayings on a number of occasions

---

[1] J. Bright, *Jeremiah*, pp. lxiii–lxxiii.
[2] *Ibid.*, p. lxxii.
[3] *Ibid.*, p. lxxii.
[4] *Ibid.*, p. lxxii.
[5] *Ibid.*, p. lxxii. See below p. 12 note 1.

which have been orally transmitted by a group of his disciples. In the course of this oral transmission the prophet's own words were forgotten; what we have in the material in question is the 'gist' of his teaching. Accordingly, in most of the passages containing these sermons and discourses Bright believes that genuine Jeremianic ideas and sentiments are expressed although in some instances he finds some development and on occasions even some misunderstanding of the prophet's teaching on the part of the circle who composed them. It may be asked, however, whether such an interpretation of these sermons almost exclusively in terms of Jeremiah's ministry and teaching is adequate. That is to say, it may be urged against Bright that in his exegesis he has not given enough consideration to a possible wider purpose behind this prose tradition, viz. that it arose out of the attempt of the circle who transmitted Jeremiah's sayings not merely to record what the prophet had said on this or that occasion but rather to relate it to certain issues, both theological and otherwise, with which they were vitally concerned in their own time. In doing so there is no need to doubt that they employed genuine Jeremianic sayings and oracles; that in many instances they did so seems quite evident, as we shall see. But their primary purpose was not, as Bright seems to suggest, to record as accurately as possible the prophet's ideas and sentiments but to draw out the significance of what he had said on certain matters during his prophetic ministry which were also relevant to their own situation or to adapt aspects of his teaching to suit that situation.[1] In other words, it is more plausible to argue that the exegetical principle which Ackroyd has discussed and to which reference has been made earlier has contributed largely to the formation and development of these Jeremianic sermons and discourses.

That such a use has been made of Jeremiah's sayings and teaching and has led to a growth in the prophetic tradition is a possibility worth much more consideration than Bright and indeed most commentators have afforded it. Thus I find it difficult to accept his suggestion that there has been some misunderstanding of the prophet's teaching by those responsible for the sermons. The question of misunderstanding does not really arise here. The instances in which Bright finds it are

---

[1] It is true that in the Introduction to his commentary (cf. p. lxxii) Bright, as we have noted, mentions the possibility of the development or adaptation of Jeremiah's thought and teaching in some of the prose sermons. In his exegesis, however, he rarely, as far as I can see, pursues this possibility and where he does find evidence of such development he simply notes it but never attempts to provide an explanation for it or to investigate what possible purpose it served for those responsible for it. See further below p. 13 note 2.

really cases of where the circle behind the prose tradition have consciously developed something which Jeremiah himself had said on certain issues with which they were concerned or, as in some instances, have claimed his prophetic authority for something which they themselves felt compelled to proclaim to their own generation. For example, with reference to the sermon on observance of the Sabbath in chapter xvii, 19–27, Bright acknowledges that the rather one-sided emphasis on the Sabbath in this passage—observance of the Sabbath is the condition of the nation's existence—cannot be attributed to Jeremiah himself. In view of this he suggests that it is 'entirely likely that we have in this passage an instance of further development—possibly the misunderstanding—of Jeremiah's thought in the circles of those who perpetuated his words'.[1] But is such a view really tenable? It is possible that there has been some development here of something Jeremiah had said on observance of the Sabbath and if this is so then some attempt must be made to explain why and in what circumstances such development took place.[2] But the very distinctive manner in which the observance of the Sabbath is formulated in this passage surely cannot be taken as merely a misunderstanding of what the prophet may have said on the matter. Here surely it is much more likely that we are dealing with the conscious attempt of those responsible for the prose to represent Jeremiah as having given expression to a belief concerning observance of the Sabbath which was an important issue in their own time.[3]

That these sermons represent a conscious and deliberate development of the prophet's teaching rather than merely the attempt to provide the 'gist' of what he had said on a number of matters is clear on other grounds also. To claim, as does Bright, that they assumed their present form largely because those who composed them could not remember the prophet's own words cannot be sustained for the following reasons. In the first place, it has become increasingly probable that much of the material in the prophetic books in our Old Testament was preserved initially to some extent at least in oral rather than written form. But at the same time such oral transmission was very probably much more reliable than Bright's argument presupposes and it is difficult to believe that the Jeremianic circle could not have

---

[1] Cf. J. Bright, *Jeremiah*, p. 120.

[2] Following Rudolph (*Jeremia*[3], pp. 102f.) and others Bright believes that underlying the sermon is the memory of something Jeremiah said on observance of the Sabbath. He offers no explanation, however, of why and in what situation the present sermon was composed.

[3] For a consideration of this sermon see below pp. 65f.

recorded the prophet's *ipsissima verba* alone if, as Bright seems to suggest, that is primarily what they were interested in. In the second place, however, evidence can be adduced to suggest that those who were responsible for the prose sermons were in fact in possession of original Jeremianic sayings and speeches, for careful examination reveals that there is in the material in question a range of very distinctive words and expressions which are peculiar to the book of Jeremiah alone and which may very plausibly be regarded as belonging to the substratum of original Jeremianic material upon which the sermons are based.[1] Indeed, in some instances what appear to be parts of the original prophetic saying can be isolated from the present texts.[2] Considerations such as these render Bright's view questionable. It is surely preferable to see these sermons as the product of a circle of traditionists who in response to the needs of the generation in which they lived either developed and presented in homiletical fashion some of Jeremiah's sayings and oracles or claimed his prophetic authority for something which they themselves wished to proclaim to those to whom they addressed themselves.

It is as the product and deposit of a living, active tradition that these sermons must be interpreted rather than as the creations of a purely literary activity at the hands of authors and editors. That is to say, more serious consideration must be given to the possibility that they took shape and assumed at least substantially their present form within the context of and as a result of a preaching and teaching ministry which was concerned with the problems and needs of a listening audience to whom those responsible for it addressed themselves.

In this connection I draw attention to Enno Janssen's work on Judah during the exile.[3] For Janssen the exilic period in Judah itself was not the barren time which Old Testament scholars have so often believed it to have been, and he is concerned to demonstrate that this period was one of considerable activity, theological, cultic and literary as well as political. For our present purposes the most important part of his study is his brief but valuable discussion of the origin and provenance of the prose sermons in the book of Jeremiah.[4] The basic position adopted by Janssen is similar to the general view outlined above, viz. that they owe their origin to a living preaching tradition and are the

---

[1] For Bright's own interpretation of this see below pp. 28ff.

[2] Attention will be drawn to this in our discussion of individual passages in our discussion in chapter 3 below.

[3] E. Janssen, *Juda in der Exilszeit*, FRLANT 69, Göttingen 1956.

[4] *Ibid.*, pp. 20–21, 105ff.

written deposit of such a tradition.[1] He believes this preaching activity to have had its first literary expression in the book of Deuteronomy in the pre-exilic period and that it survived the destruction of the Judaean state in 586 B.C. and was, as he sees it, carried on with renewed vigour during the exilic period. Here again it received literary expression in the Deuteronomistic historical work. Although it is acknowledged that this history corpus represents a carefully executed theological and literary plan, it is argued that its basic point of view—its concern with observance of the Law and its explanation of why Israel had been rejected in the catastrophic events of 721 B.C. and 586 B.C.—derived from the Deuteronomistic preaching carried out in the exilic period.[2] For Janssen the particular *Sitz im Leben* of this preaching activity was the early synagogue. It is argued that this institution had its beginnings already in the pre-exilic period and became of greater significance after the destruction of the Temple in 586 B.C.[3]

Janssen traces the prose sermons and discourses in the book of Jeremiah to these Deuteronomistic preachers who have utilized some of the prophet's oracles and sayings in their synagogue teaching.[4] This is evident, it is argued, not only from the linguistic and stylistic parallels between the Jeremianic prose material and the Deuteronomistic corpus but also from the actual form in which many of these sermons and discourses are cast, a form which is also found in a number of Deuteronomistic homilies and speeches (e.g. Josh. i, xxiii; Jud. ii. 10–15; 1 Sam. xii).[5] The view that a circle of the prophet's disciples were responsible for them is rejected on the grounds that as far as we know Jeremiah had no such circle of active disciples; he worked alone accompanied only by his scribe and companion Baruch.[6]

Janssen's basic point of view that the prose sermons in the book of Jeremiah took shape and assumed their present form for the most part at the hands of the Deuteronomists and within the context of an active preaching tradition carried out by them offers the possibility of a much

[1] *Ibid.*, pp. 21, 106ff.
[2] *Ibid.*, pp. 12ff., 105ff.
[3] *Ibid.*, pp. 107ff.
[4] *Ibid.*, pp. 105f. The suggestion that some of the Jeremianic prose sermons took shape in or were used within the context of the early synagogue had already been made by W. Rudolph, *op. cit.*, p. xviii. Before this Volz (*Jeremia*, p. 300) also found evidence of a synagogue background for some of this material, especially such prayers as that contained in xxxii 17ff. which he took as evidence of the beginnings of 'ecclesiastical prayer'. Cf. also more recently E. A. Leslie, *Jeremiah*, New York 1954, pp. 283ff., 293.
[5] Cf. E. Janssen, *op. cit.*, pp. 105, 107.
[6] *Ibid.*, p. 106.

more satisfactory solution to the problem of the provenance of these sermons than the purely literary solutions advanced by the majority of scholars hitherto. In the ensuing study the same general view is adopted, although the conclusions arrived at differ from Janssen's in some important respects.[1]

When, however, the sermons and discourses have been considered there remains a considerable amount of prose material in the book of Jeremiah which is of a different form and nature. This material consists of numerous narratives which record incidents and events in Jeremiah's prophetic ministry (esp. chapters xxvi–xxix, xxxii–xlv). In what way is this material to be interpreted and how did it evolve?

In contrast to the wide variety of views on the problem of the origin and composition of the sermons in the book, there has been, as we have already noted, widespread agreement on the authorship of the prose narratives, for scholars have generally taken the view that they were composed by Baruch. As such many have described them as a 'biography'. Others, however, have rejected or at least qualified such a description of this material largely on the grounds that the narratives in question do not cover some of the most important years in the prophet's life, particularly his early ministry during the eventful reign of Josiah.[2] Instead, a number of scholars have preferred to see in this material something in the nature of a 'passion narrative' (*Leidens-geschichte*) describing the sufferings endured by Jeremiah as Yahweh's spokesman during those years of turmoil which preceded the collapse and destruction of the Judaean state.[3] As against this, however, it must be argued that many of the narratives simply cannot be described as *Leidensgeschichte*. Thus in chapter xxvi whilst it is recorded (*vv.* 7ff.) that

---

[1] In particular, it will be seen that a serious question mark may be placed against his view that the Jeremianic prose sermons, like the Deuteronomistic history, originated in Judah rather than in Babylon during the exilic period. For a discussion see below pp. 116ff.

[2] Cf. for example recently C. Rietzschel, *op. cit.*, p. 96. It may be noted here that Mowinckel has consistently and, in the opinion of a number of scholars, correctly rejected any description of these narratives in terms of biographical writing: 'A "life of Jeremiah", a biography, he (the author of these narratives) could not have written nor have wanted to write, simply because he lacked the basic concept for such an undertaking, the concept of "a life"' (*Zur Komposition des Buches Jeremia*, p. 25). These narratives were written not just 'to tell us something about Jeremiah, much less to furnish contributions for his biography, but because the events and situations in question had provided the occasions for some of the prophet's memorable words' (*Studien zu dem Buche Ezra-Nehemia*, II, Oslo 1964, p. 91).

[3] So, for example, W. Rudolph, *op. cit.*, pp. xix, 195ff. but most notably by H. Kremers, 'Leidensgemeinschaft mit Gott im AT. Eine Untersuchung der "biographischen" Berichte im Jeremiabuch', *EvTh*, 13, 1953, pp. 122ff.

Jeremiah's Temple sermon provoked a threat to his life, it seems clear that the primary interest of the narrative, as we shall see, is not in this but in the manner in which Yahweh's Word spoken by the prophets, in this instance by both Jeremiah and the otherwise unknown Uriah, was rejected by Judah as personified in the actions of the king, Jehoiakim.[1] And chapter xxxvi, as we shall see, is concerned with the same motif.[2] Chapter xxvii and its sequel in chapter xxviii which is concerned with the conflict between Jeremiah and the prophet Hananiah centre on the problem of false prophecy, as also does chapter xxix. In none of these narratives does the fate of Jeremiah at the hands of his countrymen play any significant role whatsoever. In chapter xxxii the biographical material (vv. 1–5) is clearly intended as nothing more than a historical framework for the ensuing description of the symbolic action of the purchase of the field at Anathoth (vv. 6–15) and the dialogue between the prophet and God on the future redemption of Israel from exile (vv. 16ff.). Chapter xxxiii deals with the same theme, whilst xxxiv comprises an oracle concerning Zedekiah (vv. 1–5) and a sermon on the breach of the law demanding the septennial release of slaves (vv. 6ff.). Chapter xxxv has similarly nothing to say of the prophet's sufferings but centres rather on the comparison of the faithfulness of the Rechabites to the instruction and laws formulated (cf. vv. 6b–7)[3] by their founder, Jonadab ben Rechab, with the infidelity of Israel to the commands of Yahweh.

On these grounds, therefore, none of the individual narratives in chapters xxvi–xxxvi can with any confidence be classified as constituting part of a *Leidensgeschichte* or indeed of a general biography. In each case their primary purpose is not biographical or historical but didactic. As such they may plausibly be regarded as having evolved in a similar manner to the sermons and discourses, some of which they actually incorporate.[4] That is to say, they are properly understood as edifying stories which owe their origin to a circle of traditionists who have sought to draw out the implications of various incidents in the prophetic ministry and teaching of Jeremiah for matters with which they were vitally concerned, such as the authority of the prophetic word, the problem of false prophecy, and disobedience to the requirements of the Law. We shall turn to a consideration of this at a later stage in our study.

[1] For a discussion see below pp. 52ff.
[2] See below pp. 39ff.
[3] Cf. E. Gerstenberger, *Wesen und Herkunft des 'Apodiktischen Rechts'*, WMANT 20, Neukirchen 1965, pp. 110ff.
[4] On this see further below pp. 34ff.

This leaves us with chapters xxxvii–xliv.[1] In contrast to the individual narratives in chapters xxvi–xxxvi, these chapters form a continuous, chronologically arranged, historical cycle which narrates the fate of the prophet during the siege of Jerusalem (xxxvii–xxxviii), a brief account of the fall of Jerusalem and the capture and exile of Zedekiah together with the execution of his sons and the exile of 'the rest of the people' (xxxix. 1–10), the release of Jeremiah from prison and his favourable treatment by the Babylonian authorities (xxxix. 11–14, xl. 1–6),[2] the appointment of Gedaliah as governor of the community which the Babylonians left in Judah (xl. 7–12), the assassination of Gedaliah (xl. 13–xli. 3), the murder of the pilgrims from Shechem, Shiloh and Samaria (xli. 4–9), the rebellion of Ishmael (xli. 10–15), the flight of those who survived Ishmael's rebellion to Egypt against the counsel of Jeremiah whom they forced to go with them (xli. 16–xliii. 7), an oracle of woe against Egypt (xliii. 8–13) and finally an extended prose discourse condemning the pagan cults practised by those who fled to Egypt and announcing woe (xliv).

As a historical cycle these chapters also have been regarded as part of Baruch's biography or *Leidensgeschichte* of Jeremiah.[3] This gains some support from chapters xxxvii–xxxviii where indeed the suffering of the prophet during the siege of Jerusalem is described. Against this, however, attention must be drawn to the fact that in some of the ensuing narratives in this cycle the prophet is not even mentioned (cf. xxxix. 1–10, xl. 7–12, xl. 13–xli. 3, xli. 4–9, xli. 10–15). For this reason any description of this cycle as a *Leidensgeschichte* is inadequate and some attempt must be made to find a more comprehensive understanding of its purpose. And once again, as with the narratives in chapters xxvi–xxxvi, we shall see in the ensuing study that the primary purpose of chapters xxxvii–xliv is theological and didactic and that as such they owe their origin not to the literary activity of an individual, whether Baruch or some other 'biographer', but to a circle of traditionists.[4]

---

[1] On chapter xlv see below pp. 111ff.

[2] It is commonly agreed that the oracle of salvation addressed to Ebed-melech in xxxix. 15–18 is out of place in its present position, its proper context being chapter xxxviii, where it could be placed after v. 13 (so Rudolph, *op. cit. in loc.*) or after v. 28a (so Bright, *Jeremiah, in loc.*).

[3] Cf. especially H. Kremers, *op. cit.*

[4] The narratives about Jeremiah may in some respects be compared with those about Elijah in 1 Kings xvii–2 Kings i (ii), though there are also important differences. In the Elijah stories we learn much about the prophet and the activities, both religious and political, in which he engaged, as well as the grave danger into which his prophetic ministry brought him with the state authorities in his days and the threat to his life which this at times posed. Yet it would be quite incorrect to regard these narratives as

On the basis of our conclusions in the foregoing discussion we now turn to an examination of this Jeremianic prose tradition. This will involve us in a number of questions. In the first place we must examine the literary nature and characteristics of this Jeremianic prose material. In addition we must attempt to analyse the particular theological traditions which underly it and which it seeks to present. Finally, we must also attempt to determine the historical background of such a tradition and the religio-sociological situation in which it emerged and which it presupposes. With these and related questions we shall concern ourselves in the ensuing chapters. Our first task, however, is to discuss the vexed question of the literary characteristics of the prose in Jeremiah, since it is from here that much recent discussion of the problem of the provenance of the Jeremianic prose has proceeded.

---

biographical or, in part, a *Leidensgeschichte*, for they centre not on Elijah but on Yahweh's acts in the time of crisis in which the prophet lived and played an important part (cf. G. von Rad, *Old Testament Theology*, II, London 1965, pp. 14–25). These old stories have been incorporated relatively untouched by the Deuteronomist into his history. Only such comments as he felt necessary to fit them into his work and theological purpose have been added; the stories already embodied for the most part the particular motifs in which he was interested: the prophet's struggle against Israel's apostasy, his vehement opposition to the monarchy which played such a leading role in that apostasy, and his activity against those who broke the covenant law in both its cultic and ethical aspects. (For the Elisha stories see G. von Rad, *op. cit.*, pp. 25ff.)

2

LITERARY CONSIDERATIONS

In the preceding chapter we directed our attention to the question of the manner in which the prose material in the book of Jeremiah originated and took shape. From a negative point of view it has been argued that the discussion of this problem hitherto has been too preoccupied with considerations of an entirely or predominantly literary critical nature. As against the widely accepted view that the material in question is the result of a purely literary activity on the part of Baruch or other authors or both, the possibility that other creative processes in addition to the work of authors have contributed to the formation of the prose tradition in the book of Jeremiah has been raised. In this connection particular attention has been drawn to the number of prose sermons in the book, and it has been argued that these may plausibly be regarded as having originated in the exegetical and homiletical development and presentation of some of the prophet's original sayings or certain aspects of his teaching. With regard to the other prose material in the book, that is, the narratives in which incidents and events in the life of Jeremiah and the period in which he ministered are recorded, it has been argued that the general classification of these as biographical is an inadequate description of their real nature and purpose which must be understood as essentially theological and didactic.

On the basis of these suggestions the general thesis has been advanced that the prose material in the book is best understood as the final expression of a tradition which grew and developed around the ministry and teaching of Jeremiah and in response to the needs of the community in which those responsible for this tradition lived and worked. The investigation of the provenance of this tradition involves a consideration of a number of questions of both a literary and a theological nature and it is with these that we must now concern ourselves. In this chapter the question of the literary nature and affinities of the material in question is discussed, since this problem has formed the starting point for the assessment of the material in the attempt to understand the composition of the book of Jeremiah.

The major critical problem which arises from the sermons and
discourses in Jeremiah concerns the presence in them of a Hebrew
style and vocabulary which is closely akin to that of the Deuteronomistic corpus in Deuteronomy–2 Kings.[1] Close parallels in language
and style between these two blocks of literature have long been
recognized and broadly speaking three main solutions have been
offered to the problem although each of the three has been advanced
with considerable variation by different scholars.

1. It has been held at one time or another that Jeremiah himself
employed or indeed actually created the style. The latter view was
held by some nineteenth-century scholars who argued that Jeremiah
alone or with others was responsible for the composition of Deuteronomy.[2] Recent traditio-historical investigation into the question of the
origin of Deuteronomy and the circle responsible for it render such a
view impossible today.[3] Others have proposed the view that the
prophet coined the style which was then adopted and employed by the
authors of Deuteronomy who, they believe, worked during the exile or
early post-exilic period, that is, at a time subsequent to Jeremiah's
ministry.[4] Few today would support such a view; it is all but generally
agreed now that Deuteronomy in its original form (*Urdeuteronomium*)
was written sometime during the seventh century and before 621 B.C.
when, according to the widely accepted interpretation of the narrative
of Josiah's reformation in 2 Kings xxii–xxiii, it was discovered in the
Temple.[5] The important role of Deuteronomy in the reformation
carried out in Josiah's reign has led to the suggestion that Jeremiah,
who began his prophetic ministry at that time (cf. Jer. i. 2), was directly
influenced by the style of Deuteronomy.[6] It has even been claimed that
he took an active part in the promulgation of its demands in the course

---

[1] The circle responsible for the composition and compilation of the corpus
Deuteronomy–2 Kings will be referred to as the Deuteronomists. When referring
specifically to the authors of the original book of Deuteronomy we use the term
Deuteronomic.

[2] So, for example, J. W. Colenso, *The Pentateuch and Book of Joshua Critically Examined*,
Part VII, London 1879, pp. 12, 225–227, 259–269 and Appendix on p. 149.

[3] For a discussion of the origin of Deuteronomy see E. W. Nicholson, *Deuteronomy
and Tradition*, Oxford 1967, esp. pp. 58ff., 83ff. An excellent survey of the study of
Deuteronomy is presented in S. Loersch, *Das Deuteronomium und seine Deutungen*,
Stuttgart 1967.

[4] Cf. R. H. Kennett, 'The Date of Deuteronomy', *JTS* 7, 1906, pp. 481–500; J. N·
Schofield, 'The Significance of the Prophets for the Dating of Deuteronomy' in *Studies
in History and Religion*, ed. E. A. Payne, London 1942, pp. 44–60.

[5] Cf. E. W. Nicholson, *op. cit.*, pp. 1–17.

[6] So, for example, S. R. Driver, *Deuteronomy*[3], ICC, Edinburgh 1902, pp. xviiff.

of that reformation.[1] According to another view Deuteronomy had formed part of his early education in the priestly circles at his home in Anathoth.[2] The suggestion has been made that the prophet was influenced by the Deuteronomic style as the dominant prose style of the period in which he lived.[3] Another form of this particular suggestion is that the *Gattung* of the sermon had been increasingly employed in the seventh century and that Jeremiah adopted it as an already well established form of address used by both prophets and priests.[4] Similar to this is the suggestion that the prophet derived the form and style of the prose sermon from the preaching tradition of the covenant festival in the Jerusalem Temple from which also, it is maintained, the Deuteronomic parenetic style itself was derived.[5]

2. The various suggestions noted above all proceed from the basic view that Jeremiah himself employed this prose style and that accordingly the passages in which it is found are to be attributed to the prophet himself. Contrary to this standpoint, however, many scholars have attributed these passages to authors or editors other than him. As far as I am aware Duhm first proposed such a theory, arguing that the style and terminology of many of them represents the work of a Deuteronomistic *Ergänzer* who edited the material which had come from Jeremiah and Baruch.[6] Hölscher adopted a similar point of view as also did Skinner,[7] whilst Mowinckel, followed closely by Rudolph and others,[8] believed the passages in question to have constituted a special Deuteronomistic source employed by the compilers of the book. Hyatt has assigned them directly to the Deuteronomists, suggesting that they represent an attempt to create the impression that the great

---

[1] Cf. T. K. Cheyne, *Jeremiah: His Life and Times*, London 1888, pp. 56ff.; W. Erbt, *Jeremia und seine Zeit*, Göttingen 1902.

[2] Cf. Y. Kaufmann, *The Religion of Israel*, London 1961, pp. 416f.

[3] Cf. W. O. E. Oesterley and T. H. Robinson, *Introduction to the Books of the Old Testament*, London 1934, p. 304.

[4] So O. Eissfeldt, *The Old Testament: An Introduction*, Oxford 1965, pp. 15f., 352.

[5] Cf. A. Weiser, *Das Buch des Propheten Jeremia* (1955), p. 482 note 1; *idem*, *Introduction to the Old Testament*, London 1961, pp. 217f. It should be noted, however, that Weiser holds the view that those who transmitted Jeremiah's words also employed this liturgical style, so that it is not always possible to separate the original wording of Jeremiah's sermons from later liturgical elaboration. Cf. also, J. W. Miller, *Das Verhältnis Jeremias und Hesekiels sprachlich und theologisch untersucht*, Assen 1955, pp. 23ff.

[6] B. Duhm, *Das Buch Jeremia* (1901), pp. xviff.

[7] G. Hölscher, *Die Profeten*, Leipzig 1914, pp. 382f. and 'Komposition und Ursprung des Deuteronomiums', *ZAW* 40, 1922, pp. 233–239; J. Skinner, *Prophecy and Religion: Studies in the Life of Jeremiah*, Cambridge 1922, p. 102.

[8] S. Mowinckel, *Zur Komposition des Buches Jeremia* (1914); W. Rudolph, *Jeremia*³ (1968), pp. xviff.; F. Horst, 'Die Anfänge des Propheten Jeremia', *ZAW* 41, 1923, pp. 94–153.

prophet had actively supported the Deuteronomic reformation of his own time.[1] Bentzen similarly believed that they come from the Deuteronomists who, it is claimed, have attempted to use the prophet's teaching for their own 'propaganda'.[2] Nielsen suggests that the passages present a conscious revision of original Jeremianic sayings by the Deuteronomists who, it is argued, were interested in certain aspects of his teaching.[3] In his work on Judah during the exilic period to which we have already referred, Janssen has advanced the view that the prose sermons owe their origin to Deuteronomistic preachers at that time who employed some of Jeremiah's original sayings in their teaching and preaching which was carried out, according to Janssen, in the early synagogue.[4] Rietzschel has recently taken a similar view.[5] H. G. May has proposed that the passages in question are the work of a biographer of Jeremiah who was influenced not only by the Deuteronomistic style but also by that of Second Isaiah and the editor of the book of Ezekiel.[6]

3. The third main type of solution proceeds to a greater or lesser extent from the view that these passages are the work of Jeremiah's disciples who were influenced by Deuteronomistic ideas and language. This was advocated by Mowinckel in a later work than that in which he advanced the view noted in (2) above.[7] Lindblom holds essentially the same view.[8] Pfeiffer suggested that Baruch prepared an edition of the book and revised or rewrote many of his master's speeches in the Deuteronomistic style.[9] In his recently published commentary Bright, as we have already seen, argues that the prose tradition of Jeremiah's preaching developed on the basis of the prophet's own words and seeks to present a record of his message as understood by a group of his followers who came strongly under the influence of the Deuteronomistic circle.[10] The role played by Jeremiah's disciples with regard to the origin of these sermons was stressed some thirty years ago by Birkeland.[11] Following and further developing the principles already formulated by

[1] J. P. Hyatt, 'The Deuteronomic Edition of Jeremiah' in *Vanderbilt Studies in the Humanities*, vol. I, Nashville 1951, pp. 71–95 and *The Book of Jeremiah*, IB 5 (1956).

[2] A. Bentzen, *Introduction to the Old Testament*[2], Copenhagen 1952, p. 119.

[3] E. Nielsen, *Oral Tradition* (1954), pp. 77f.

[4] E. Janssen, *Judah in der Exilszeit* (1956), pp. 105ff.

[5] C. Rietzschel, *Das Problem der Urrolle* (1966), pp. 9–24.

[6] H. G. May, 'Towards an Objective Approach to the Book of Jeremiah: The Biographer', *JBL* 61, 1942, pp. 139–155 and 'Jeremiah's Biographer', *JBR* 10, 1942, pp. 195–201.

[7] S. Mowinckel, *Prophecy and Tradition* (1946), pp. 62ff.

[8] J. Lindblom, *Prophecy in Ancient Israel*, Oxford 1962, Additional Note V, pp. 425f.

[9] R. H. Pfeiffer, *Introduction to the Old Testament* (1948), p. 505.

[10] J. Bright, *Jeremiah* (1965), p. lxxii.

[11] H. Birkeland, *Zum hebräischen Traditionswesen* (1938).

Nyberg,[1] Birkeland argued that we have in the book of Jeremiah two different stages in the Jeremianic tradition. On the one hand there are poetic oracles which were fixed in writing at an early stage. On the other hand, however, are the prose speeches which represent the written deposit of a process of oral transmission among the circles of the prophet's disciples by whom some of his sayings were developed and adapted.[2]

The relevance of these sermons and discourses for the understanding of Jeremiah's message is quite clearly dependent upon which particular view of their origin is adopted. Thus Duhm, for example, dismissed them as of no value whatsoever.[3] This view was also taken by Mowinckel,[4] Hölscher[5] and Horst.[6] The material in question was dated by each of these scholars in the post-exilic period, ranging from the beginning of it, as proposed by Horst (530–500 B.C.), down to a time not earlier than 400 B.C., as suggested by Mowinckel. In a number of articles May advanced a similar view, suggesting that the book in its present form represents the work of a biographer of the prophet who was not Baruch but one who lived not earlier than 500 B.C.[7] In compiling the book this biographer employed genuine Jeremianic oracles and sayings, memoirs and material traditionally ascribed to Jeremiah. In addition, however, according to May he also inserted into the book speeches which he himself freely composed and which have no value in attempting to assess the prophet's message and teaching. At the other extreme to such views as these is that of, for example, Eissfeldt and a number of other commentators who regard these sermons and discourses as genuine utterances of Jeremiah and as such first-hand evidence concerning his prophetic ministry and teaching.[8] On these grounds also it has been held that some of them were probably already present in the *Urrolle* in 605/4 B.C.[9]

[1] H. S. Nyberg, *Studien zum Hoseabuch*, Uppsala 1935.

[2] H. Birkeland, *op. cit.*, p. 42. Cf. more recently, I. Engnell, *Svenskt Bibliskt Uppslags-verk*[2], vol. I, 1962, cols. 1105–1106.

[3] B. Duhm, *op. cit.*, pp. xviif.

[4] S. Mowinckel in his earlier work *Zur Komposition des Buches Jeremia*, p. 57 where he says of the prose discourses (his source C): 'Its Jeremiah bears little relationship to the real Jeremiah'.

[5] G. Hölscher, *Die Profeten*, pp. 379f.

[6] F. Horst, *op. cit., passim*.

[7] H. G. May, 'Towards an Objective Approach to the Book of Jeremiah: the Biographer', *JBL* 61, 1942, pp. 139–155.

[8] O. Eissfeldt, *op. cit.*, pp. 16, 352; cf. T. H. Robinson, 'Baruch's Scroll', *ZAW* 42, 1924, pp. 209–221; J. W. Miller, *op. cit.*, pp. 28ff.

[9] Cf. O. Eissfeldt, *op. cit.*, p. 352; T. H. Robinson. 'Baruch's Scroll'; J. W. Miller, *op. cit.*, pp. 21f. *et passim*.

Of the three main views of the origin of the prose sermons in Jeremiah outlined above, the first raises formidable difficulties which render it very improbable. The most recent, thoroughgoing attempt to sustain the view that the prose sermons are for the most part genuine speeches of Jeremiah has been made by J. W. Miller.[1] Following Bright,[2] Miller stresses the differences in vocabulary between the prose sermons in Jeremiah and the Deuteronomistic literature and concludes that in spite of the well-known similarities there are too many differences in the range of vocabulary in the two blocks of material to warrant the view that they both derive from the same author.[3] The similarities in style and vocabulary between the prose sermons in Jeremiah and the Deuteronomistic corpus are to be explained rather as being due, it is argued, to the use made by both the Deuteronomic/Deuteronomistic authors and Jeremiah himself of a common liturgical style and form which made its appearance in the seventh century and which found expression in the Jerusalem Temple after the discovery of Deuteronomy in 621 B.C.[4] In addition, Miller finds differences in theme between the Jeremianic material and the Deuteronomistic literature.[5] On these grounds, therefore, it is argued that the prose sermons in Jeremiah represent for the most part the prophet's *ipsissima verba*, and Miller assigns many of them to the *Urrolle* compiled in 605 B.C. which he believes to have consisted solely of such prose sermons.[6]

Several criticisms may be raised against Miller's view. His argument, following Bright, that the differences in vocabulary between the prose in Jeremiah and the Deuteronomistic literature render the view that the former was composed by the Deuteronomists untenable, is not

---

[1] J. W. Miller, *op. cit.*

[2] J. Bright, 'The Date of the Prose Sermons of Jeremiah', *JBL* 70, 1951, pp. 15–35.

[3] J. W. Miller, *op. cit.*, pp. 23–24.

[4] *Ibid.*, pp. 24ff.

[5] *Ibid.*, pp. 27f. and in his exegesis of individual passages on pp. 29ff.

[6] Miller argues (*op. cit.*, pp. 21ff.) on the basis of Jer. xxxvi that the *Urrolle* was a document of 'fundamental clarity and striking single-mindedness' (*ibid.*, p. 21) and on this basis contends that it was composed in prose as a more effective means of conveying the message intended than poetic oracles the effect of which, it is suggested, would have been weak in the situation in which the scroll was to be read. It may be agreed that the contents of the scroll would have been expressed clearly, but to infer from this that it must therefore of necessity have been composed in prose is quite untenable. We have simply no sound grounds for maintaining that poetic oracles would have been less effective than prose in the situation in which Baruch read the prophet's scroll. On the contrary, the normal form of prophetic address was in verse and, furthermore, the fact that the Psalms, for the most part composed in verse, were most probably written for use in the cultic assembly in the Jerusalem Temple would seem to indicate that such an assembly to which Jeremiah's scroll was read would have been more than familiar with a poetic form of address.

C

compelling, for, as we shall see, the peculiarly Jeremianic vocabulary in the sermons can be explained on the grounds that whoever composed them was working on the basis of authentic material from the prophet himself which has been incorporated wholly or partly in the present sermons.[1] Secondly, even a superficial reading reveals that the prose sermons in Jeremiah differ widely in their range of vocabulary and peculiar expressions from the poetic oracles in the book. The differences are so striking that both blocks of material cannot reasonably be regarded as having come from one and the same person. Had Jeremiah himself composed them both, then surely there would have been a definite and clearly observable overlapping between the range of vocabulary in the prose and poetry. In a recent article W. L. Holladay has drawn attention to some linguistic points of contact between the two blocks of material,[2] but these are significantly few and, once again, can be understood as indicating that whoever was responsible for the prose sermons was in possession of a collection or collections of the prophet's own oracles and sayings.

Furthermore, and perhaps more important, the differences between the two types of material in the book is not one of language and style alone, for there are some prose passages which contain or reflect ideas which cannot seriously be attributed to Jeremiah. Perhaps the best example of this is the sermon in chapter xvii. 19–27, to which we have already referred, which shows a one-sided concern for observance of the Sabbath which almost certainly does not represent the thought of Jeremiah.[3] Miller concedes this and regards the passage as unauthentic and secondary.[4] But this itself places a question mark against his own view, for this sermon is composed in the same style and contains a number of the same characteristic expressions as the prose sermons elsewhere in the book. Miller himself acknowledges this, but argues that the passage betrays its secondary nature by proclaiming Judah's salvation or judgement to be dependent upon observance of one particular law in contradistinction to other sermons (e.g. Jer. vii. 5ff.) which demand in more general terms the moral behaviour of the people.[5] Against this, however, it may be argued that the sermon in Jer. xxxiv. 8ff., regarded by Miller as a genuine sermon of Jeremiah,[6]

---

[1] For a discussion of Bright's views see below pp. 28ff.

[2] W. L. Holladay, 'Prototype and Copies: a new approach to the poetry-prose problem in the Book of Jeremiah', *JBL* 79, 1960, pp. 351–367.

[3] See further below pp. 66 note 1.

[4] J. W. Miller, *op. cit.*, pp. 53f.

[5] *Ibid.*, p. 53.

[6] *Ibid.*, pp. 61f.

announces judgement upon Judah precisely for disobeying one particular law, in this instance the law demanding the septennial release of slaves. We shall see at a later stage in our study that both these sermons centre on a theme which constitutes one of the dominant characteristics of the Jeremianic prose tradition as a whole.[1]

Other objections to Miller's thesis will emerge during the course of our examination of individual prose passages in Jeremiah. In anticipation of these, however, one example may here be mentioned which involves a passage which Miller not only ascribes to Jeremiah but also believes to have been amongst those passages which Baruch is said to have added to the *Urrolle* (cf. Jer. xxxvi. 32).[2] The passage in question is the well-known sermon concerning the two baskets of good and bad figs in Jeremiah xxiv. The vivid imagery of this sermon makes it very probable that it is at least dependent upon a genuine saying of the prophet himself. In its present form, however, it not only pronounces judgement upon Zedekiah and those who remained in Judah after the first deportation in 597 B.C. but upon those 'who dwell in the land of Egypt' (*v.* 8). But this already presupposes the period *after* 586 B.C. and the flight to Egypt of the community set up by the Babylonians under Gedaliah who had subsequently been assassinated (Jer. xli. 1–3; xliii–xliv).[3] In view of this it seems much more plausible to see in the present sermon the development of something which Jeremiah had said and its adaptation to a later situation than that in which he spoke. At a later stage in our study we shall see that such an approach to this sermon offers a much more satisfactory interpretation of it than one solely in terms of Jeremiah's ministry.[4]

One further observation may be made. It is well known that the prose material in the MT of Jeremiah is considerably longer than that in the LXX.[5] This seems to indicate a fluidity in this material which cannot simply be due to the manner in which the Greek translators have dealt with the Hebrew text on which they worked (though this may explain many of the variations) but is rather to be taken as evidence that this prose material represents a tradition which evolved over a period of time and of which the LXX at least in some places very

[1] See below pp. 63ff.

[2] J. W. Miller, *op. cit.*, p. 61.

[3] This seems to me much more likely than the view of Rudolph, who regards this passage as genuine (*Jeremia*[3], pp. 157ff.) and takes 'those who dwell in the land of Egypt' to refer to fugitives who fled there on the approach of Nebuchadnezzar in 597 B.C.

[4] See below pp. 110f.

[5] The differences between MT and LXX, where important, are discussed in our examination of individual passages in Chapter III.

probably represents an earlier stage in its fixation in writing than the textual tradition behind the MT.[1]

In view of these considerations it may be concluded that the correct procedure in dealing with the problem of the origin of the prose sermons in Jeremiah is to accept them as having arisen out of the circumstances in which the oracles and sayings originally delivered by Jeremiah himself were transmitted and subjected to the influence of a distinctive theological tradition.

If this view is accepted then the problem becomes one of deciding between the second and third main views outlined above, viz. between the view that the sermons assumed their present form at the hands of the Deuteronomists and the view that they derive from the circle of the prophet's disciples. We may begin our discussion of this problem with a consideration of the case for the second of these two suggestions.

In his contribution to this problem in an article some years ago Bright argued that whilst there are undoubtedly close and important parallels between the language of these sermons in Jeremiah and that of the Deuteronomistic literature, there are also marked differences and that when the latter are given the weight they deserve in the analysis of the style of these sermons it will emerge that it is a style in its own right dependent only to some extent upon that of the Deuteronomists.[2] In an appendix to his article Bright offered a table of words and expressions characteristic of the prose in Jeremiah to demonstrate his argument.[3] On the basis of this it was argued that the prose sermons in the book represent the work of a circle of Jeremiah's disciples who were strongly influenced by the Deuteronomistic style and theology. As we have already seen, Bright adopts this position in his recently published commentary on Jeremiah.

[1] Cf. A. Weiser, *Introduction to the Old Testament*, p. 218; J. Bright, *Jeremiah*, p. lxxii. This view finds some support from the discovery at Qumran of a Hasmonaean manuscript (4QJer[b]) containing a shorter text of Jeremiah identical with the LXX. We may cite the words of F. M. Cross, 'The Contribution of the Qumran Discoveries to the Study of the Biblical Text', *IEJ* 16, 1966, pp. 81–95: 'Study of the two textual traditions (i.e. MT and LXX) in the light of the new data makes clear that the Proto-Massoretic text was expansionist, and settles an old controversy. . . . The Septuagint faithfully reflects a conservative Hebrew textual family. On the contrary, the Proto-Massoretic and Massoretic family is marked by editorial reworking and conflation, the secondary filling out of names and epithets, expansion from parallel passages, and even glosses from biblical passages outside Jeremiah.' (*Ibid.*, p. 82.)

[2] J. Bright, *JBL* 70, 1951, pp. 15–35. Of 56 expressions which occur frequently in the prose sermons in Jeremiah, according to Bright '23 do not occur in Dtr. at all and of the 33 which do 13 occur not over twice in all that literature, and so are hardly typical of it'. (*Ibid.*, p. 25).

[3] *Ibid.*, pp. 30–35.

Two observations may be made concerning this view. The first concerns the way in which Bright has assessed the Deuteronomistic language in the sermons and the second the manner in which he has interpreted the presence in them of non-Deuteronomistic words and expressions peculiar to the Jeremianic prose tradition alone.

The position here adopted by Bright, viz. that the Deuteronomistic phraseology in the prose in Jeremiah arose out of the influence of the Deuteronomistic tradition on those who composed this material, has been advanced, as we have seen, by a number of scholars.[1] The possibility of such influence can be argued on the general grounds that the Deuteronomists were very clearly active during the period of the prophet's own lifetime and in the years after it when the circle who, on this hypothesis, were responsible for the sermons worked. The weakness in a view such as this is that it is impossible to determine the provenance of these sermons on the basis of their linguistic and stylistic usage alone; it is only when other considerations such as the question of the structure and form as well as the theological interests of the material have been examined that this can properly be achieved. Nevertheless, it may legitimately be asked whether the view advanced by Bright and others does not greatly underestimate the very pronounced nature of the Deuteronomistic language itself in these sermons. When all considerations have been weighed, it remains true that there is an impressive array of parallels between the phraseology of these sermons in Jeremiah and that of the Deuteronomistic literature. Some of these phrases appear to have belonged to a common stock of well-worn clichés employed by the Deuteronomic and Deuteronomistic authors.[2] There are, however, in addition to these a number of expressions of a strikingly individualistic nature which occur only once or twice and never more than three times in the whole of the Deuteronomistic corpus and elsewhere, with minor variations in some instances, only in the prose in Jeremiah.[3] In these instances the balance of probability between their having been due to Deuteronomistic influence rather than the actual

---

[1] See above pp. 23f.

[2] For example, 'to go after other gods', 'to provoke (God) to anger', 'unto this day', or 'as at this day', 'by a mighty hand and an outstretched arm', etc.

[3] These are as follows: 'Their dead bodies will be food for the birds of the air and for the beasts of the earth (and none will frighten them away)' in Jer. vii. 33, xvi. 4, xix. 7, cf. xxxiv. 20, elsewhere only in Deut. xxviii. 26; 'and I will make them a horror to all the kingdoms of the earth' in Jer. xv. 4, xxiv. 9, xxix. 18, xxxiv. 17, elsewhere only in Deut. xxviii. 25; 'in the siege and in the distress with which their enemies shall afflict them' in Jer. xix. 9, elsewhere only in Deut. xxviii. 53, 55, 57; 'his ears will tingle' in Jer. xix. 3, elsewhere in 1 Sam. iii. 11; 2 Kings xxi. 12; 'from the iron furnace' in Jer. xi. 4, elsewhere only in Deut. iv. 20 (cf. 1 Kings viii 51).

involvement of the Deuteronomists themselves in the composition of the passages in which they occur surely lies with the latter. At a later stage in our study some attempt will be made, however, to show that the affinities in language and style between the Jeremianic material and the Deuteronomistic literature are accompanied by other distinctive literary affinities.[1]

Before turning to a consideration of these, however, something must be said concerning the manner in which Bright has assessed the presence in the Jeremianic prose sermons of non-Deuteronomistic vocabulary and phraseology which is peculiar to the book of Jeremiah alone. Is the presence of such words and expressions in the prose sermons really incompatible with the view that they assumed their present form at the hands of the Deuteronomists? That this is not so may be argued on the following grounds. What Bright appears to have failed to recognize is the fact that in arguing for a Deuteronomistic provenance of these sermons it is not implied that they are in every instance *ad hoc* creations of the Deuteronomists. On the contrary, it seems clear that underlying many of them are sayings and oracles which the prophet himself uttered. In other words, the circle responsible for these sermons were working on the basis of genuine Jeremianic material and it is therefore only to be expected that the sermons contain elements of that original material together with a substratum of the original language in which it was couched.

In order to substantiate this, attention may here be drawn to the manner in which traditional material, both prophetic and otherwise, has been handled and presented in the Deuteronomistic literature. It is well known that the Deuteronomists were intensely concerned with prophecy.[2] This is most in evidence in the prophecy-fulfilment schema which forms one of the most striking features of their history work.[3] This schema consists of a series of prophetic predictions each of which is recorded as having been fulfilled. Of particular importance for our present purposes is the manner in which the Deuterononomists presented these prophecies. They are for the most part couched in the familiar style and terminology of the Deuteronomistic literature. In a number of instances they appear to be free compositions by the Deuteronomists based perhaps only on the memory of an original

---

[1] Lists of parallels between the language in the book of Jeremiah and Deuteronomy and the Deuteronomistic literature are presented in S. R. Driver, *Deuteronomy*[3], p. xciii; J. E. Carpenter and G. Harford, *The Composition of the Hexateuch*, London 1902, pp. 147ff.; G. Hölscher, *Die Profeten*, pp. 382ff.

[2] See below pp. 45ff.

[3] Cf. G. von Rad, *Studies in Deuteronomy*, London 1953, pp. 78ff.

saying if indeed there was one (e.g. 1 Kings xi. 30ff.). In other instances elements of traditional oracles have been utilized (e.g. 1 Kings xiv. 10–11, xvi. 4; 2 Kings ix. 8–10). In yet other instances the nucleus or at least snatches of the original oracles can be discerned in the present text (e.g. 2 Sam. vii. 8–16; 2 Kings xxii. 15–20).[1] Of particular significance is the manner in which the Deuteronomists have in one place recorded what appears to be a genuine Isaianic saying (2 Kings xix. 20ff.) together with a saying which they themselves probably composed and attributed to him (2 Kings xx. 16ff.). And apart from prophetic material, there is yet another striking example of the manner in which the Deuteronomic authors handled traditional material in their possession, for it has been shown that in Deuteronomy itself they have worked over old series of apodeictic laws together with other legal material and presented them in characteristic parenetic fashion.[2]

On the basis of these considerations and examples it is entirely plausible to argue that the Deuteronomists have handled and presented the Jeremianic material in a similar manner. This at least would explain the presence in the prose sermons in the book of a range of peculiar words and expressions to which Bright has drawn attention as well as, in some instances, elements of the original sayings or oracles of the prophet. On the question of the peculiar vocabulary of these sermons some consideration may here be given to an important contribution to this problem by W. L. Holladay who has drawn attention to a number of parallels between this vocabulary and the poetic oracles in the book.[3] Holladay's suggestion is that in such cases the poetic use of the phrase is the 'prototype' of the prose usage. In other words, it is suggested that Jeremiah himself coined the phrase which was subsequently taken up and employed by the authors of the prose in the book. In a number of cases the phrase in the prose is exactly the same as in the poetic oracle whilst in others there has been some slight degree of alteration. Examples of the former are afforded by such expressions as 'the gates of Jerusalem' which occurs in prose in xvii. 19, 21, 27 and in poetry in i. 15, xxii. 19;[4] 'deliver from the hand of the oppressor him who has been robbed', occurring in prose in

---

[1] Possibly the nucleus of Nathan's oracle is to be found in 2 Sam. vii. 11b, 16. Cf. L. Rost, *Überlieferung von der Thronnachfolge Davids*, BWANT III: 6, Stuttgart 1926, pp. 47ff. On Huldah's oracle in 2 Kings xxii. 15–20 see E. W. Nicholson, *op. cit.*, pp. 14f.

[2] Cf. G. von Rad, *op. cit.*, pp. 11–24.

[3] W. L. Holladay, *op. cit.*

[4] This phrase occurs elsewhere only in Lam. iv. 12. It occurs in Neh. vii. 3, xiii. 19 but with reference to specific gates.

xxii. 3 and in poetry in xxi. 12;[1] 'according to the fruit of his/your doings', in poetry in xvii. 10, xxi. 14 and prose in xxxii. 19.[2] In some instances there appears to be a combination in the prose of two or more expressions which occur separately in the poetic oracles. An example of this is 'the cities of Judah and the streets of Jerusalem' (prose: vii. 17, 34, xi. 6, (13), xxxiii. 10, xliv. 6, 17, 21) of which 'the streets of Jerusalem' occurs once in poetry in v. 1 and 'the cities of Judah' in iv. 16, ix. 10. These parallels between the prose and poetic oracles in Jeremiah indicate that whoever was responsible for the sermons was in possession of a collection of the prophet's oracles and sayings. The possibility that the circle by whom the sermons received their present form at times employed a striking word or phrase from the poetic oracles in developing the original material must certainly be acknowledged. On the other hand, it is very probable that the prose uses are not in every case 'copies' of the poetic usage elsewhere in the book but were already present in the actual sayings or speeches of the prophet upon which the sermons are in a number of instances based. But whichever view is preferred, the presence of words and expressions in the prose which are peculiar to the book of Jeremiah alone is only evidence that those who were responsible for the sermons were working on the basis of the original Jeremianic tradition and were probably in possession of the original scroll and other sayings of the prophet.[3]

On these grounds, therefore, it is plausible to argue against Bright that the presence of non-Deuteronomistic language and material in these prose sermons in Jeremiah is not incompatible with their having assumed their present form at the hands of the Deuteronomists. On the contrary, it may be taken as further evidence in favour of such a Deuteronomistic origin, for, as we have seen, the manner in which original prophetic material has here been taken up and developed is precisely the way in which similar material has been handled and presented in the Deuteronomistic literature.

This view finds additional support from an examination of the literary structure of a number of these prose sermons in the book of Jeremiah and the various elements which they comprise, for here again striking similarities with speeches and sermons in the Deuteronomistic corpus can be discerned.[4] The importance of ancient near eastern vassal treaties for our understanding of the nature and form of covenant

---

[1] This phrase occurs only in these two passages in the Old Testament.
[2] The three instances here cited are the only occurrences of this phrase.
[3] For this see below ch. 3 *passim*, pp. 128ff.
[4] Cf. E. Janssen, *op. cit.*, pp. 105ff.

texts in the Old Testament is now widely recognized and it has been shown, notably by D. J. McCarthy,[1] that in the Old Testament this form finds clearest expression in the book of Deuteronomy, which follows the pattern thus:[2] (1) an introduction constituting a hortatory prologue with a marked historical content (v–xi); (2) a long section setting forth the covenant stipulations (xii–xxvi); (3) a list of blessings and curses which will ensue faithfulness or unfaithfulness to these stipulations respectively (xxviii). Of particular significance for our present purposes, however, is the manner in which the elements of this structure have provided a basis for individual sermons and speeches in the Deuteronomistic corpus as a whole.[3] Because such homiletical use has been made of the covenant structure there is a certain degree of overlapping in these sermons between the various elements which it comprises. Nevertheless, in many of the passages in question the basic structure of the form is followed, as the following examples indicate:

Chap.	Introduction	Historical retrospect and/or hortatory prologue	Yahweh's command; call to obedience; warning against apostasy or description of apostasy already committed	Blessings and curses
Deut. vi	1	2–3	4–14	15
			16–17	18–19
Deut. vii		1–2a	2b–8	9–11, 12–15
Deut. viii	1	2–10	11–17	18–20
Josh. i	1–2	3–5	6–8a	8b–9
Josh. xxiii	1–2	3–5	6–11	12–16
Jud. ii	10a	10b	11–13	14–15
2 Kings xvii	13aα	(7, 8)	13aβ–17 (7–12)	18–20

It seems clear, as the following table seeks to indicate, that a number of the prose sermons in the book of Jeremiah are based upon this covenant form so frequently employed by the Deuteronomic and Deuteronomistic authors, the major difference being that the historical retrospect occupies a more important place in the Deuteronomic and Deuteronomistic passages cited above. The other elements, however, are clearly present and, apart from the recitation of the historical prologue, the Jeremianic sermons in question follow the basic structure thus:

[1] D. J. McCarthy, *Treaty and Covenant*, Analecta Biblica 21, Rome 1963, pp. 109–130.

[2] It is widely agreed that the book of Deuteronomy in its original form comprised substantially chapters v–xi, xii–xxvi, xxviii of the book in its present form. For this see E. W. Nicholson, *op. cit.*, pp. 18–36.

[3] Cf. D. J. McCarthy, *op. cit.*, pp. 111ff., 131ff., 141ff.

Chap.	Introduction	Yahweh's command; call to obedience	Description of Israel's apostasy and disobedience	Judgement announced
vii	1–2	3–7	8–12	13–15
vii	1–2	3–7	16–19	20
vii	21–22	23	24–28	29[1]
vii	21–22	23	30–31	32–viii 3
xi	1–2	3–7	8–10	11–17
xvii	19–20	21–22	23	24–27[2]
xxv	1–2	3–6	7	8–11[3]
xxxiv	8–12	13–14	15–16	17–22
xxxv	1–12	13	14–16	17 (18–19)

On the basis of our discussion thus far it may be concluded that the prose sermons in the book of Jeremiah exhibit striking similarities to the literary features of the Deuteronomistic literature. There is, as we have noted, an impressive array of parallels in vocabulary and phraseology between the two blocks of material. In addition, the style in which the Jeremianic sermons are composed has undoubtedly its closest parallel in the Deuteronomistic style with its pronounced homiletical nature and its fondness for repetition, all of which is aimed at inculcating the message being delivered into the minds of those to whom they were addressed. Furthermore, we have seen that the manner in which these sermons embody in many instances elements and phraseology of the original prophetic material which they seek to develop is strikingly reminiscent of the way in which the Deuteronomic and Deuteronomistic authors have handled and presented similar material in the Deuteronomistic corpus. Finally, we have also seen that the form and structure of a number of the Jeremianic sermons reveals close similarities to the structure and various elements of specifically Deuteronomistic sermons and speeches.

We now turn to a brief examination of the literary nature of the other prose material in the book of Jeremiah, that is, the so-called biographical narratives. At an earlier stage in our study the possibility was advanced that this material also assumed its present form at the hands of the Deuteronomistic circle. Most commentators have, however, adopted the view that the two different types of prose material in

[1] This verse is possibly an authentic saying of Jeremiah himself.

[2] Instead of the usual announcement of judgement, these verses, following the Deuteronomistic pattern outlined above, set out blessings and curses. See below pp. 66f.

[3] That these verses form an independent unit within this chapter is argued by C. Rietzschel, op. cit., pp. 25ff. Even if various verses within this unit are regarded as secondary, the basic form remains the same (cf. C. Rietzschel, ibid., p. 35).

Jeremiah had different origins and were composed for different purposes. This twofold division in the prose in the book was advocated by B. Duhm at the beginning of this century[1] and some years later more thoroughly worked out by Mowinckel.[2] Mowinckel made a classification of the material in the book into three major sources as follows:[3] (A) a source consisting of prophetic oracles, for the most part in poetic form; (B) a source comprising narratives in prose; (C) prose sermons and speeches in the Deuteronomistic style and forming yet another source in the hands of the final editors of the book. This classification has been adopted by a number of commentators, notably by Rudolph and Bright,[4] though with a number of variations in the material allocated to each source, especially B and C.

Some objections of a general nature have already been raised against the description of the prose narratives in the book (Mowinckel's source B)[5] as a biography of the prophet or, as more precisely defined by some scholars, a passion-narrative (*Leidensgeschichte*) describing his sufferings.[6] It can scarcely be questioned that these narratives do in fact provide us with considerable information concerning the prophetic activity of Jeremiah and the hardship and suffering he often endured in the exercise of his ministry. In this way we know more about him than about any other prophetic figure in the Old Testament. But neither of these classifications offers an adequate or comprehensive description of the material in question, for, as we have seen, this material is on the one hand too incomplete to constitute a biography in the proper sense of the word, whilst on the other hand to describe it as a *Leidensgeschichte* cannot accommodate the fact that many of the narratives it comprises are simply not concerned with the prophet's sufferings. The real weakness in such classifications is that they arise from a preoccupation with the purely historical information provided by the narratives, important though this information is, to the exclusion of any attempt to determine their theological interests and purpose. The view which will be presented in this study is that the primary concern of these narratives is theological rather than purely historical or biographical and that such a theological understanding offers a more comprehensive evaluation of their

[1] B. Duhm, *op. cit.*, pp. xivff.

[2] S. Mowinckel, *Zur Komposition des Buches Jeremia* (1914); for Mowinckel's later view of the problem see his *Prophecy and Tradition* (1946) pp. 62ff.

[3] Mowinckel also classified xxx–xxxi. 28 (the so-called 'Book of Consolation') as a further source D. Cf. *Zur Komposition des Buches Jeremia*, pp. 45ff.

[4] W. Rudolph, *Jeremia*[3], pp. xivff.; J. Bright, *Jeremiah*, pp. lxiiiff.

[5] Mowinckel himself did not refer to these narratives as biographical. See above p. 16 note 2.

[6] See above pp. 16ff.

origin and composition and their relationship one with another. To be more specific, the view here proposed is that the twofold division of the prose in Jeremiah as held by most commentators cannot be sustained and that the so-called biographical material assumed its present form, like the prose sermons and discourses, at the hands of the Deutero-nomistic circle. That is to say, the Jeremianic prose tradition must for the most part be understood as the attempt of the Deuteronomists to present a theological interpretation of the prophetic teaching and ministry of Jeremiah.

That both the sermons and the prose narratives assumed their present form at the hands of the Deuteronomists is evidenced largely by a consideration of their theological nature and interrelationships and with these we shall be concerned at a later stage in our study. Even on the literary level, however, the sharp distinction which has so often been drawn between the two blocks of material is very questionable. There are to be sure differences, but these are more often than not dictated by the obvious difference in subject matter with which each is concerned. Such a difference, however, is already discernible in the Deuteronomistic corpus itself where both homiletical passages and historical narratives stand side by side. Thus, for example, in 2 Kings xvii such a difference can be observed between the specifically historical sections in the chapter describing the events which led to and followed the destruction of the northern state (vv. 1–6, 24–34) and the homi-letical material presenting a theological interpretation of the events thus described (vv. 7–23, 35ff.). In the book of Jeremiah many of the narratives provide nothing more than the historical framework for a prose sermon.[1] How much difference, it may be asked, is there between the occurrence of this in the Jeremianic prose material and in the Deuteronomistic corpus where the same relationship between historical narrative and homiletical material can clearly be observed? In other words, the fact that there is a difference in literary style between the two types of prose material in Jeremiah is in itself no basis on which to advocate a different origin and authorship for each of them.

We can indeed go further and point to an overall marked similarity between the prose narratives in Jeremiah and the Deuteronomistic literature. This is perhaps best demonstrated by the fact that almost

---

[1] This in itself places a question mark against the usual separation of these two types of material and certainly against their allocation to originally separate sources which have been subsequently interwoven (so Mowinckel, Rudolph, Bright). For this reason also a number of scholars now question the distinction commonly drawn between the prose sermons and the narratives. Cf. F. Augustin, 'Baruch und das Buch Jeremia', ZAW 67, 1955, pp. 50f.; W. L. Holladay, op. cit., p. 354.

any of the Jeremianic narratives could well be inserted into the Deuteronomistic history of the last years of Judah in 2 Kings and from a purely literary point of view would not reveal any real difference from the surrounding material.[1] The manner in which the Jeremianic narratives are in almost every instance prefaced with details concerning the particular time in which the events described took place—in a number of instances both year and month are cited—as well as the listing of the various personalities, royal and state officials and otherwise, who participated in these events is entirely typical of the Deuteronomistic method as observable in the books of Kings (cf. Jer. xxi. 1, xxiv. 1, xxv. 1f., xxvi. 1, xxvii. 1, xxviii. 1, xxix. 1f., xxxii. 1f., xxxiv. 1f., 6f., 8ff., xxxvii. 1f., xxxviii. 1, etc.).

From a literary point of view, therefore, there is no compelling reason in favour of the view that the prose sermons in the book of Jeremiah had a different origin and authorship from the prose narratives. On the contrary, there is some evidence to suggest that, like the sermons and discourses, the narratives also owe their composition to the Deuteronomists. Some attempt must now be made to determine whether the literary parallels between the Jeremianic prose material and the Deuteronomistic literature are accompanied by theological affinities between the two blocks of material. It is with a consideration of this question that we concern ourselves in the next chapter.

[1] M. Noth, *Überlieferungsgeschichtliche Studien I* (Halle 1943, Tübingen 1957³), pp. 86f. has suggested that 2 Kings xxv. 1–26 was composed by the Deuteronomist on the basis of Jer. xxxix–xli (which he ascribes to Baruch).

3

THE PROVENANCE OF THE PROSE
TRADITION IN JEREMIAH:
THEOLOGICAL CONSIDERATIONS

In our discussion of the literary nature and characteristics of the prose sermons and discourses in the book of Jeremiah some attempt has been made to reassert and substantiate the view, long held by many Old Testament scholars, that they reflect strongly the influence of the Deuteronomistic circle and assumed their present form at the hands of that circle. The literary evidence suggests, as we have seen, that the Deuteronomists, in keeping with their exegetical method and technique observable in the literature which derives from them, have here subjected traditional prophetic material in their possession to homiletical and theological expansion and development. At the same time, however, we also examined briefly the literary nature of the prose narratives in the book and it has been argued that these also can plausibly be regarded as having derived from the Deuteronomists. In other words, the view here advanced is that the division of the prose in Jeremiah into two separate sources with different origins as held by most commentators cannot be sustained and that both the homiletical material as well as the narratives (the so-called biographical passages) assumed their present form at the hands of one and the same circle, that is, the Deuteronomists.

On the basis of our discussion thus far, therefore, the prose material in Jeremiah is to be regarded as the deposit of a tradition which centres on the prophetic life and preaching of Jeremiah and which in its literary nature and form shows all the signs of having been developed by the Deuteronomists. We must now turn to an investigation of the theological interests and concerns which underly this Jeremianic prose tradition and which it seeks to present. If these also can be identified with the theological purposes and intrests of the Deuteronomists as represented in the corpus of literature which derives from them, then we shall have a plausible solution to the problem of the provenance of the Jeremianic prose tradition.

I

At an earlier stage in our investigation we saw that the narrative in chapter xxxvi concerning the compilation in 605/4 B.C. of a scroll of Jeremiah's early oracles has been regarded by most commentators as having been composed by Baruch as a description of how the written collection of the prophet's oracles and sayings had its beginnings. Against this, however, we contended that any interpretation of this narrative solely or even primarily in terms of biographical writing is inadequate, even though it does provide us with valuable historical information. Rather, it has been argued that its primary purpose is theological, and some suggestions in favour of this have been briefly stated.[1] In what follows some attempt is made to substantiate this view and to show that this very narrative contributes significantly to the particular understanding of the provenance of the Jeremianic prose tradition which is advanced in this study.

From a literary point of view the chapter comprises three distinct but mutually interdependent sections which describe the three main stages in the 'episode of the scroll' here narrated.[2] The first (vv. 1–8) takes the form of an introduction which narrates that in the fourth year of Jehoiakim (605/4 B.C.) Yahweh commanded Jeremiah to compile a scroll containing all the oracles which he had uttered 'against Israel and Judah'[3] since his call in the reign of Josiah until that time. Already in v. 3 the purpose of this is stated:

> Perhaps if the house of Judah hears all the disaster which I plan to bring upon them, they will turn each one of them from his evil way; then I will forgive their wrongdoing and sin.

Thus we learn immediately that not only are the prophet's oracles to be committed to writing but they are also to be proclaimed, or rather, reproclaimed. For both the writing of the scroll and the public reading of it in the Temple Jeremiah commissions the scribe Baruch (vv. 4–6)— for some reason of which we are not informed the prophet himself was banned from the Temple precincts[4]—and once again though in different

---

[1] See above pp. 16f.

[2] For a discussion of this chapter see also E. Nielsen, *Oral Tradition* (1954), pp. 64ff.; M. Kessler, 'Form-Critical Suggestions on Jer. 36', *CBQ* 28, 1966, pp. 389ff.

[3] See above p. 1 note 2.

[4] It has been suggested that the prophet was banned from the Temple because of levitical impurity (so e.g. B. Duhm, *Das Buch Jeremia* (1901), p. 290) or, alternatively, that he was unable to enter the Temple because he was under some sort of cultic 'taboo' at this time (cf. W. Robertson Smith, *The Religion of the Semites*[3], (edit. S. A. Cook), London 1927, p. 456, followed by A. Guillaume, 'The Root אזן in Hebrew', *JTS* 34, 1933, pp. 62–64. Cf. the remarks of K. Marti on עצרה in Isa. i. 13 in his *Das*

words the purpose of these actions is stated (*v. 7*). It is characteristic of Hebrew narrative art, of which this chapter offers an excellent example, that already at the end of this first unit in the narrative it is recorded that Baruch fulfilled the prophet's command to read the scroll in the Temple (*v. 8*). This 'obedience formula'[1] has the effect both of rounding off the introduction and at the same time of anticipating the second section in the narrative which provides a detailed account of the events which ensued the reading of the scroll (*vv. 9–26*).[2]

Here we are told that an opportunity was afforded Baruch for reading the scroll on the occasion of a fast which was proclaimed in the following year, the fifth year of Jehoiakim's reign (*vv. 9–10*). At this point, however, the narrative moves quickly on, for although we are told that the scribe read the contents of the scroll 'in the hearing of all the people' not a word is said of their reaction. Instead, attention is immediately focused on the reaction of one man, Micaiah ben Gemariah ben Shaphan. By this means the narrative acquires a new urgency and the reader's anticipation of the ensuing course of events is greatly heightened. Micaiah goes to the palace and reports what he has heard to a group of state officials to whose ranks he himself evidently belonged (*vv. 11–13*). Having heard Micaiah's account of what had happened, these officials decide to hear the contents of the scroll for themselves and send for Baruch who is brought before them and reads it to them (*vv. 14–15*). At this point the alarm which we already sense in the actions of the *śārîm* comes to a head and we read that when they heard the words of the scroll 'they feared'.[3] Thereupon they decide that the matter must be reported to the king himself. Here again, however, we note the skilful manner in which the king's reactions are anticipated, for before going to report to him the *śārîm* are recorded as having warned Baruch and through him the prophet to go into hiding (*v. 19*). Nielsen's words are apt here: 'Even though one knew nothing of king Jehoiakim before, and though one had no concrete ideas of the contents

---

[1] Cf. M. Kessler, *op. cit.*, p. 393 and footnote 17 on the same page.

[2] Against the suggestion of J. Bright, *Jeremiah*, p. 180 that 8b is perhaps a gloss, or the view of, for example, P. Volz. *op. cit.*, pp. 324, 325 note (e) that *v.* 9 should precede *v.* 5. Duhm was surely correct in seeing 8b as a conscious anticipation of what follows (*op. cit.*, p. 291. Cf. W. Rudolph, *op. cit.*, p. 232; A. Weiser, *op. cit.*, p. 333).

[3] See below p. 43 note 2.

Buch Jesaja, Tübingen 1900, *in. loc.*). Others argue that it was due simply to the opposition of the Temple priesthood and cite such passages as Jer. xx. 1ff., xxvi. 7ff. in support of this (so e.g. C. H. Cornill, *Das Buch Jeremia* (1905), p. 389; P. Volz, *Der Prophet Jeremia* (1922), p. 328; W. Rudolph, *Jeremia*[3] (1968), p. 233; A. Weiser, *Das Buch der Propheten Jeremia* (1955), p. 332; J. Bright, *Jeremiah* (1965), p. 179).

of the roll, we now suspect that the possibility of a conflict is present. And with this suspicion we listen to the climax of the drama'.[1] And the reader's suspicions are further heightened by the notice in the following verse (*v.* 20) that the officials did not actually bring the scroll with them to the king but left it in the room in which they had made their deliberations. Jehoiakim, however, demands to see it and we are told that as it was read to him he cut off three or four columns at a time and, in spite of the protests and intercessions of the officials who had brought it to him,[2] burned the scroll piece by piece (*vv.* 23–25). In addition, the king gave orders for the arrest of both Jeremiah and Baruch, but without success (*v.* 26).

There then follows the third and final section of the narrative. Once more the scene has changed; we have left the court and the king and his *śārīm* and are again in the company of Jeremiah himself. Again we note, however, how skilfully what is now described is linked to what has preceded, for the unit begins with a brief recapitulation of the previous two sections in the narrative:

> Now after the king had burned the scroll and the words which Baruch had written at the dictation of Jeremiah, the word of Yahweh came to Jeremiah saying. . . .
>
> (*v.* 27)

In this final section Jeremiah is commanded by Yahweh to have the oracles rewritten. At the same time a fresh oracle against Jehoiakim is given; in the light of what has happened there can now be no hope, and the purpose for which the scroll was compiled in the first place (cf. *vv.* 3, 7) has been abrogated by the king's actions. Hence, both he and the people whose representative he is are faced with inevitable doom (*vv.* 30–31). Once again the artistic craft of the author is observable, for it is only now in the final verses of the narrative that we are told explicitly and with characteristic terseness what the contents of the scroll were which provoked the dismay of the *śārīm* and the wrath of the king (*v.* 29):

> And concerning Jehoiakim king of Judah, you shall say: 'Thus says Yahweh: "You have burned this scroll saying: 'Why have you written in it that the king of Babylon will surely come and ravage this land, exterminating from it both man and beast?'" '

Finally, and again typical of Hebrew narrative art at its best, this last

---

[1] Cf. E. Nielsen, *op. cit.*, p. 68.

[2] LXX^BN in *v.* 25 read that the officials actually asked the king to burn the scroll. As far as I am aware no commentator has supported this reading. Cf. the comments of Duhm, *op. cit.*, pp. 294f.

D

section is rounded off with a further obedience formula recording the rewriting of the scroll in fulfilment of Yahweh's command (*v.* 32).

On the basis of this brief survey and examination of the narrative and its literary form we may now proceed to an investigation of its dominant motifs and the indications it affords as to its origin and authorship. We may begin by affirming what has in effect become clear from our discussion above, viz. that this narrative cannot seriously be classified as part of a 'biography', for both as a whole and in its component parts it centres not on Jeremiah but on the scroll of his oracles. To be more specific, the narrative has for its primary purpose a description of the rejection of the Word of Yahweh, here enshrined in the scroll of the prophet's oracles, in the actions of the king who is the personification of the nation. Thus, as we have seen, the narrative moves with increasing intensity to its climax in the destruction of the scroll by Jehoiakim, the immediate consequence of which is a fresh oracle of doom against both king and people, an oracle which in itself forms the anticlimax and dénouement to the hope of repentance and forgiveness expressed at the beginning of the narrative (*vv.* 3, 7). It is precisely here in fact that we are provided with what must be considered a strong indication of the circle responsible for this narrative, for there is unquestionably a striking similarity between the manner in which the burden of responsibility for Israel's rejection of the Word of Yahweh and the judgement which this brings is placed firmly upon the shoulders of the king and the way in which in the Deuteronomistic history the judgement which both kingdoms underwent is attributed directly to the failure of the kings to obey the demands of the Law.[1]

The possibility of the Deuteronomistic authorship of Jeremiah xxxvi to which this similarity in motif gives rise can, however, be substantiated by a number of considerations, for there is considerable evidence to suggest that the narrative in question was consciously composed as a parallel to 2 Kings xxii with the primary intention of pointing to the contrast between the reaction of Jehoiakim to the Word of God and that of his revered father Josiah whose humble obedience to the Book of the Law and the reformation which he carried out in response to its demands are there recorded—a contrast which, we may note, is echoed elsewhere in the book of Jeremiah (cf. xxii. 13ff.). Thus even a cursory reading of both narratives reveals a marked degree of parallelism in the broad outline of the events recorded, even though there is much variation in detail. In both of them we read of a scroll, in the one a

[1] For this see especially G. von Rad, *Old Testament Theology*, I, London 1962, pp. 337ff.

scroll of the Law and in the other a scroll of prophetic oracles, which began its public history, so to speak, in the Temple (2 Kings xxii. 8; Jer. xxxvi. 10). In both instances the scroll first comes into the hands of a state official, the Law scroll to Hilkiah the high priest and Shaphan, and Jeremiah's scroll to Micaiah ben Gemariah ben Shaphan (2 Kings xxii. 9ff.; Jer. xxxvi. 10f.). Both narratives record the reaction of the king (2 Kings xxii. 11ff.; Jer. xxxvi. 23ff.) and both give a prominent place to a prophetic oracle which ensued that reaction (2 Kings xxii. 15ff.; Jer. xxxvi. 28ff.). That these formal parallels between the two narratives do not arise simply from the actual pattern of the historical events recorded is evidenced by other internal parallels between them. There appears to be a very deliberate contrast drawn between Josiah's penitence on hearing the Book of the Law and Jehoiakim's attitude and reaction to Jeremiah's scroll:[1]

And when the king heard the words of the Book of the Law, he rent his garments.	But neither the king nor any of his servants who heard all these words was afraid, nor did they rend their garments.
(2 Kings xxii. 11. Cf. 19)	(Jer. xxxvi. 24)

Furthermore, it is certainly not without significance that at least some of those *śārīm* who are described as having reacted reverently towards Jeremiah's scroll and who took steps to protect the prophet and his scribe from Jehoiakim's anger belonged, as their names (Micaiah ben Gemariah ben *Shaphan* and Elnathan ben *Achbor*) indicate, to the circle of officials who participated actively in the events of Josiah's reformation (Jer. xxxvi. 11ff. Cf. 2 Kings xxii. 12). The emphasis here placed on the role of these 'Josian' officials in the events recorded and their pious attitude towards the prophet's words may be regarded as having been intended by the authors of this narrative to sharpen further the contrast which they sought to draw between Jehoiakim and Josiah.[2]

---

[1] Cf. P. Volz, *op. cit.*, p. 329; E. Nielsen, *op. cit.*, p. 69. Cf. M. Kessler, *op. cit.*, p. 396 who observes: 'Ingeniously, the narrator states how instead of "rending" (*qr'*) his *garments* as in mourning (as Josiah did upon hearing the *sēper hattôrâ* read, 2 Kings xxii. 11), Jehoiakim "rent" (*qr'*) the *scroll* from which the oracles were read'.

[2] There has been some controversy over precisely what motivated the actions of the *śārīm* referred to in *vv.* 11ff., 25. Many commentators, including Volz, Duhm, Rudolph and Weiser, maintain that they identified themselves with Jeremiah's message. Such an interpretation is rejected by W. McKane, *Prophets and Wise Men* (1965), pp. 118ff., who argues that these *śārīm* are included among those who together with Jehoiakim are condemned in *v.* 24 and who, therefore, however much they themselves venerated Jeremiah, also rejected his message. Their reason for doing so, it is argued, was that they were unable to accept the prophet's word as valid 'counsel' (עצה) for the conduct of affairs of state. As for the 'fear' which they experienced (*v.* 16), this 'did not flow from piety . . . but from deep misgivings about the consequences on the morale of the

In addition to these specific parallels between Jeremiah xxxvi and 2 Kings xxii, however, there are yet other marked Deuteronomistic features in the Jeremiah narrative. Thus in the introductory section (*vv.* 1–8) words are employed to express the hope that Judah on hearing the scroll would 'turn again' (repent) (שוב) and that their 'supplication' (תחנה) would be accepted by Yahweh who would 'forgive' (סלח) which are highly characteristic of the Deuteronomistic literature.[1] In addition, the prose rendering of Jeremiah's oracle

[1] Note in particular the concentration of all three words in Solomon's prayer in 1 Kings viii where שוב occurs in *vv.* 33, 35, 47, 48, תחנה in *vv.* 28, 30, 38, 45, 49, 52

---

population of what they must have regarded as a deplorable intervention by Jeremiah' (p. 120). Against this, however, it may be argued that there is what appears to be a careful avoidance of the use of the word *śārīm* in *v.* 24, where 'servants' (עבדיו) is used instead (cf. M. Kessler, *op. cit.*, p. 395 note 27) and this suggests that the authors of the narrative are deliberately contrasting two opposing groups involved in the events recorded, on the one hand the 'Josian' officials and on the other the king and his 'servants' (whether these also were *śārīm* or not). This contrast is further evidenced by that drawn between those who wished to destroy the scroll and those who wished to preserve it (*vv.* 20, 23, 25) as also between those who attempted to arrest and (probably) execute the prophet and those who sought to protect him (*vv.* 19, 26). In view of this it seems clear to me that the same contrast is intended by the use of the verb 'to fear' (פחד) in *vv.* 16, 24 to designate those who accepted Yahweh's Word as spoken by the prophet and those who rejected it. It remains possible of course that the sharp contrast here drawn between the 'Josian' officials on the one hand and the king and his 'servants' on the other is due largely to the authors of this narrative, for the reason stated above in the text, and that from a historical point of view it was by no means as pronounced as the narrative suggests. That is to say, McKane may well be correct in asserting that whilst these 'Josian' *śārīm* may have respected the prophet and have been anxious to protect his person, they would have been unable *as statesmen* to accept his words as valid counsel in affairs of state and would thus have sided with the king in rejecting them. But this interpretation must be arrived at on the basis of other considerations; the intention of the authors of Jeremiah xxxvi appears to have been to describe these *śārīm* as having accepted the prophet's words in contradistinction to Jehoiakim who rejected them. However, in view of the sympathy which members of the house of Shaphan are described elsewhere in the book of Jeremiah (xxvi. 24, xxix. 3) as having shown to Jeremiah, it is possible that they had remained loyal to the principles of the Deuteronomic reformation carried out by Josiah and because of this were well disposed towards the prophet. W. Johnstone, 'The Setting of Jeremiah's Prophetic Activity', *TGUOS* xxi, 1965/66, pp. 47–55, believes that the house of Shaphan was closely related to the Deuteronomic circle and argues that Jeremiah's association with members of that house indicates that he himself 'was from the start, and continued to be, a member of the Deuteronomic circle' (*ibid.*, p. 52). Even if such a close relationship between the house of Shaphan and the Deuteronomic circle is conceded, however, it still does not follow that the support of members of that house for Jeremiah indicates that the prophet belonged to the Deuteronomic circle. It need indicate no more than that the house of Shaphan, because of its attachment to the theology of the Deuteronomic circle with its intense interest in prophecy, acknowledged the divine authority of the word which Jeremiah spoke. Any relationship between Jeremiah and the Deuteronomic circle would have to be argued on grounds other than those of his association with members of the house of Shaphan.

against Jehoiakim (*vv.* 29–31), composed in the characteristic style and phraseology of the prose sermons in the book, is typical of the Deuteronomistic method, referred to at an earlier stage in our study, of handling original prophetic material. Finally, one possible Deuteronomistic feature of this oracle generally overlooked by the commentators is the curse here pronounced against Jehoiakim that 'he shall have none to sit upon the throne of David' (*v.* 30) which has all the appearance of being the application of the condition of monarchical succession laid down in the law dealing with kingship in Deuteronomy xvii. 14ff. where it is commanded that the king is to conduct his life according to the demands of the Book of the Law 'so that he may continue long in his kingdom, *he and his sons*, in Israel' (*v.* 20. Cf. 1 Kings ii. 4, viii. 25, ix. 4ff.).

If all this is accepted then it may be concluded that the central concern of this narrative is not with a description of how the book of Jeremiah had its beginnings, much less with a mere recording of an incident, albeit an important one, in the prophet's life, but rather with the manner in which Yahweh's Word as proclaimed by the prophet was rejected by Israel as personified in the king and actualized in his deeds. In this way, as we have suggested, it is strikingly similar to the manner in which the burden of responsibility for the judgement which both kingdoms underwent is attributed in the Deuteronomistic history to the failure of the kings to obey the demands of the Law. In this as in other ways, therefore, the narrative may plausibly be regarded as having been composed by the Deuteronomists. We can, however, go further and show that the authority with which the prophetic word is here endowed and the place of supreme importance which it is conceived of as having had in the life of Israel also finds a ready basis in the theology of the Deuteronomists, specifically in their concept of the role and function of prophecy in Israel.

The basis of the Deuteronomistic interpretation and presentation of the role and function of the prophets is contained in Deuteronomy xviii. 9–22. At the centre of this pericope stands a statement concerning the means whereby Yahweh, after the death of Moses, will continue to reveal his will to Israel:

> I will raise up for them from among their brethren a prophet like you; and I will put my words in his mouth and he will speak to them all that I command him.   (Deut. xviii. 18)

(twice), 54, and סלה in *vv.* 30, 34, 36, 39, 50. For the significance of שוב in the Deuteronomistic theology see H. W. Wolff, 'Das Kerygma des deuteronomistischen Geschichtswerks', *ZAW* 73, 1961, pp. 171–186, now in his *Gesammelte Studien*, München 1964, pp. 308–324.

It has long been recognized by scholars that this can no longer be interpreted, as in traditional Jewish and Christian theology,[1] as referring to some eschatological figure.[2] Rather, it is now widely agreed that it is to be understood historically as referring to a succession of prophets through whom and by whom Yahweh's Word would come to Israel. That is to say, the noun נָבִיא (prophet) in *vv.* 15, 18 has a distributive meaning just as in *vv.* 20, 22 it designates every and any (false) prophet who may arise.[3]

The role which Deuteronomy portrays Moses as having exercised is that of teacher and preacher of the Law and the one through whom it was mediated to Israel at Horeb/Sinai and again, as the authors of Deuteronomy assert, on the plains of Moab. In two passages in the book, including the pericope on prophecy, this mediating role is specifically mentioned (Deut. v. 4–5; xviii. 16). These passages together with Exodus xx. 18–21 (E),[4] with which they are closely parallel, have been regarded by a number of scholars as dependent upon an aetiology of the office of covenant mediator.[5] Whether or not this is so, the unique element in the Deuteronomic description of the role of Moses is that it is associated with prophecy: Moses is the first of a succession of prophets whom Yahweh promises to raise up to proclaim his divine will to Israel:

> Yahweh your God will raise up for you a prophet like me from among your brethren[6]—him you shall heed—in accordance with what you asked of

---

[1] For a discussion of this see H. M. Teeple, *The Mosaic Eschatological Prophet, JBL* monograph series, vol. 10, 1957.

[2] Although in his earlier work 'Die falschen Propheten', *ZAW* 51, 1933, pp. 109ff. von Rad accepted the distributive interpretation of 'prophet' in this text, he has more recently expressed doubts about it, advancing the possibility that the authors may in fact have had an eschatological figure in mind. He suggests that in view of the resemblances, observed by a number of scholars, between the Suffering Servant in Deutero-Isaiah and the figure of Moses in Deuteronomy, it is possible that both the Deuteronomic authors and Deutero-Isaiah stood within a tradition which looked for a prophet 'like Moses' (cf. G. von Rad, *Old Testament Theology*, II, London 1965, pp. 260ff.; *Deuteronomy*, London 1966, pp. 122ff.). But the evidence for the distributive interpretation is very impressive and I remain convinced that it is the more plausible view. Whether Deutero-Isaiah himself had the Deuteronomic 'prophet like Moses' in mind in his concept of the Servant, as von Rad suggests, is a question which I feel unable to attempt to answer.

[3] For a fuller discussion see S. R. Driver, *Deuteronomy*[3] (1902), pp. 227–229.

[4] Cf. W. Beyerlin, *Origins and History of the Oldest Sinaitic Traditions*, Oxford 1965, pp. 12f.

[5] Cf. G. von Rad, *The Problem of the Hexateuch*, London 1966, p. 30; H.-J. Kraus, *Die prophetische Verkündigung des Rechts in Israel*, Zollikon 1957, pp. 12ff.; *idem, Worship in Israel*, Oxford 1966, pp. 106ff.; W. Beyerlin, *op. cit.*, p. 139; M. Newman, *The People of the Covenant*, New York-Nashville 1962, p. 119.

[6] Following the reading of LXX instead of MT 'from your midst, from your brethren.'

Yahweh your God at Horeb on the day of assembly, when you said: 'I will no more hear[1] the voice of Yahweh my God or see again this great fire, lest I die.' And Yahweh said to me: 'What they have said is good. I will raise up for them, from among their brethren, a prophet like you; and I will put my words in his mouth and he will speak to them all that I command him.'

(Deut. xviii. 15–18)

The question arises what the historical reality is which lies behind this 'promise' of prophets like Moses. Some scholars, notably H.-J. Kraus and H. Graf Reventlow,[2] see in it a reference to a succession of prophetic office-bearers who exercised the function of covenant mediator within a cultic context, that is, the festival of the renewal of the covenant.[3] It is very questionable, however, whether the Deutero-nomic authors had any such well-defined office in mind and much more probable that they were concerned with prophecy in general.[4] There is no necessity to see in it anything more than a promise that Yahweh would send prophets as occasion would demand who would make known his divine will and proclaim his Word to Israel. As such, this formu-lation, though presented in Deuteronomy as a promise placed on the lips of Moses right at the beginning of Israel's history, undoubtedly presupposes the activity and preaching of the prophets down through the centuries. Indeed it is entirely possible that those who were responsible for it were the bearers or at least heirs of a tradition in which the prophets were already believed to be the successors of Moses who was at the same time regarded as the first and greatest of the prophets (cf. also Deut. xxxiv. 10).[5] Whether or not this is so, however,

[1] Not as in most English Versions 'Let me not hear. . . .' Cf. S. R. Driver, *op. cit.*, p. 228.

[2] Cf. H.-J. Kraus, *Die prophetische Verkündigung des Rechts in Israel*, pp. 14ff.; *idem*, *Worship in Israel*, pp. 106ff.; H. Graf Reventlow, 'Prophetenamt und Mittleramt', *ZTK* 58, 1961, pp. 269–284.

[3] For a critique of the views of Kraus, Reventlow and others concerning a prophetic 'office' in Israel see especially H. Gross, 'Gab es in Israel ein prophetisches Amt?', *TTZ* 73, 1964, pp. 336–349.

[4] Kraus (*Die prophetische Verkündigung des Rechts in Israel*, p. 15 note 16) argues that the pericope deals with two different types of prophet, on the one hand official, prophetic law-preachers (*Rechtspropheten*) in *vv.* 15–19, and on the other prophets of the 'foretelling' type (*Geschichtspropheten*) in *vv.* 20–22. Such a distinction cannot be sus-tained, however, for the warning against false prophets in *vv.* 20–22 arises immediately from *vv.* 15–19 and attempts to meet the problem of how Israel is to discern those prophets whom Yahweh has 'raised up' from those not sent by him. This clearly indicates that the same type of prophet is intended throughout the pericope.

[5] In my own work on Deuteronomy (*Deuteronomy and Tradition*, Oxford 1967) I argued in favour of the view that Deuteronomy owes its composition to a prophetic circle. My attention has since been drawn to a number of important contributions, which I unfortunately overlooked in preparing my work, which have pointed to wisdom elements in Deuteronomy: cf. especially M. Weinfeld, 'The Dependence of

it is clear that the Deuteronomic authors themselves have here given expression to such a belief. Thus prophecy is seen to have been established at Sinai in the person and function of Moses. In this way it is endowed with the greatest possible authority and we are left in no doubt that the Deuteronomic authors regarded it as the means *par excellence* whereby Yahweh made his will known to Israel. In so far as the authors have here employed the old aetiology of covenant mediator, if such it is, this most probably indicates that they saw the prophets as having been in their preaching the spokesmen of the covenant and as such the successors of Moses through whom it was mediated to Israel at the beginning of her existence as Yahweh's people. In other words, the prophets are here regarded as having exercised the role and functions of covenant mediator charismatically, as men 'called' by Yahweh, and not as specifically designated cultic officials.[1]

The pericope as a whole must be seen as having been intended to emphasize the centrality and supreme importance of prophecy as the channel of divine revelation in Israel. Thus it begins (Deut. xviii. 9–14) with a condemnation of the various mantic and cultic practices whereby the nations seek to ascertain the will of their gods—by diviners, soothsayers, augurers, sorcerers, charmers, mediums, wizards and necromancers. Israel is to have no part in these; they are 'abominable practices' (תוֹעֵבוֹת) to Yahweh:

> For these nations which you are about to dispossess give heed to soothsayers and diviners; but as for you, not so has Yahweh your God granted you.
>
> (Deut. xviii. 14)

[1] H. Gross, *op. cit.*, p. 346; M. Noth, 'Office and Vocation in the Old Testament', *The Laws in the Pentateuch and Other Essays*, London 1966, p. 247.

Deuteronomy upon Wisdom' (Hebrew), in *Yehezkel Kaufmann Jubilee Volume*, ed. M. Haran. Jerusalem 1960; *idem*, 'The Source of the Idea of Reward in Deuteronomy' (Hebrew with an English summary), *Tarbiz* 30, 1960, pp. 8–15; *idem*, 'The Origins of Humanism in Deuteronomy', *JBL* 80, 1961, pp. 241–247; J. Malfroy, 'Sagesse et Loi dans le Deutéronome', *VT* 15, 1965, pp. 49–65. More recently see also M. Weinfeld, 'Deuteronomy: the Present State of the Enquiry', *JBL* 86, 1967, pp. 249–262; J. L. McKenzie, 'Reflections on Wisdom', *JBL* 86, 1967, pp. 1–9. But wisdom ideas and language are so pervasive in the Old Testament literature that it is not really clear what significance should be placed upon their presence in Deuteronomy. I would regard as very questionable any view which would attribute the provenance and composition of Deuteronomy to exclusively wisdom circles. At the same time and in view of the contributions cited above, I now regard it as probable that the Deuteronomic movement contained within its active adherents some who belonged to the circles of the Wise in Israel. In fact we should perhaps understand the Deuteronomic circle to have been a comprehensive movement of reform in which people of varying traditions, prophetic, priestly and wisdom, were actively engaged (cf. J. W. McKay, *Josiah's Reformation: Its Antecedents, Nature and Significance* (Ph.D. dissertation, unpublished), Cambridge 1969, pp. 239–322).

'It is precisely in this strategic context', as Muilenburg so aptly puts it,[1] 'that the impressive words about the prophet appear (*vv.* 15–19). Prophecy stands over against all these alien practices, and the revelation which the prophet receives in Israel is of a radically different order from that of the nations. It is the Word of Yahweh which surpasses all other ways of revealing.' Thus Yahweh himself provides the means of communicating his divine will to Israel by raising up prophets who will proclaim his Word. It is to them and not to the practitioners of mantic techniques that Israel must take heed; disobedience to the words which they will speak in Yahweh's name will incur judgement (*v.* 19):

And anyone who will not listen to my words which he shall speak in my name, I myself will require it of him.

But prophecy itself is not without grave danger for Israel, for not all prophets who speak in Yahweh's name do so at his command; the word which they proclaim is not his Word. Accordingly, in the final section of the pericope (*vv.* 20–22) the Deuteronomic authors warn Israel of this danger, condemning such prophets and providing a means of identifying them. In this way this section is clearly closely related to what precedes (*vv.* 15–19) and arises immediately from it in response to the problem which the promise there involves, viz. how Israel is to discern the prophets whom Yahweh sends from those whom he has not sent, that is, how she is to recognize his Word from the words of the prophets who speak 'presumptuously'.

In view of all this it is wrong to argue, as some scholars do, that the prophetic element in Deuteronomy is merely a form of expression employed to describe Moses as the ideal man of God[2] or an attempt of the authors from an ideological standpoint to fit the phenomenon of prophecy within the schema of offices in general.[3] On the contrary, it seems clear from what we have said above that for the Deuteronomic circle prophecy was of central and supreme importance in the life of Israel.

This is further evidenced by the very considerable importance attached to the prophets in the Deuteronomistic history where the description of their activity and preaching is governed to a marked degree precisely by the principles already formulated in Deuteronomy itself. Thus the authority and power of the prophetic word forms the

---

[1] J. Muilenburg, 'The "Office" of Prophet in Ancient Israel', in *The Bible in Modern Scholarship*, ed. J. P. Hyatt, London 1966, pp. 86f.

[2] So G. von Rad, *Studies in Deuteronomy* (1953), p. 69.

[3] So M. Noth, *op. cit.*, p. 247 note 46.

basis of one of the most characteristic features of the corpus as a whole,
viz. the prophecy-fulfilment schema to which attention has already
been drawn.[1] Furthermore, their function as preachers of the Law is
exemplified in the many instances in which they are described as having
confronted those who transgressed it with its demands, and inveighed
against the constant failure to obey them; one has only to think in this
connection of Samuel's confrontation of Saul (1 Sam. xiii), Nathan's
attack against David concerning the Bathsheba affair (2 Sam. xii),
Ahijah's condemnation of Solomon's apostasy (1 Kings xi. 30ff.) and
his subsequent invective against Jeroboam I (1 Kings xiv. 7ff.), Jehu
ben Hanani's words of judgement against Baasha (1 Kings xvi 1ff.)
and of course the bitter conflict of Elijah and his successor Elisha with
the house of Omri (1 Kings xviii, xxi). Most significant of all, however,
is the summary statement in 2 Kings xvii. 13–14 which presents *in nuce*
the Deuteronomistic interpretation of the role and function of the
prophets and which together with the context to which it belongs
forms what has been described by O. H. Steck as the Deuteronomistic
Prophetenaussage which became the basis for the tradition developed in
later Judaism concerning the sufferings endured by the prophets as
Yahweh's spokesmen at the hands of Israel:[2]

> Yet Yahweh warned Israel and Judah by every prophet and seer:[3] 'Turn
> from your evil ways and keep my commandments and[4] statutes according to
> the whole Law which I commanded your fathers and which I sent to you by
> my servants the prophets.' But they would not listen but were more[5] stubborn
> than their fathers who were not faithful to Yahweh their God.

A number of important factors emerge from this which are of
relevance for our investigation of the provenance of the Jeremianic
prose tradition and with these we shall be concerned in the ensuing
pages. For our present purposes, however, some further observations
may now be made concerning the narrative in Jeremiah xxxvi. It has
already been shown that the central theme of this narrative is Israel's
rejection of the Word of Yahweh as spoken by the prophet Jeremiah
and enshrined in a scroll of his oracles. In this connection it has been
argued that the way in which Israel is here personified in the person of

---

[1] See above p. 30.
[2] O. H. Steck, *Israel und das gewaltsame Geschick der Propheten*, WMANT 23, Neukirchen 1967, pp. 64ff.
[3] For this reading see C. F. Burney, *Notes on the Hebrew Text of the Books of Kings*,
Oxford 1903, p. 332; J. A. Montgomery and H. S. Gehman, *Kings*, ICC Edinburgh,
1951, p. 468.
[4] Inserting 'and' with LXX and other versions.
[5] For this reading see C. F. Burney, *op. cit.*, p. 332.

Jehoiakim and her rejection of Yahweh's Word actualized in his destruction of the scroll is a strong indication that the narrative was composed by the Deuteronomists, since it is strikingly similar to the manner in which they attributed the judgement inflicted upon both kingdoms to the failure of the kings to obey the Law. In the light of our discussion above, however, it seems clear that the theme of Israel's refusal to obey the words of the prophets and the judgement which this brought is itself best understood as Deuteronomistic, for it is evidently based on the belief in the divine authority of the prophetic word which as the Word of Yahweh demands obedience and when disobeyed entails judgement, all of which is, as we have seen, highly characteristic of the Deuteronomistic theology of prophecy (Deut. xviii. 15, 19). Furthermore, there can be little doubt that this theme is closely paralleled in the sermon on the fall of the Northern Kingdom in 2 Kings xvii in the course of which, as the text cited from it above indicates, the judgement which befell Israel and Judah is attributed to their constant failure to obey the prophetic call to repentance. Indeed, closer examination reveals a striking similarity in structure between Jeremiah xxxvi and 2 Kings xvii. 13ff. Each comprises three sections, the first narrating the proclamation of the Word of Yahweh by the prophets, the second recording Israel's rejection of the Word and the third stating the consequence of this in terms of judgement upon Israel:[1]

	Yahweh's Word comes to Israel by the prophets	Israel's rejection of the words of the prophets	Judgement announced
2 Kings xvii	13	14–17	18
Jer. xxxvi	1–8	9–26	27–31

We may now briefly summarize our conclusions concerning Jeremiah xxxvi. We have seen that this narrative cannot seriously be regarded as biographical, for both as a whole and in its individual parts it centres not on Jeremiah himself but on the scroll of his oracles. As such its central theme is Israel's rejection of Yahweh's Word as proclaimed by the prophet and the judgement which this incurred. Attention has been drawn to a number of marked Deuteronomistic features in the narrative and most of all to the strongly Deuteronomistic character of its dominant motif with its emphasis on the authority of the prophetic word and the judgement which failure to obey it brought upon Israel. In this way the narrative is best classified not as part of a biography but

[1] Cf. O. H. Steck, *op. cit.*, p. 67.

as an 'edifying' story which, in common with one of the central themes of the Deuteronomistic history, sought to explain why Judah suffered Yahweh's judgement in the tragic events of 586 B.C.

In the light of our discussion of Jeremiah xxxvi we now turn to a brief examination of another narrative in the book, chapter xxvi. Once again we note that this narrative also is regarded by the majority of commentators as having been composed by Baruch as part of his biography or *Leidensgeschichte* of the prophet.[1] At first sight such a view seems entirely plausible, for the narrative describes in some detail the disturbance which Jeremiah's Temple sermon (already recorded in vii. 1–15 and here briefly summarized in *vv.* 4–6) provoked and the ensuing demand for his execution on the grounds of blasphemy. Once again, however, it may be argued that such an interpretation rests upon a too superficial reading of the chapter and that closer examination reveals that it is not a particular incident in the life of the prophet or the suffering he endured which forms the main theme of this narrative, but that it is dominated by the same motif which we found to be central to the narrative of the scroll in chapter xxxvi. In what follows some attempt is made to show that, as in the case of chapter xxxvi, this narrative is to be classified as an edifying story which owes its composition also to the Deuteronomists.

The narrative begins with a brief recapitulation of the occasion of the famous Temple sermon (*vv.* 1–2), a statement of the purpose for which it was preached (*v.* 3), and a summary of its contents (*vv.* 4–6). We are struck immediately by two very significant parallels between this section and the narrative in chapter xxxvi. Firstly, the purpose for which the sermon is to be preached is couched for the most part in the same terminology in which the purpose of the reading of the scroll is described in xxxvi. 3:

> Perhaps they will listen and will turn each one of them from his evil way; then I will be relieved[2] of my plan to bring disaster upon them because of their evil deeds.
>
> (Jer. xxvi. 3)

Secondly, this introductory section in chapter xxvi displays the same structure which we found to underlie chapter xxxvi and which, as we

---

[1] So B. Duhm, *op. cit.*, pp. 210ff.; C. H. Cornill, *op. cit.*, pp. 298ff.; P. Volz, *op. cit.*, pp. 92ff.; W. Rudolph, *op. cit.*, pp. 168ff.; A. Weiser, *op. cit.*, pp. 238ff.; J. Bright *Jeremiah*, pp. 171f. J. P. Hyatt, *Jeremiah*, (IB 5, 1956), p. 1005 takes it as having been composed by the Deuteronomists on the basis of Baruch's memoirs.

[2] Not 'I will *repent* of the evil . . .' as in most English Versions. The translation of נחמתי given above is based upon the discussion of נחם by D. Winton Thomas, *ExpT* 44, 1933, pp. 191–192.

have seen, is clearly parallel to the Deuteronomistic *Prophetenaussage* in 2 Kings xvii. 13ff.[1] On the basis of these parallels it can plausibly be concluded that this chapter also owes its composition to the Deuteronomists.

In the following section of the narrative it is recorded that as a result of his sermon Jeremiah was set upon by 'the priests and the prophets and all the people'[2] who accused him of blasphemy and demanded his execution (*vv.* 7–9). At this point, however, a number of the royal *śārîm* intervene (*v.* 10) and there follows a law court hearing in which the Temple personnel, the priests and the prophets, formally indict the prophet and demand the death penalty for his alleged crime (*v.* 11), against which Jeremiah makes his defence (*vv.* 12–15) and is finally acquitted by the court (*v.* 16).

If, as Rietzschel has cogently pointed out,[3] the chapter ended here, then it would be entirely plausible to regard it as a straightforward biographical narrative describing the perilous situation in which the prophet was involved because of his provocative words on this occasion. There are, however, two further and closely interrelated sections in the chapter which bring the narrative to its climax and raise the possibility of a quite different understanding of its central motif from the merely biographical interpretation advanced by most commentators.

In the first of these two final sections (*vv.* 17–19) it is narrated that 'certain of the elders of the land'[4] cited as a precedent for Jeremiah's threatening words against Jerusalem those spoken by Micah a century or more before (*v.* 18. Cf. Mic. iii 12), recounting at the same time that far from executing Micah for his woeful oracle 'Hezekiah and all Judah' were moved to repentance and sought to appease Yahweh and forestall the judgement thus pronounced against them (*v.* 19). It is clear that this constitutes a speech on behalf of the defence of Jeremiah (a *Verteidigungsrede*).[5] As such it belongs naturally, from the point of view of court procedure, before the verdict of the court (*Urteilsspruch*)

---

[1] Cf. O. H. Steck, *op. cit.*, p. 72.

[2] W. Rudolph, *op. cit.*, p. 170 deletes 'and all the people' in *v.* 8b as a gloss from *v.* 7a, taking the priests and the prophets alone to have been the accusers (*vv.* 11, 16) and regarding the people as having belonged to those who acquitted the prophet (*vv.* 11,16). Such a view is hypercritical; there is no difficulty in understanding the people referred to in *vv.* 11, 16 as having belonged to the court as distinct from those who formed the mob which assailed the prophet in the Temple. See below note 4.

[3] C. Rietzschel, *Das Problem der Urrolle* (1966), p. 98.

[4] I understand these elders as having belonged, together with the *śārîm*, to the court and as being the 'people' referred to in *vv.* 11, 16. Cf. H. J. Boecker, *Redeformen des Rechtslebens im Alten Testament*, WMANT 14, Neukirchen 1964, p. 95.

[5] Cf. H. J. Boecker, *ibid.*, pp. 95–96.

which, as we have seen, is already recorded in *v.* 16.[1] Its present
position is quite deliberate, however, and arises directly from the
purpose for which we must see the narrative as a whole to have been
composed, viz. to describe not merely an incident in Jeremiah's
prophetic ministry but rather the manner in which the Word of
Yahweh which he proclaimed to Judah was rejected. Thus having
already described (*vv.* 7–11) how Jeremiah's words were rejected by
'the priests and the prophets and all the people' and indeed actually
regarded as blasphemous, the author in this new section (*vv.* 17–19)
now focuses the entire decision for that rejection upon the person of the
king, for although Jehoiakim is not mentioned in these verses the whole
force of the reference to Hezekiah is surely, as Rietzschel again has
argued,[2] to contrast that king's humble and penitent response to the
Word of Yahweh spoken by Micah with Jehoiakim's rejection of the
words of Jeremiah. And this is confirmed by the next and final section
of the narrative (*vv.* 20ff.) which records how another prophet, Uriah,
who 'prophesied against this city and this land in words like all those of
Jeremiah' was hounded down and executed by Jehoiakim. That
Jeremiah did not suffer the same fate was due only to the intervention
of Ahikam ben Shaphan (*v.* 24).[3]

With these two sections, therefore, the narrative reaches its climax
by providing the antithesis to the hope expressed in *v.* 3 that Judah on
hearing Jeremiah's words would repent and be delivered, for it was
ultimately the king, as the personification of the nation and the one
upon whom its well-being depended, who was responsible for the
rejection of the call to repentance proclaimed by the prophets, both
Jeremiah and Uriah, and the judgement which this entailed for Judah.
It is characteristic of the interpretation of this narrative solely or
predominantly in terms of biographical writing that these two final
sections raise difficulties, the first (*vv.* 17–19) because its most obvious
position in a narrative regarded as being concerned primarily with
recounting the trial of Jeremiah on a charge of blasphemy and the
threat to his life which this involved is before rather than after *v.* 16,[4]

---

[1] Cf. H. J. Boecker, *ibid.*, p. 95; C. Rietzschel, *op. cit.*, p. 98.

[2] C. Rietzschel, *op. cit.*, pp. 98–99.

[3] There is no need, with Rietzschel (*op. cit.*, p. 99), to regard *v.* 24 as a secondary
insertion. On the contrary, it belongs closely with what precedes it and asserts that
Jeremiah, in spite of his legal acquittal, was, like Uriah, rejected but saved from the
same fate as his unfortunate contemporary.

[4] W. Rudolph, *op. cit.*, p. 171 recognizes the difficulty and suggests that the verbs in
v. 17 are to be understood as pluperfects, that is: 'And some of the elders of the land
had stood up and *had* addressed the whole assembly of people, saying'. But this is only
to recognize that the section belongs properly before *v.* 16 and emphasizes that the

and the second (*vv.* 20–24) because, again, in a narrative taken as being part of a biography of Jeremiah it is concerned not with his fate but with the martyrdom of the otherwise unknown prophet Uriah.[1] These difficulties do not arise, however, when it is recognized that the narrative is primarily concerned not with an incident in the life of Jeremiah but rather with the record of the rejection of the Word of Yahweh spoken by 'his servants the prophets' and the judgement which this entailed for Judah. It is in fact, as we have suggested, precisely because this is the central theme of the narrative that these two sections have been placed in the position which they occupy.[2]

If all this is accepted then it is clear that chapter xxvi is occupied with the same motif which we found to be central to the narrative of the scroll in chapter xxxvi. This together with the other parallels which we have observed between these two narratives confirms that both have a common provenance and authorship. Finally, the affinities, both linguistic and otherwise, which both of them share with the Deuteronomistic corpus and the fact that they are constructed wholely (xxxvi) or partly (xxvi. 1–6) according to the form of the Deuteronomistic *Prophetenaussage* in 2 Kings xvii. 13ff. leaves us in little doubt as to the identity of the particular circle to which they owe their composition.

But if these two narratives can be said to be based upon the Deuteronomistic *Prophetenaussage*, concerned with its theme and constructed to a more or less marked degree upon its form, there are a number of passages in the Jeremianic prose tradition which are quite simply direct reproductions of it as the following tabulation indicates:[3]

[1] Cf. C. Rietzschel, *op. cit.*, p. 99.

[2] For these reasons I find unacceptable the view of Rudolph, *op. cit.*, pp. 168f. (cf. M. Kessler, 'Jeremiah Chapters 26–45 Reconsidered', *JNES* 27, 1968, p. 83) that the chapter as the first in the complex xxvi–xxxvi seeks to show Jeremiah's legitimation as a true prophet of Yahweh vindicated by Jerusalem's highest court and recognized by the people. The court certainly did recognize that he 'spoke in the name of Yahweh' but very evidently the Jerusalem cultic authorities, the people generally and the king himself did not share the court's verdict (cf. *v.* 24!). The complex, chapters xxvi–xxxvi is, as we shall see, best understood as a history of the Word of Yahweh proclaimed by Jeremiah and rejected by Judah and coming as it does at the beginning of this complex, chapter xxvi sets the tone for the succeeding chapters. See below pp. 105ff.

[3] Cf. O. H. Steck, *op. cit.*, p. 72.

---

purpose of the author was not merely to record an incident in the prophet's career but to make that incident the basis of his own understanding of the events of history and the judgement which his people had suffered.

	Yahweh warns Israel by 'his servants the prophets'	Israel rejects the words of the prophets	Yahweh's judgement upon Israel
2 Kings xvii	13	14–17	18
Jer. vii	25 (27)	26 (27)	32–34
Jer. xxv	4b–6 (3)	4a, 7 (3)	8–11[1]
Jer. xxvi	4–5abα (2)	5bβ (3)	6
Jer. xxix	19b	19a	17–18
Jer. xxxv	15a (13, 14)	15b (14)	17
Jer. xxxvi	1–8	9–26	27–31
Jer. xliv	4	5	6 (2, 11ff.)

We may now briefly summarize our findings thus far. From our examination of Jeremiah xxvi and xxxvi it has emerged that these two narratives are not dominated by a biographical interest as most scholars have argued. This is not to deny that they provide us with valuable information about incidents in the prophet's life; but they were not composed solely or even primarily with this end in view. Rather, as we have seen, they are to be classified as edifying stories centring on the theme of Judah's rejection of the Word of Yahweh spoken by the prophet Jeremiah and the judgement which this rejection entailed. In this respect it has been shown that they are closely related to the Deuteronomistic *Prophetenaussage* in 2 Kings xvii. 13ff. the threefold literary structure of which is adopted (Jer. xxxvi) or actually reproduced (Jer. xxvi. 1–6) by both of them. We have also seen that the authority of the prophetic word which these narratives presuppose is, as with 2 Kings xvii. 13ff., based upon the Deuteronomic theology of the role and function of prophecy (Deut. xviii. 9–22). In addition, further similarities, both literary and linguistic, have been observed between the Jeremianic narratives and the Deuteronomistic corpus. Finally, attention has been briefly drawn to the fact that a number of other passages in the Jeremianic prose tradition are also based upon the theme and reproduce the literary form of the Deuteronomistic *Prophetenaussage* (Jer. vii. 25–34; xxv. 3–11, xxix. 17–19, xxxv. 13–17, xliv. 4–6). In view of all this it can confidently be concluded that these narratives and passages in the book of Jeremiah owe their composition to the Deuteronomists. Furthermore, it is of the utmost significance that the material in question has been found not only in the sermons and discourses (Jer. vii, xxv, xliv) but also in chapters widely assigned to the so-called biography or *Leidensgeschichte* composed by Baruch (Jer. xxvi, xxix, xxxv, xxxvi). This substantiates the view expressed at

---

[1] On this unit in Jeremiah xxv see C. Rietzschel, *op. cit.*, pp. 27–37.

an earlier stage in our study that the division of the prose in Jeremiah into two separate sources with different origins and authors cannot be sustained and that both types of material, the homiletical and the 'biographical', share a common provenance and authorship.

II

The second major theme in the prose in Jeremiah with which we must now concern ourselves is that in which the prophets, including and especially Jeremiah himself, are presented as spokesmen and preachers of the Law. This is a theme which has for the most part been neglected by commentators but which, as the following discussion seeks to show, provides further strong evidence of the Deuteronomistic origin of the prose material in the book of Jeremiah.

The basis of the ensuing investigation has already been set forth in our discussion of the place of prophecy in the Deuteronomistic corpus as contained primarily in the pericope on prophecy in Deuteronomy xviii. 9–22, and 2 Kings xvii. 7–18. Of particular significance for our present purpose is the latter, the Deuteronomistic *Prophetenaussage*, which has already proved to be of decisive importance in our study thus far. The passage in question comprises four elements as follows:[1] (A) a description of Israel's infidelity (*vv.* 7–12); (B) Yahweh sent 'his servants the prophets' to warn Israel (*v.* 13); (C) but Israel rejected the words of the prophets (*vv.* 14–17) and (D) as a result of this incurred judgement (*v.* 18). Of these, the second (B) is of special interest for us now, for there the message addressed by the prophets to Israel is summarized as a call to obedience to the Law, and in the Deuteronomistic corpus this clearly designates the Law of Moses as set forth in Deuteronomy:[2]

> Yet Yahweh warned Israel and Judah by every prophet and seer: 'Turn from your evil ways and keep my commandments and statutes according to the whole Law which I commanded your fathers and which I sent to you by my servants the prophets.'[3]

[1] Cf. O. H. Steck, *op. cit.*, p. 67.

[2] In the light of Noth's work on the Deuteronomistic history corpus in Deuteronomy–2 Kings (*Überlieferungsgeschichtliche Studien I* (1943 and 1957)) it can scarcely be doubted that התורה in this verse is to be understood as referring to Deuteronomy. Accordingly, the view that 'law' is here used in a 'pre-nomistic' sense, that is, as mediated by the prophets without reference to Moses (cf. J. A. Montgomery and H. S. Gehman, *The Book of Kings*, ICC, Edinburgh 1951, *in loc.*) is to be rejected (cf. also 1 Kings ii. 3; 2 Kings xiv. 6, xxiii. 25).

[3] For this translation see above p. 50.

E

Several observations may be made concerning this verse. Firstly, the theme of Israel's disobedience to the Law of Moses forms one of the dominant motifs of the Deuteronomistic history where the catastrophes which befell Israel in the tragic events of 721 B.C. and 586 B.C. are interpreted as divine judgement upon such disobedience. Secondly, this in turn reflects the centrality of the Law in the Deuteronomistic theology, a centrality which has for its background the situation brought about by the exile when, robbed of both Temple and cult, Israel's relationship with and worship of Yahweh became more and more orientated towards observance of the Law by which means also, we may note, the Old Testament canon had its beginnings and began to emerge. Thirdly, the presentation of the prophets as the spokesmen of the Law has at its basis the Deuteronomic pericope on prophecy (Deut. xviii. 9–22) where, as we have seen, the prophets are conceived of as the successors of Moses, the first and greatest of the prophets (cf. Deut. xxxiv. 10) through whom the Law was revealed and given by Yahweh to Israel. As to the reality behind this, we have argued against the view that the Deuteronomic authors had here in mind a succession of prophetic office-bearers who exercised the function of covenant mediator within a cultic context such as the festival of the renewal of the covenant. Rather, it is much more probable that the Deuteronomic circle were here concerned with prophecy in general and regarded (or at least were heirs of a tradition which already regarded) the prophets as having been in their condemnation of Israel's apostasy the representatives of the covenant and in their preaching the spokesmen of the obligations which it imposed upon Israel as formulated in the Law of Moses. Accordingly, just as the prophets are regarded as the successors of Moses so also the words which they addressed to Israel are regarded as complementing and sustaining the 'words of Moses' (cf. Deut. i. 1); just as Yahweh first revealed his will through his 'servant Moses' so he continued to do so through 'his servants the prophets' (Deut. xviii. 15ff.). Hence the authority attached to the words of Moses is also attached to the words of the prophets (Deut. xviii. 19) and just as Israel is enjoined to obey the Law so also is she to obey the will of Yahweh as proclaimed in the words of the prophets. Thus in the Deuteronomistic theology the Law and the Prophets belong together.

It is of the utmost significance that this twofold theme of the prophetic preaching of the Law and Israel's rejection of it is represented to a very pronounced degree in the Jeremianic prose tradition, and it is to a consideration of this that we now turn.

We may begin by examining a number of texts in the prose in

Jeremiah which are closely similar to two passages in the Deuteronomistic corpus and which, like them, present *in nuce* the theme referred
to above which sets forth the interpretation of the catastrophes of
721 B.C. and 586 B.C. in terms of judgement upon Israel's failure to live
in accordance with the requirements of the Law. The relevant passages
in the Deuteronomistic literature are Deuteronomy xxix. 21–27 (EVV
22–28) and I Kings ix. 8–9 (=2 Chron. vii. 21–22):

And the generation to come, your children who will succeed you, and the
foreigner who comes from a distant land, will say, when they see the
afflictions and diseases of that land … all the nations will say (ואמרו
כל־הגוים): 'Why has Yahweh done thus to this land (על־מה עשה יהוה ככה
לארץ הזאת)? What has caused such fierce anger?' Then men will say:
'It is because they forsook the covenant of Yahweh, the God of their fathers
(על אשר עזבו את־ברית יהוה אלהי־אבתם), which he made with them when
he brought them out of the land of Egypt, and went and served other gods
and worshipped them (וילכו ויעבדו אלהים אחרים וישתחוו להם), gods whom
they had not known and whom he had not allotted to them. Therefore Yahweh's anger was kindled against this land, bringing upon it all the
curses written in this book; and Yahweh uprooted them from their land in
anger and rage and great wrath, and cast them into another land, as at this
day.'   (Deut. xxix. 21–27)

And this Temple will become ruins;[1] every one who passes by it (כל עבר
עליו) will be appalled and will hiss. And they will say: 'Why has Yahweh
done thus to this land (על־מה עשה יהוה ככה לארץ הזאת) and this Temple?'
Then men will say: 'It is because they forsook Yahweh (על אשר עזבו
את־יהוה) their God who brought their fathers out of the land of Egypt,
and laid hold on other gods and worshipped them and served them (ויחזקו
באלהים אחרים וישתחו להם ויעבדום). Therefore Yahweh brought all this
disaster upon them.'   (I Kings ix. 8–9)

In addition to their obvious parallels in phraseology, both these
passages display the same structure thus:
(I) the question (Deut. xxix. 21–23; I Kings ix. 8);
(II) the answer and explanation (Deut. xxix. 24–25; I Kings ix. 9a);
(III) a restatement of the circumstance which prompted the question
(Deut. xxix. 26–27; I Kings ix. 9b).

The relevant passages in the book of Jeremiah which we now
compare with these two from the Deuteronomistic literature are as
follows:

And when they say:[2] 'Why has Yahweh our God done all these things to us
(תחת מה עשה יהוה אלהינו לנו את־כל־אלה)?', you shall say to them: 'As

[1] For this reading see C. F. Burney, *Notes on the Hebrew Text of the Books of Kings*,
Oxford 1903, pp. 132f. Cf. J. A. Montgomery and H. S. Gehman, *op. cit.*, p. 213.
[2] The context requires 'they say' instead of the MT 'you say'.

you have forsaken me (כאשר עזבתם אותי) and served foreign gods (ותעבדו
אלהי נכר) in your own land, so shall you serve strangers in a land that is not
yours.'

(Jer. v. 19)

Why (על ־מה) is the land ruined and laid waste like a desert where no one
travels? And Yahweh said: 'Because they have forsaken my Law (על ־עזבם
את ־תורתי) which I set before them, and have not obeyed my voice, or
walked in accord with it, but have stubbornly followed their own evil heart
and have gone after the Baalim (וילכו אחרי הבעלים) of which their fathers
taught them.' Therefore, thus says Yahweh of Sabaoth, the God of Israel:
'Behold, I will feed this people with wormwood and give them poisonous
water to drink; and I will scatter them among the nations whom neither
they nor their fathers have known; and I will send the sword after them
until I have exterminated them.'

(Jer. ix. 11b–15. EVV 12b–16)

And when you tell this people all these things, and they say to you: 'Why
(על ־מה) has Yahweh pronounced all this great disaster against us? What
is our iniquity? What is our sin that we have committed against Yahweh our
God?', then you shall say to them: 'Because your fathers have forsaken me
(על אשר ־עזבו אבותיכם אותי), says Yahweh, and have gone after other gods
and have served and worshipped them (וילכו אחרי אלהים אחרים ויעבדום
וישתחוו להם), but have forsaken me (ואותי עזבו) and have not kept my
Law (ואת ־תורתי לא שמרו), and because you have done worse than your
fathers, for every one of you stubbornly follows his own evil heart, refusing
to obey me. Therefore I will hurl you out of this land into a land which
neither you nor your fathers have known, and there you shall serve other
gods day and night, for I will show you no favour.'

(Jer. xvi. 10–13)

And many nations will pass by (ועברו) this city, and every one will say to
the other: 'Why has Yahweh done thus to this great city (על ־מה עשה יהוה
ככה לעיר הגדולה הזאת)?' Then men will say: 'It is because they forsook the
covenant of Yahweh their God (על אשר עזבו את ־ברית יהוה אלהיהם) and
worshipped other gods and served them (וישתחוו לאלהים אחרים ויעבדום).

(Jer. xxii. 8–9)

From the point of view of phraseology, Jeremiah xxii. 8–9 clearly
bears a close resemblance to Deuteronomy xxix. 21ff. Of the remaining
three passages, xvi. 10ff. is also striking, whilst v. 19 and ix. 11b–15,
though displaying fewer linguistic parallels with the two Deuteronomistic texts, from a stylistic point of view are nonetheless Deuteronomistic. Equally significant as the parallels in terminology, however,
is the fact that the Jeremianic texts reproduce the same literary form
which, as we noted above, underlies the Deuteronomistic texts:

	I	II	III
Deut. xxix	21–23	24–25	26–27
1 Kings ix	8	9a	9b
Jer. v	19a	19bα	19bβ
Jer. ix	11b	12–13	14–15
Jer. xvi	10	11–12	13
Jer. xxii	8	9	—

A number of scholars have drawn attention to a remarkable parallel between this form in the Old Testament and a passage in the Annals of Asshur-ban-apal concerning a certain king Uate who had evidently broken his treaty-oath of allegiance to the Assyrian monarch:[1]

> All the curses mentioned in the treaty tablet fell upon him, and the people of the Arabu asked each other: 'Why did this evil matter happen to the land of the Arabu?' and (replying) they said: 'Because we did not guard the great treaty made with Asshur and sinned against the goodness of Asshur-ban-apal, the beloved king of Ellil.'

In view of this parallel it has been argued by some that the Biblical authors were familiar with the Assyrian text in question.[2] There is to be sure some evidence that the Deuteronomists were in possession of Assyrian texts, especially treaty documents,[3] but the argument in this particular instance is strained. From the point of view of content there is obviously nothing so extraordinary about Deuteronomy xxix. 21ff. and its parallel texts in the Old Testament which requires explanation on the basis of any external source, whether Assyrian or otherwise. On the contrary, it has a perfectly natural background in the tragic events of 586 B.C. in Judah. Clearly it is the form of the Biblical passages rather than their content which constitutes the real parallel to the Assyrian document. In this also, however, there is no need to regard the Biblical authors as having been dependent upon the Assyrian text since the form is well attested in the Old Testament itself. It will be recalled that the passages in question comprise for the most part three elements: (I) the question; (II) the answer and explanation; (III) a restatement of the circumstance or factor which prompted the question. This same threefold structure is found elsewhere in the Old Testament. Thus, for example, Deuteronomy vi. 20ff. follows the pattern thus:

---

[1] See ANET², pp. 299f.

[2] Cf. R. Frankena, 'The Vassal-Treaties of Esarhaddon and the Dating of Deuteronomy', *OTS* 14, 1965, pp. 153f.; W. L. Moran, 'The Ancient Near Eastern Background of the Love of God in Deuteronomy', *CBQ* 25, 1963, pp. 83f.

[3] Cf. especially M. Weinfeld, 'Traces of Assyrian Treaty Formulae in Deuteronomy', *Biblica* 46, 1965, pp. 417–427; R. Frankena, *op. cit.*, pp. 140ff.

(I) the question:

> When your son asks you in time to come: 'What is the meaning of the testimonies and the statutes and the ordinances which Yahweh our God has commanded you?', then you shall say to your son:

(II) answer and explanation:

> 'We were Pharaoh's slaves in Egypt; and Yahweh brought us out of Egypt with a mighty hand; and Yahweh wrought signs and wonders, great and grievous, against Egypt, against Pharaoh and all his household, before our eyes; and he brought us out from there, that he might bring us in and give us the land which he swore to our fathers.'

(III) restatement of the factor which prompted the question:

> 'Therefore Yahweh commanded us to do all these statutes, to fear Yahweh our God, for our good always, that he might preserve us alive, as at this day. And it will be righteousness for us, if we are careful to do all this commandment before Yahweh our God, as he has commanded us.'

A further example is to be found in Exodus xiii. 14–15 concerning the sacrifice of the first-born:

(I) the question:

> And when your son asks you in time to come: 'What does this mean?', you shall say to him:

(II) answer and explanation:

> 'By strength of hand Yahweh brought us out of Egypt, from the house of bondage. For when Pharaoh stubbornly refused to let us go, Yahweh slew all the first-born in the land of Egypt, both the first-born of man and the first-born of cattle.'

(III) restatement of the factor which prompted the question:

> 'Therefore I sacrifice to Yahweh all the males that first open the womb; but all the first-born of my sons I redeem.'

These together with other examples of the form may be tabulated as follows:[1]

	I	II	III
Exod. xii	26	27	—
Exod. xiii[2]	14a	14b–15a	15b
Deut. vi	20	21–23	24–25
Josh. iv	6	7a	7b
Josh. iv	21	22–23	(24)

[1] It may be noted that the passages in Exodus here cited are usually assigned to Deuteronomic or Deuteronomistic editing (cf. M. Noth, *Exodus*, London 1962, p. 93).
[2] Cf. also Exod. xiii. 8.

In view of this the argument that Deuteronomy xxix. 23ff. and its parallel texts in the Old Testament are dependent upon an Assyrian prototype must be rejected. On the contrary, it seems clear that the Deuteronomists have here employed a form with which they were already familiar within their own tradition. The similarity between the Biblical texts and the Assyrian text is best explained as having arisen from their use of a common form, a form which may be classified as aetiological and which originated within the context of instruction of a catechetical nature.[1]

In the light of all this we can now draw some conclusions about the four passages in the Jeremianic prose tradition with which we are here primarily concerned (Jer. v. 19, ix. 11b–15, xvi. 10–13, xxii. 8–9). We have observed that in both phraseology and form they are Deuteronomistic through and through. Furthermore, like their two parallels in Deuteronomy xxix. 21ff. and 1 Kings ix. 8–9, they present *in nuce* that interpretation of the events of 586 B.C. in terms of Yahweh's judgement upon Israel's failure to obey the Law which forms one of the central themes of the Deuteronomistic corpus as a whole. Finally, the ascription of such words concerning obedience or disobedience to the Law to Jeremiah is entirely in keeping with the characteristically Deuteronomistic standpoint according to which, as we have again seen, the prophets were conceived of as the spokesmen and representatives of the Law (cf. 2 Kings xvii. 13). Accordingly, it is plausible to conclude that the passages in question owe their composition to the Deuteronomists.

Yet another passage in the Jeremianic prose tradition which may be examined in this connection is chapter xxxiv. 8–22. Here also, as the ensuing considerations seek to show, we have a prose sermon which shows all the signs of having been composed by the Deuteronomists. Once again, this passage, like those considered above, may be examined from the point of view of language, form and content.

As to the first of these, the style of the sermon is entirely typical of the prose in Jeremiah with its characteristic repetitious nature and favourite words and expressions, many of which are familiarly Deuteronomistic. Of these, two are particularly striking, 'I will make you a horror to all the kingdoms of the earth' (*v.* 17) and 'their dead bodies shall be food for the birds of the air and the beasts of the earth' (*v.* 20), both of which are curse formulae which occur elsewhere in the Jeremianic prose (xv. 4, xxiv. 9, xxix. 18 and vii. 33, xvi. 4, xix. 7) but

---

[1] For a discussion see J. A. Soggin, 'Kultätiologische Sagen und Katechese im Hexateuch', *VT* 10, 1960, pp. 341–347; B. O. Long, *The Problem of Etiological Narrative in the Old Testament*, BZAW 108, Berlin 1968, pp. 78ff.

otherwise only in Deuteronomy xxviii. 25 and 26 respectively. For these reasons Mowinckel, followed by Rudolph and others, has attributed this passage to the Deuteronomists.

In addition to its characteristic Deuteronomistic phraseology, however, this sermon follows the same form as that which we have already seen to underly sermons and passages in the Deuteronomistic literature and elsewhere in the prose tradition in Jeremiah. Thus, after an introduction in *vv.* 8–12, the sermon exhibits the threefold pattern with which we are already familiar: (A) proclamation of Yahweh's law (*vv.* 13–14); (B) Israel's disobedience (*vv.* 15–16); (C) Yahweh's judgement upon Israel (*vv.* 17–22).

In both language and form, therefore, the sermon in xxxiv. 8–22 shows impressive evidence of having taken shape at the hands of the Deuteronomists. And when we turn to a consideration of its purpose this conclusion is further strengthened, for, like the texts referred to above, it is concerned with the theme of Yahweh's judgement upon Israel, infidelity to the Law, except that in this instance a specific example of such infidelity is described, viz. a breach of the law of the septennial release of slaves. The law requiring the release of slaves who have served six years is formulated in both Exodus xxi. 2–6 and Deuteronomy xv. 12–18. It is clear, however, that the sermon in Jeremiah xxxiv is dependent upon the latter, for the release here, as there, is extended to female slaves (Jer. xxxiv. 9; Deut. xv. 12) whilst the Exodus text mentions only the male slaves.

We may conclude therefore that Jeremiah xxxiv. 8–22 owes its composition to the Deuteronomists. This does not mean, however, that its historicity is to be questioned.[1] Nor need it be doubted that Jeremiah himself would have condemned such an act of treachery on the part of those responsible. There is little point, however, in attempting to isolate the prophet's *ipsissima verba* from the text, for, as we have seen, the sermon owes its present form to the Deuteronomists who, working at a later time, have here developed something which Jeremiah had said on the occasion described, with the twofold purpose of presenting to those to whom they addressed themselves an explanation of why Israel had suffered Yahweh's judgement and at the same time pressing home upon their consciences that they themselves must live according

---

[1] The Deuteronomic law concerns the release of slaves who have served six years. Since the release implemented by Zedekiah appears to have been a general release it is difficult to know whether it was prompted by a desire to conform to the law in Deut. xv or by some other factor (cf. J. Bright, *Jeremiah*, p. 223). In its present form, however, the sermon is clearly thinking in terms of the requirement of the law in Deut. xv 12ff. and the breach of it by Zedekiah and the nobles on the occasion described.

to the requirements of the Law which their fathers had so failed to observe and obey. At a later stage in our study we shall be concerned with the background of this Jeremianic prose tradition and it will be argued there that it was in Babylon during the exilic period that this tradition emerged and developed.[1] In anticipation of this, however, one further observation may here be made concerning the sermon in chapter xxxiv. 8–22. In the law in Deuteronomy xv. 12ff. concerning the release of Hebrew slaves one of the motives given to exhort obedience to this law is that Israel herself had once been slaves in Egypt (Deut. xv. 15. Cf. Deut. v. 15, x. 19, xxiv. 18, 22). If we are correct in regarding the Jeremianic prose material as having been composed in Babylon during the exilic period, then it is possible that the sermon in Jeremiah xxxiv. 8ff. had an ironic and poignant element in it, for those who had so failed to accord their slaves the humanitarian rights required by the Law now found themselves once again in bondage in an alien land; they were now themselves back in 'Egypt'!

Yet another passage in the prose in Jeremiah which falls for consideration in this connection is the sermon on the observance of the Sabbath in Jeremiah xvii. 19–27 to which we have referred at an earlier stage in our study.[2] Here also the style and language of this sermon are typical of the Jeremianic prose and display the usual affinities with the Deuteronomistic literature. And once again, the form of the sermon, though differing somewhat from that in xxxiv. 8–22 examined above, is nevertheless still based, perhaps even more directly, upon the Deuteronomistic homiletical form now familiar to us. It will be recalled that a number of sermons in the Deuteronomistic corpus are constructed upon the covenant form with the following elements: (1) a hortatory prologue and/or historical retrospect; (2) a proclamation of and/or call for obedience to Yahweh's Law; (3) promises of blessings and threats of curses conditional upon Israel's obedience or disobedience to the Law. We have noted that this covenant form is a favourite with the Deuteronomistic circle, providing not only the form upon which the central corpus of Deuteronomy itself is constructed,[3] but also 'the basis for oratorical efforts at inculcating obedience to the basic demands of Yahwistic religion'.[4] As we have observed, such passages as Deuteronomy vi. 1–19, vii. 1–15, viii. 1–20, Joshua xxiii, etc. follow this form whilst others, for example 2 Kings xvii. 7–20, are clearly based upon it. And similarly, the sermon on the Sabbath in Jeremiah xvii. 19–27 with which we are particularly

[1] See below pp. 116ff.   [2] See above pp. 13, 26.
[3] See above pp. 32–33.   [4] Cf. D. J. McCarthy, op. cit., p. 170.

concerned here displays the same structure omitting only the first element (1), the prologue. Apart from this, however, we find the form thus: (2) the proclamation of the Law (in this instance specifically the law of the Sabbath) in *vv*. 20ff. and (3) promises of blessing for obedience (*vv*. 24–26) and a threat of judgement in the event of disobedience (*v*. 27). Accordingly, like the sermon in xxxiv. 8–22 examined briefly above, this sermon also in both style and language as well as in structure and in its call for obedience to the Law may plausibly be regarded as having assumed its present form at the hands of the Deuteronomists.

How then are we to understand this sermon? Whilst it is possible, as a number of commentators have argued,[1] that Jeremiah himself said something on the observance of the Sabbath, any exegesis of this passage solely or even primarily in terms of his prophetic ministry and teaching is inadequate. Nor can it be understood, as Bright suggests, as merely a mistaken interpretation of something he had said. Rather, it must be understood as the work of those who developed the Jeremianic tradition. As such it clearly presupposes a situation in which observance of the Sabbath had come to the forefront of religious life and practice. This means that for those to whom it was addressed it constituted not primarily a literary record of the teaching of Jeremiah for his contemporaries but an urgent exhortation to them in their own situation. What that situation was we shall discuss at a later stage in our investigation.[2] By way of anticipation, however, we may observe that since it was very probably in the exilic period that the observance of the Sabbath acquired or began to acquire the significance and importance which it had in post-exilic Judaism and which this sermon presupposes (cf. Exod. xxxi. 12–17 (P); Isa. lvi, lviii. 13f.; Ezek. xx, xxii. 8, xxiii. 38, xliv, 24, xlvi).[3] it is probable that it was at this time that this sermon took shape and assumed its present form.[4]

[1] Cf. for example W. Rudolph, *op. cit.*, p. 120; A. Weiser, *Jeremia*, p. 155; J. Bright, *Jeremiah*, p. 120. That Jeremiah may have said something on observance of the Sabbath need not be questioned, for it is important to remember that such observance was already strictly enjoined in the pre-exilic period (cf. Exod. xx. 8–10, xxiii. 12, xxxiv. 21; Deut. v. 12–14. Cf. also Amos viii. 5). At the same time there is much evidence to suggest that during the exilic period and subsequently the Sabbath occupied a place of increasing importance in Judaism (see below pp. 124f.) and the strong emphasis placed upon it in Jeremiah xvii. 19ff., where Israel's continued existence as Yahweh's people is actually made dependent upon observance of the Sabbath, is best understood against this later background rather than that of an earlier period.

[2] See below pp. 124f.

[3] On the Sabbath in the exilic and post-exilic period see H.-J. Kraus, *Worship in Israel* (1966), pp. 87f.

[4] See also below pp. 124f.

We now turn to a consideration of the sermon in chapter xi calling for obedience to 'the words of this covenant', a passage which perhaps more than any other has been at the centre of the discussion of the origin of the Jeremianic prose tradition. Some have regarded it as an authentic sermon preached by Jeremiah actively supporting the reformation carried out by Josiah on the basis of Deuteronomy in 621 B.C.[1] Others have taken it as nothing more than the attempt of the Deuteronomistic circle to present the great prophet as having identified himself with the aims and principles of Deuteronomy.[2] Some scholars have adopted the view that the sermon whilst not preserving the prophet's *ipsissima verba* is nevertheless based upon a sound tradition according to which he called for obedience to the demands of the Sinai covenant, not the Deuteronomic Law.[3] Since, however, the covenant described and formulated in Deuteronomy is nothing less than a ratification of the Sinai covenant, others, notably Bright,[4] reject such a view and whilst agreeing that the sermon is a later composition believe that it is based upon a tradition of Jeremiah's support for the Deuteronomic reformation. In the light of our discussion above this last point of view is the most plausible. Once more, however, it must be stressed that the sermon did not originate as an attempt merely to preserve a literary record of the tradition of what Jeremiah had said but as an exhortation to obedience to the Law by the traditionists responsible for it to the community in which they lived and ministered. To put it another way, the sermon represents the actualization for a later generation of the Word of Yahweh spoken by the prophet Jeremiah to an earlier generation.

That this sermon owes its composition to the Deuteronomists, as many have suggested, cannot seriously be questioned. The passage as a whole is one of the most Deuteronomistic in style and language in the entire book and characteristic Deuteronomistic words and expressions simply abound, some of the more striking being: 'the words of this covenant' (*vv.* 2, 3, 6, 8. Cf. Deut. xxviii. 69 (EVV xxix. 1), xxix. 8 (EVV *v.* 9), 2 Kings xxiii. 3);[5] the formula 'cursed be' with its response 'Amen'! (*vv.* 3, 5) is found in Deuteronomy xxvii. 15ff., whilst from its

[1] See most recently, J. W. Miller, *Das Verhältnis Jeremias und Hesekiels sprachlich und theologisch untersucht* (1955), pp. 42ff.

[2] Cf. J. P. Hyatt, Jeremiah, IB 5 (1956), pp. 905f.

[3] Cf. W. Rudolph, *op. cit.*, pp. 77f.; A. Weiser, *Jeremia*, pp. 101f.

[4] Cf. J. Bright, *Jeremiah*, p. 89.

[5] We may also compare this with 'the words of this law' in Deut. xvii. 19, xxvii. 3, 8, 26, xxviii. 58, xxix. 28, xxxi. 24, xxxii. 46. On this expression see B. Lindars, 'Torah in Deuteronomy', in *Words and Meanings*, Essays presented to D. Winton Thomas, ed. P. R. Ackroyd and B. Lindars, Cambridge 1968, pp. 128f.

content 'cursed be the man who does not heed the words of this covenant' closely resembles Deuteronomy xxvii. 26; 'from the iron furnace' (*v.* 4. Cf. Deut. iv. 20; 1 Kings viii. 51); 'a land flowing with milk and honey' (*v.* 5. Cf. also xxxii. 22) whilst occurring elsewhere in the Old Testament (cf. Exod. iii. 8, 17, xiii. 5, xxxiii. 3; Lev. xx. 24; Num. xiii. 27, xiv. 8, xvi. 13, 14; Ezek. xx. 6, 15) is frequent in the Deuteronomistic literature (Deut. vi. 3, xi. 9, xxvi. 9, 15, xxvii. 3, xxxi. 20; Josh. v. 6); 'to go after other gods' (*v.* 10 and also vii. 6, 9, xiii. 10, xvi. 11, xxv. 6, xxxv. 15) is very much a characteristic Deuteronomistic expression (Deut. vi. 14, viii. 19, xi. 28, xiii. 2, xxviii. 14, etc., etc.), though also found elsewhere.

In addition to this, however, once again this sermon displays the same threefold structure observed elsewhere:[1] (A) proclamation of Yahweh's Law (*vv.* 3–7); (B) Israel's disobedience (*vv.* 8–10); (C) Yahweh's judgement upon Israel (*vv.* 11–17). Finally, in its presentation of the prophet as the spokesman of the Law and the central place which the Law thus occupies in it, we have still further impressive evidence that this sermon took shape at the hands of the Deuteronomists and emerged not as the result of a purely scribal and literary activity but rather within the context of a teaching ministry which addressed itself to the needs of a community to which it presented at one and the same time an explanation of why Judah suffered Yahweh's judgement in 586 B.C. and a solemn exhortation to obedience to the Law.

We now turn to yet another passage in the Jeremianic prose tradition which may be classified under the theme of the prophetic proclamation of the Law, vii–viii. 3. Although in its present form this passage purports to be as a whole Jeremiah's famous Temple sermon for which, as chapter xxvi records,[2] he was tried for heresy and blasphemy, it is widely recognized that only *vv.* 1–15 can properly be related to that sermon,[3] the remaining material comprising a number of separate units which have been grouped together with it in the course of transmission. Looked at from this point of view, the section comprises the following units: (1) a sermon (*vv.* 1–15) condemning as false the belief that the mere presence of the Temple in Jerusalem was a guarantee against Yahweh's judgement upon Judah's sins; (2) a saying inveighing

---

[1] The LXX omits all of *vv.* 7–8 with the exception of the last two words 'but they did not do (them)'. Even if the LXX text is accepted the structure of the sermon remains the same.

[2] See above pp. 52ff.

[3] Cf. for example, W. Rudolph, *op. cit.*, pp. 51f.; J. Bright, *Jeremiah*, p. 58.

against the practice of the cult of the queen of heaven and other gods (*vv.* 16–20); (3) an oracle condemning the offering of sacrifices as no substitute for obedience to the covenant law (*vv.* 21–29); (4) a further saying condemning various pagan practices including the Molech cult (*vv.* 30–31), followed by an oracle of woe (*vv.* 32–34) which has been supplemented by the addition of viii. 1–3.

All four units have it in common that they each, with the partial exception of the third in which verse 29 is poetry, are composed in the style and language typical of the Jeremianic prose with recognizably Deuteronomistic words and expressions throughout. At the same time, and perhaps more than in any other prose section in the book, snatches of what were probably the original sayings of the prophet can be isolated here and there, although it is very questionable whether any of these original sayings can be reconstructed in anything approaching its entirety.[1] Nevertheless, such expressions as the threefold cry of 'the Temple of Yahweh' (*v.* 4) or the striking simile likening the Temple to a 'robbers' hideout' (*v.* 11) as well as the decalogue-type list of offences (*v.* 9. Cf. Hos. iv. 2) and the fragment of a poetic oracle in *v.* 29 strike the eye as belonging to the original sayings upon which the present text has been based and developed by the traditionists.

As with other prose sermons which we have examined, here we are dealing with material which owes its present form to the Deuteronomists. This is already evident from the familiar style and phraseology of the text and from the actual form upon which the separate units have been constructed and combined. Thus the first, the Temple sermon in *vv.* 1–15, follows the pattern (A) proclamation of Yahweh's Word and Law (*vv.* 1–7); (B) description of Judah's apostasy and rejection of the Word (*vv.* 8–12); (C) announcement of judgement (*vv.* 13–15). To this has been added the second unit (*vv.* 16–20) which comprises (B) a further description of Judah's apostasy (*vv.* 16–19) and (C) a further announcement of judgement (*v.* 20). The third section contains (A) proclamation of Yahweh's Word and Law (*vv.* 21–23); (B) description of apostasy (*vv.* 24–28); (C) announcement of judgement (*v.* 29), which has been supplemented by the fourth and final unit (B) further description of apostasy (*vv.* 30–31) and (C) further announcement of judgement (*vv.* 32–34, viii. 1–3).

[1] G. Fohrer, 'Jeremias Tempelwort (Jer. 7 1–15)', *ThZ* 5, 1949, pp. 401–417 reprinted in his *Studien zur Alttestamentlichen Prophetie*, BZAW 99, Berlin 1967, pp. 190–203 attempts to reconstruct the Temple sermon in vii. 1–15 as an original composition in *Kurzvers*. But his arguments necessitate excising, in most instances arbitrarily, many phrases from the sermon in its present form. For a criticism see W. Rudolph, *op. cit.*, p. 51 note 2.

It has sometimes been argued that the Deuteronomists could not have been responsible for such a discourse in which both the Temple and the offering of sacrifice come in for such sharp criticism.[1] This must be rejected, however, for the following reasons. In the first place, everything suggests that for the Deuteronomists it was above all obedience to the requirements of the Law which would guarantee Israel Yahweh's blessing; the parenesis which constitutes the most characteristic feature of Deuteronomy itself as well as the main theme of the Deuteronomistic history evidence this. Neither the Temple nor the mere offering of sacrifice (nor, we may add, the promises to David!) could ever have been accepted by them as a guarantee of Yahweh's blessing and protection apart from faithfulness to the Law. Secondly, in the period after 586 B.C. when the Deuteronomistic history assumed its final form and when also, as we believe, the Jeremianic prose sermons were developed (at least substantially), the destruction of the Temple was a bitter reality which demanded explanation, an explanation which the Temple sermon in Jeremiah vii. 1–15 together with other discourses and narratives in the Jeremianic prose tradition unquestionably provide. And thirdly, and most significant of all, the Deuteronomists leave us in no doubt that the Temple was no guarantee of safety from judgement if Israel was unfaithful to Yahweh and disobeyed his Law:

> If you and your children at all turn back from following me and do not keep my commandments and my statutes which I have set before you, but go and serve other gods and worship them, then I will cut off Israel from the land which I have given them, and the Temple which I have consecrated for my name I will cast out of my sight. . . .
>
> (1 Kings ix. 6f.)

Accordingly, far from being objections to the Deuteronomistic origin of Jeremiah vii–viii. 3, the sayings which this prose complex contains concerning the Temple and the offering of sacrifice, with the corresponding emphasis upon obedience above all else to the requirements of the Law and the implicit explanation of why the Temple like the ancient shrine at Shiloh had been destroyed, are entirely in keeping with the Deuteronomistic standpoint and are readily understood as having taken shape and assumed their present form in the exilic period, when such matters would clearly have been of pressing concern to those who had survived the judgement wrought by Yahweh upon Judah and Jerusalem in 586 B.C.

We may summarize our discussion in this section. We have examined

---

[1] Cf. for example, A. Weiser, *op. cit., in loc.*

a number of passages in the Jeremianic prose tradition and it has emerged that in language, style, and literary structure they show all the signs of having been composed by the Deuteronomists. In addition, we have seen that the passages in question are concerned primarily with the significance and relevance of the Law in the life of Israel and it has been argued that in this also they point for their origin and composition to the same circle. It has been maintained throughout, however, that such passages are not to be thought of as an attempt to provide a record of something which Jeremiah had said or the 'gist' of something he had said even though, as we have seen, snatches of original prophetic sayings are observable in some of them. Rather, they must be viewed as the product of a tradition which addressed itself to the needs of a community. As such, and when taken together, these passages served a threefold purpose. First of all they sought to show how Yahweh's prophet Jeremiah, like his prophetic predecessors (cf. Jer. xxvi. 4–5), called his generation to obedience to the Law and warned his contemporaries of the disastrous consequences of infidelity to its requirements. Secondly, in doing so they provided an explanation of why Judah had experienced the catastrophe of 586 B.C., interpreting it as Yahweh's judgement upon his people's disobedience and apostasy. And thirdly, addressed as they were to those who had survived that judgement but lived in its shadow, they constituted an earnest exhortation to them that they themselves should live in accordance with the requirements of the Law which would assure them Yahweh's blessing.

Viewed in this manner, these sermons and discourses are both didactic and kerygmatic, for they not only instructed those to whom they were addressed about the events of the past but also announced to them a word of hope for the future, a future in which they had the opportunity of realizing again their role as Yahweh's people. This gives rise, however, to a further problem, for it has been questioned whether the Deuteronomists to whom we have attributed these passages in the Jeremianic prose tradition afforded any place within their theology for such a kerygmatic element. In order to substantiate the view expressed above it therefore becomes necessary to show that such a kerygmatic element can legitimately be ascribed to the Deuteronomists; and it is to this that we now turn.

III

It will already have become apparent from our investigation thus far that one of the most important contributions to our study of the Old

Testament during the past generation has been Martin Noth's thesis that the corpus Deuteronomy-2 Kings is not the final outcome of a process of literary redaction and expansion of an original book or series of books,[1] but represents the attempt of an author to write the history of Israel from Moses to the exile and to present a theological interpretation of that history.[2] This Deuteronomistic historian wrote in the shadow of 721 B.C. and 586 B.C. and was concerned mainly with providing an explanation of why Yahweh had rejected his people, first the Northern Kingdom and finally Judah, in these catastrophes. In writing his history this author[3] had at his disposal a great deal of material deriving from very varied sources and periods in Israel's history, all of which he has knit together into a structural unity by means of a literary framework which together with frequent insertions and comments set forth his own theological understanding of the events he records.

This Deuteronomistic history is divided into five parts. The first is the period of Moses, which is covered by the book of Deuteronomy as the Law of Yahweh mediated through Moses on the plains of Moab as a ratification of the covenant on Horeb/Sinai.[4] Noth believes that the central purpose of the historian was to show how Israel time and time again refused and failed to conform to the will of Yahweh as set forth

---

[1] The generally accepted view of scholars in the later 19th century was that the books of Joshua, Judges, Samuel, and Kings (or Samuel-Kings) were already in existence by the exilic period as separately composed and independent books. During the exilic period they were edited by a Deuteronomistic redactor (for a statement of this view see J. Wellhausen, *Prolegomena to the History of Israel*, Edinburgh 1885, pp. 228–294). This later gave way to the view that the Pentateuchal sources J and E continue through the Former Prophets, J up to the reign of Solomon and E up to the fall of the Northern Kingdom or beyond, so that by the time of the exile there was already a connected work comprising Joshua, Judges, Samuel and Kings which was then edited by a Deuteronomistic redactor (see, for example, G. Hölscher, 'Das Buch der Könige: seine Quellen und seine Redaktion', in *Eucharisterion. Festschrift für Gunkel*, FRLANT 18, Göttingen 1923, pp. 158–213). Both these views still have their advocates, the latter favoured by O. Eissfeldt, *The Old Testament: An Introduction* (1965), pp. 241ff. and the former by G. Fohrer, *Introduction to the Old Testament*, Nashville and New York 1968, pp. 196–237. But such views fail to offer a more satisfactory solution to the problem than Noth's theory which is widely accepted as accounting for more of the problems involved in studying this corpus of literature in Deuteronomy-2 Kings.

[2] M. Noth, *Überlieferungsgeschichtliche Studien I*, (1943, 1957[2]).

[3] Noth (*ibid.*, pp. 109f.) thinks in terms of a single author for this history. Even if this is accepted, however, it is clear that such an author stood within a tradition and in writing this history was representing the circle of traditionists to which he belonged. Cf. P. R. Ackroyd, *Exile and Restoration*, London 1968, pp. 63f.

[4] Cf. M. Noth, *op. cit.*, pp. 27–40. For details of Noth's understanding of the stages of composition and growth of the material in the history as a whole the reader is referred to the relevant sections in Noth's work here cited.

in the Law until he finally rejected her. The second division is contained in the book of Joshua which covers the period of the conquest of Canaan under the leadership of Joshua.[1] This is followed by the history of the judges which ends with the establishment of the monarchy and Samuel's speech in 1 Samuel xii.[2] The history of the monarchy follows in 1 Samuel xiii–2 Kings xxv and comprises two sections. The first narrates the rise of the monarchy under Saul and its zenith under David and Solomon with the building of the Temple (1 Sam. xiii–1 Kings viii),[3] and the second describes the increasing apostasy under the monarchy in both northern and southern kingdoms and the eventual downfall of both states in 721 B.C. and 586 B.C.[4]

According to Noth the main way in which the author has achieved an overall unity in his work is by means of speeches which he freely composed and either placed on the lips of leading figures in Israel's history or simply inserted into the narrative at crucial moments and transition points in the history. Thus Joshua i contains a speech on the eve of the conquest whilst Joshua xii presents a summary of the victories of the tribes during the conquest and Joshua xxiii contains a speech of Joshua at the end of the conquest. The history of the period of the judges is summarized in Judges ii. 11–23 and the transition from the period of the judges to the monarchy is accompanied by a speech placed on the lips of Samuel (1 Sam. xii). The downfall of the Northern Kingdom is the occasion of yet another homily in 2 Kings xvii. 7ff.[5]

On the question of the *terminus ad quem* for the composition of the Deuteronomistic history, the final verses of 2 Kings xxv recording the release of Jehoiachin from prison in exile offer valuable information, for we know that this release took place in 561 B.C. Furthermore, the fact that no indication is given that the second Temple had been or was being rebuilt establishes 520 B.C. as the latest date. All this suggests that the Deuteronomistic history assumed at least substantially its final form before 520 B.C. and after 561 B.C. although if the verses recording the release of Jehoiachin are taken as a later addition the work may already have been finished even before 561 B.C.[6] On the question of the *terminus a quo*, however, there has been considerable

---

[1] *Ibid.*, pp. 40–47.

[2] *Ibid.*, pp. 47–61.

[3] *Ibid.*, pp. 61–72.

[4] *Ibid.*, pp. 72–87.

[5] D. J. McCarthy, 'II Samuel 7 and the Structure of the Deuteronomic History', *JBL* 84, 1965, pp. 131–138 has argued forcibly that II Sam. vii is a key Deuteronomistic passage to be included with those singled out by Noth, since it also represents a transition point.

[6] But see the discussion of 2 Kings xxv below pp. 131f.

F

discussion, some scholars arguing that there was a Deuteronomistic history already in existence in the pre-exilic period which was then edited during the exilic period,[1] others, including Noth himself, arguing that it was composed in its entirety after the destruction of Jerusalem in 586 B.C.[2] The difficulty here can be avoided to some extent if we see the history as the written deposit of a teaching ministry which was carried on by the Deuteronomists and which had its beginnings in the late pre-exilic period in Judah when it would have centred largely on inculcating the warning for Judah to be derived from the tragedy which had befallen the Northern Kingdom and thereby exhorting those who had providentially escaped Yahweh's judgement to obedience to his will as set forth in the book of Deuteronomy which had at that time already made its appearance. Such a teaching and preaching ministry would have been carried on after the collapse of the state when it would have been given a new direction now that Judah also had fallen under Yahweh's judgement. If this view is accepted we must understand the Deuteronomistic history as coming at the end of a long process in the course of which material of diverse origin was collected and utilized by the Deuteronomists in their teaching activity. But the Deuteronomistic history as a literary production set out in the ordered, one might even say chapter by chapter fashion as outlined above would thus have been composed during the exilic period but on the basis of much material which had already taken shape at an earlier time at the hands of the Deuteronomistic preachers.

According to Noth the central purpose of the Deuteronomistic historian was to provide an explanation why Yahweh had rejected Israel in the tragic events of 721 B.C. and 586 B.C. Together with the promulgation of the Law by Moses had come the stern warning of the curse which would befall Israel if she failed to obey Yahweh's will as set forth in this Law. The threat of this curse is already expressed at the earliest time by Moses (e.g. Deut. iv. 25–27) and repeated by Joshua after the conquest has been completed (Josh. xxiii. 16), whilst throughout Israel's history, according to the Deuteronomist, Yahweh warned Israel 'by every prophet and seer' (2 Kings xvii. 13), constantly calling her to obedience, but to no avail (cf. 1 Sam. xii. 14ff., 25; 1 Kings ix. 6ff.; 2 Kings xvii. 23; xxi. 14f.). Now in the period in which the Deuteronomistic history made its appearance the threat which had come with the giving of the Law and in the preaching of the prophets

---

[1] For example, R. H. Pfeiffer, *Introduction to the Old Testament* (1948), pp. 410ff.; J. Gray, *Kings*, London 1964, pp. 13ff.

[2] M. Noth, *op. cit.*, pp. 91ff.

had been violently realized and Israel which had rejected Yahweh's Law and ignored the warnings of 'his servants the prophets' had fallen under the curse of the Law. What had occurred in the events of 721 B.C. and 586 B.C. was thus described as the judgement of a righteous God upon a wayward and disobedient people.

It must be asked, however, whether Noth's assessment of the motivation and purpose of the Deuteronomists is entirely adequate or complete. That the interpretation of the downfall of Israel forms a central aspect of the history is indisputable. But is this word of judgement all they had to say to the generation to whom they addressed themselves? Or had they some additional purpose in mind? To be more precise, had the Deuteronomistic circle any concern for the future of those who had undergone Yahweh's judgement and anything to declare concerning what was now to be done by Yahweh and what they in turn should do in the new situation brought about by the destruction of the state and the ensuing exile? Noth himself denies that the Deuteronomists had any concern for the future; what had happened was seen by them as 'something final and complete' and they were unconcerned with what future possibilities lay open for Israel.[1] Viewed in this manner, however, the purpose of the Deuteronomists in writing their history amounted to something approaching mere academic interest and one is left wondering what need there could have been to address such a work to a generation which, *ex hypothesi*, had to all intents and purposes been written off by Yahweh.[2]

But did the Deuteronomists really regard what had occurred in 586 B.C., as Noth seems to suggest, as the great *finitum est* of Israel as Yahweh's people? There is much evidence to suggest that they did not and that far from declaring only a word of judgement to their contemporaries they also proclaimed the means whereby the breach between Yahweh and Israel could be healed so that they could once more realize their existence as his people.[3] This kerygmatic element in the Deuteronomistic history is expressed in terms of a condition: if Israel 'turns again' (שׁוּב) to Yahweh then he will have compassion on her and restore her well-being. The basis of this promise of forgiveness must be understood in terms of a renewal of the covenant. In the Deuteronomistic corpus as it now stands any suggestion that Yahweh would

[1] M. Noth, *op. cit.*, pp. 107f.
[2] Cf. G. von Rad, *Old Testament Theology*, I (1962), p. 346.
[3] Cf. H. W. Wolff, 'Das Kerygma des deuteronomistischen Geschichtswerks', *Gesammelte Studien* (1964), pp. 308–324; H. Timm, 'Die Ladeerzählung (1 Sam. 4–6; 2 Sam. 6) und das Kerygma des deuteronomistischen Geschichtswerks', *EvTh* 26, 1966, pp. 509–526; P. R. Ackroyd, *Exile and Restoration*, pp. 78–83.

irrevocably terminate Israel's election has been removed.[1] The responsibility for the complete termination of the covenant would lie with Israel herself, for the covenant would remain in force so long as she remained faithful to the obligations which it placed upon her. Thus Yahweh's judgement fell upon Israel time and time again in the course of her history, but it was never a final judgement or rejection. This could come only if Israel refused to 'turn again' to Yahweh (cf. I Sam. vii. 3; I Kings viii. 33, 35; 2 Kings xvii. 13, xxiii. 25). In other words, the curse of the Law could be avoided if Israel obeyed or, in the event of disobedience, revoked by Israel's turning again to Yahweh. That such a possibility of forgiveness and renewal remained after the calamity of 586 B.C. is expressed in a number of passages in the Deuteronomistic corpus. Thus we have already seen how in Deuteronomy iv. 25–27 Moses warns Israel of the consequences of apostasy. But this section continues with the promise that even after judgement if Israel 'turned again' to Yahweh he would forgive her:

> There you will seek Yahweh your God, and you will find him, if you search after him with all your heart and with all your soul. When you are in distress and all these things happen to you in the latter days, you will turn again (ושבת) to Yahweh your God and obey his voice, for Yahweh your God is a merciful God; he will not desert or destroy you or forget the covenant with your fathers which he made with an oath.
>
> (Deut. iv. 29–31)

In a second passage in Deuteronomy which is of particular importance in this connection the same promise is proclaimed:[2]

> And when all these things come upon you, the blessing and the curse, which I have set before you, and you call them to mind among all the nations where Yahweh your God has driven you, and you turn again (ושבת) to Yahweh your God, you and your children, and obey his voice in all that I command you this day, with all your heart and with all your soul; then Yahweh your God will restore your well-being[3] and have compassion upon you; and he will gather you again from all the peoples where Yahweh your God has scattered you. If your exiles are in the farthest parts of the heaven,

---

[1] It is probable that Deuteronomy in its original (i.e. pre-exilic) form presented Israel with a straightforward either-or, that is, either faithfulness to the covenant stipulations which would bring blessing, or disobedience which would entail the termination of the covenant without any suggestion of a renewal of Israel's election. When, however, the worst actually happened in 586 B.C. such an extreme position would no longer have been maintained and hope for renewal and restoration would have come to the forefront during the exilic period. The passages in Deuteronomy (Deut. iv. 29ff., xxx. 1ff.) cited below in which we find such hope expressed derive from the Deuteronomistic historian and did not belong to *Urdeuteronomium*.

[2] On this passage see also below pp. 118f.

[3] For this translation of the expression שוב שבות see A. R. Johnson, *The Cultic Prophet in Ancient Israel*[2], Cardiff 1962, p. 67 and note 4 on the same page.

from there Yahweh your God will gather you, and from there he will fetch you; and Yahweh your God will bring you into the land which your fathers possessed, that you may possess it; and he will make you more prosperous and numerous than your fathers. And Yahweh your God will circumcise your heart and the heart of your offspring, so that you will love Yahweh your God with all your heart and with all your soul, that you may live.

(Deut. xxx. 1–6)

And in the unquestionably Deuteronomistic 'prayer of Solomon' (1 Kings viii. 22–53) the same promise is set forth:

If they sin against thee—for there is no man who does not sin—and thou art angry with them, and dost give them to an enemy, so that they are carried away captive to the land of the enemey, far off or near; yet if they lay it to heart in the land to which they have been carried captive, and turn again (ושבו) and seek thy grace in the land of their captors, saying: 'We have sinned and committed iniquity and evil'; if they turn again (ושבו) to thee with all their heart and with all their soul in the land of their enemies who carried them away captive, and pray to thee toward their land which thou gavest to their fathers, the city which thou hast chosen, and the Temple which I have built for thy name; then hear thou in heaven thy dwelling place their prayer and supplication, and maintain their cause and forgive thy people who have sinned against thee, and all their transgression which they have committed against thee; and grant them compassion in the sight of those who carried them away captive, that they may have compassion on them.

(1 Kings viii. 46–50)

Here then are three passages in which the Deuteronomists have clearly given expression to a word of hope to those who had undergone judgement; if Israel 'turns again' to Yahweh it will secure his forgiveness of her sins so that she can once more realize her existence as his people. Accordingly, Noth's view that the Deuteronomists concerned themselves only with Yahweh's judgement upon Israel must be rejected.[1]

[1] When this book was finished my attention was drawn to Professor Walter Brueggemann's important article 'The Kerygma of the Deuteronomistic Historian', *Interpretation* 22, 1968, pp. 387–402. Brueggemann takes his starting point from Wolff's work outlined above but goes on to show that the Deuteronomistic appeal to Israel to 'turn again' to Yahweh has its basis in the belief in Yahweh's fidelity to Israel which is expressed in terms of Yahweh's 'good' (טוב) in the Deuteronomistic theology. This 'good' or graciousness of Yahweh supports the call for repentance. There is evidence that the term 'good' was employed within the context of international treaties with reference to the making and honouring of such treaties and although in the Deuteronomistic literature it has many nuances it is also there used to express fidelity to the covenant relationship on the part of Yahweh and Israel. Brueggemann argues that it was used by the Deuteronomists in exile (a) to indicate that 586 B.C. happened because Israel was not 'good' toward Yahweh, (b) to affirm that Yahweh still shows 'good' to Israel, and therefore (c) to urge Israel to 'turn

At this point we may examine briefly what part, if any, the promises to David occupy in the Deuteronomists' hopes for Israel's future. We look in vain for any developed messianic hope within the Deuteronomistic corpus or any clear statement that after judgement Yahweh would reactivate his promises to the house of David. Nevertheless, in view of the prominent place which they have afforded the sacral traditions centring on the Davidic dynasty in their history it would be passing strange if at least some element of hope arising from these traditions was not expressed, if only in a veiled manner.[1] That such a hope is expressed, however, has been adduced by a number of scholars from the passage at the end of the Deuteronomistic history which narrates the release of Jehoiachin from prison in exile (2 Kings xxv. 27–30).[2] That this event would have been the object of renewed expectations among the exiles in Babylon is very probable, for it seems clear, especially from the book of Ezekiel, that Jehoiachin was regarded by the exiles as king of Judah throughout the exilic period.[3] It is surely reasonable to see the record of this event in 2 Kings xxv. 27ff. as having been prompted, at least to some extent, by such expectations. Noth rejects such an interpretation, arguing that the phrase 'all the days of his life' (v. 30) indicates that Jehoiachin had died and that this record in itself was directed against precisely those who looked for renewal and restoration through Jehoiachin.[4] Against this it has been argued, however, that the expression 'all the days of his life' means 'in perpetuity'[5] and this more positive understanding of it is reinforced, it is further argued, by the note (v. 29) that Jehoiachin 'put off his prison

---

[1] If McCarthy's view (*JBL* 84, 1965, pp. 131–138) that 2 Sam. vii is to be regarded as one of the key passages in the structure of the Deuteronomistic history is accepted, it provides further evidence of the importance attached to the Davidic covenant traditions in the Deuteronomists' theology. It would also indicate the continued interest of the Deuteronomists in these traditions during the exilic period.

[2] Cf. G. von Rad, *Old Testament Theology*, I (1962), pp. 343ff.; P. R. Ackroyd, *Exile and Restoration*, pp. 78ff.; E. Zenger, 'Die deuteronomistische Interpretation der Rehabilitierung Jojachins', *BZ* 12, 1968, pp. 16–30.

[3] Cf. W. Zimmerli, *Ezechiel*, BKAT 13, 1956ff., pp. 43ff.; P. R. Ackroyd, *Exile and Restoration*, p. 114.

[4] M. Noth, *Überlieferungsgeschichtliche Studien I*, p. 108 and especially his response to von Rad in 'Zur Geschichtsauffassung des Deuteronomisten', *Proceedings of the XXII Congress of Orientalists, Istanbul* 1951, vol. II, Leiden 1957, pp. 558–566.

[5] Cf. P. R. Ackroyd, *Exile and Restoration*, p. 80 following S. Talmon, 'Double Readings in the Massoretic Text', *Textus* I, 1960, pp. 144–184.

---

again', to repent, in the light of Yahweh's continuing 'goodness' (*op. cit.*, p. 389). Thus 'in the light of this ('good') motif the kerygma of the Deuteronomist is that Yahweh stands by his promise, that he can be trusted, and therefore it is safe for Israel to repent, change, and invest in the future' (*ibid.*).

garments', an expression which elsewhere in the Old Testament (Gen. xlv. 22. Cf. Zech. iii. 4f.) indicates a change (for the better) in situation and the bestowal of honour or divine favour.[1] But even if it is conceded that the record in 2 Kings xxv. 27ff. does presuppose the death of Jehoiachin, it is still entirely possible to interpret it as giving expression to renewed hopes centring on the promises to David by announcing the restoration of the Davidic line through Jehoiachin *and his successors*. This is all the more probable when it is fully appreciated what precisely the event described involved, for E. Zenger has recently argued very persuasively on the basis of a detailed exegesis of 2 Kings xxv. 27ff. that this event took place as part of the enactments implemented by Amel-Marduk in his accession year (561 B.C.) as king of Babylon and constituted nothing less than the rehabilitation by the Babylonian authorities of Jehoiachin as officially recognized king of Judah and vassal to the Babylonian king.[2] These considerations mean, first of all, that the release of Jehoiachin in 561 B.C. marked a very significant turning point in the fortunes of the exiles in Babylon and would almost certainly have led to a renewed hope of national restoration through the Davidic dynasty now reinstated and officially recognized by the Babylonian powers. But second, and of greater relevance for our present purposes, it seems clear from these considerations that in 2 Kings xxv. 27ff. the Deuteronomists were not, as Noth seems to suggest, merely

[1] Cf. P. R. Ackroyd, *Exile and Restoration*, p. 81. See below note 2.

[2] E. Zenger, *op. cit.*, pp. 18ff. Zenger arrives at this conclusion on the basis of the following considerations: (a) שנת מלכו (2 Kings xxv. 27) refers to the accession year of Amel-Marduk and this coupled with the probability that the accession of a new monarch necessitated or provided the opportunity for a re-affirmation of the oath of vassaldom on the part of Babylon's vassal kings renders it likely that the release of Jehoiachin took place on such an occasion and for such a purpose. (b) This finds further support in the expression (v. 27) נשא את־ראש יהויכין (lit. 'he lifted up the head of Jehoiachin') which Zenger, on the basis of an examination of the phrase in both the Old Testament and Accadian texts, argues does not mean simply 'Amel-Marduk freed Jehoiachin from prison' but, in this context, 'summoned Jehoiachin from prison for an audience before the king'. (c) Furthermore, Zenger following W. L. Moran, 'A Note on the Treaty Terminology of the Sefire Stelas', *JNES* 22, 1963, p. 174, shows that the expression וידבר אתו טבות (v. 28) is incorrectly translated 'he spoke kindly with him' and refers rather to 'friendship, good relations' with specific reference to the amity established by treaty. (d) Zenger also finds a context for Amel-Marduk's action in placing Jehoiachin's throne 'above the thrones of the kings who were with him in Babylon' (v. 28) within the context of the royal enthronement ritual in Babylon at which the vassal kings were present to witness the accession of their overlord. Zenger suggests also, however, that the choice of the word כסא 'throne' may have been a deliberate allusion on the part of the Deuteronomists to the words of Nathan in 2 Sam. vii (cf. esp. vv. 13, 16). (e) It is also suggested that the note that Jehoiachin 'put off his his prison garments' (v. 29) may indicate that Jehoiachin was re-robed in his royal apparel.

narrating the closing chapter of the Davidic dynasty but were on the contrary recording its survival. Furthermore, the very fact that they have done so is surely of considerable significance and most probably indicates that they also saw in this event at least the possibility of national restoration under a Davidic king and the continuing reality, in spite of everything, of the promises to David. At the same time it remains true that it is only in this short passage at the end of their history that the Deuteronomists have 'hinted' at such messianic expectations and their more fully developed hopes for Israel's future centre not on the promises to David but on Israel's 'turning again' to Yahweh and on her obedience to his Law.

When now we turn again to the passages in the Jeremianic prose tradition which we examined above and which have been ascribed to the Deuteronomists, then it is plausible to conclude that in calling for obedience to the Law they presuppose and have at their basis this Deuteronomistic kerygma according to which Israel's 'turning again' to Yahweh and her obedience to his Law would guarantee her renewed existence as his people. It means also, however, that a number of other passages in the prose tradition in Jeremiah which express more directly a word of hope for Israel's future can now be investigated and to these we may now direct our attention.

The first passage which we may consider briefly in this connection is Jeremiah xviii. 1–12. This passage has all the appearance of having been developed on the basis of an original saying of Jeremiah which has been preserved to some extent at least in *vv.* 6, 11a. On the other hand, *vv.* 7–10 together with the appeal to 'turn again' in *v.* 11b as well as the record of Israel's refusal to do so in *v.* 12 come directly from the traditionists to whom we owe the passage in its present form. It is with *vv.* 7–10 that we are mainly concerned here:

> If at any time I declare concerning a nation or a kingdom, that I will pluck up and break down and destroy it, and if that nation, concerning which I have spoken, turns again (וָשָׁב) from its evil, I will be relieved from my plan to bring disaster upon it. And if at any time I declare concerning a nation or a kingdom that I will build and plant it, and if it does evil in my sight not obeying my voice, then I shall be relieved of my intention to do good to it.

Once again, accepting this passage as belonging to the Jeremianic prose tradition which developed subsequent to the destruction of Judah in 586 B.C., we ask the question: what was such a passage intended for and what did it mean for those to whom it was addressed? The passage begins by postulating a situation in which 'a nation or kingdom' stands under Yahweh's judgement and offers the possibility that such judgement can be averted if that nation 'turns again'. In the next part of the text the position is reversed. Here a situation is presented in which 'a nation or a kingdom' is to be the recipient of Yahweh's blessing, but a blessing which would be annulled if they refused 'to obey'. As a discourse placed on the lips of Jeremiah himself it sets forth the choice which lay before those to whom he addressed himself in the days before the catastrophe of 586 B.C. In the period in which the text was actually composed, however, that is, in the period after 586 B.C. it would have offered an explanation of why Judah had suffered judgement. But at the same time, and most important of all, it would have offered a word of hope to those who had undergone Yahweh's judgement; those who had experienced the bitter reality of having been 'plucked up and broken down and destroyed' were now offered the possibility of being 'built and planted' if they 'turned again' and 'obeyed'. In this it seems clear that this passage is a direct expression of the Deuteronomistic kerygma which we examined above and which also announces Yahweh's forgiveness and blessing in response to Israel's 'turning again'.

Two further passages in the Jeremianic prose tradition which reflect this same Deuteronomistic kerygma are xxiv. 4–7 and xxix. 10–14, both of which are concerned with the forgiveness and restoration which will ensue Israel's 'turning again'. In these instances, however, a considerable advance has been made upon xviii. 7–10, for whilst it is still Israel's 'turning again' which will secure forgiveness and restoration, such a 'turning again' is now assured by Yahweh himself who now takes the initiative so that Israel *will* 'turn again' (xxiv. 7; cf. xxix. 12). That is to say, the conditional 'if' has now receded and the element of promise has come to the forefront of the kerygma. Furthermore, in xxiv. 7 this element of promise is further extended, for not only is forgiveness and restoration envisaged but Yahweh himself will endow his people with the will to obey him; he will 'give them a heart to know me that I am Yahweh; and they shall be my people and I will be their God' (*v*. 7).

The promise here set forth is, however, carried further and fully developed in two other passages in the Jeremianic prose tradition which proclaim that not only will Yahweh himself take the initiative in renewing the broken relationship with his people but that in doing so he will graciously endow them with the will and the ability to live in accordance with his Law, a will and an ability which they hitherto lacked and for which they suffered judgement. Can these passages also be attributed to the Deuteronomists?

The most important of these two passages is Jeremiah xxxi. 31–34 on the 'new covenant', a passage which has been described as one of the profoundest and most moving in the entire Bible.[1] With only a few exceptions[2] scholars have regarded it as a genuine saying of Jeremiah though some, whilst believing that it embodies his thought, concede that it does not in its present form preserve his *ipsissima verba*.[3] There are impressive reasons, however, for rejecting such a view and in favour of regarding this passage as pointing for its composition to the Deuteronomists.[4]

To begin with, in both language and style it belongs clearly to the Jeremianic prose tradition. Its repetitious nature is immediately apparent,[5] whilst, for example, the covenant formula 'I will be their God and they shall be my people' (*v.* 33) occurs elsewhere in the Jeremianic prose in vii. 23, xi. 4, xxiv. 7, xxxii. 38.[6] In addition, the notion of the Law being in Israel's 'heart' (*v.* 33) is found in such passages as Deuteronomy vi. 6, xxx. 14 and has at its basis the frequent Deuteronomistic exhortation to love Yahweh 'with all the heart and soul' (cf. Deut. iv. 29, vi. 5, x. 12, xi. 13, xiii. 3, xxvi. 16, xxx. 2, 6, 10; Josh. xxii. 5; 1 Sam. xii. 20, 24; etc.). Similarly, the statement that Yahweh himself would place his Law within Israel's 'heart' (*v.* 33. Cf. xxiv. 7, xxxii. 39) is clearly akin to Deuteronomy xxx. 6, where it is said that he would 'circumcise' Israel's heart (cf. Jer. ix. 25 (EVV 26)) and is paralleled by other Deuteronomistic texts in which Yahweh is described as effecting a change in the 'heart' (cf. Deut. ii. 30, xxix. 3 (EVV 4); 1 Sam. x. 9; 1 Kings iii. 9, 12, x. 24).

As to the 'new covenant' which Yahweh would make with Israel, the following observations are pertinent.[7] In the Deuteronomistic corpus covenant ceremonies appear at crucial moments in Israel's history. Thus the book of Deuteronomy itself purports to be the Law delivered by Moses within the context of a covenant ceremony (cf. Deut. xxvi. 16ff.) on the plains of Moab after the forty years' wandering in the wilderness and on the eve of the entry into the promised land. When the conquest has been completed Joshua leads the tribes in a similar

---

[1] Cf. J. Bright, *Jeremiah*, p. 287.

[2] Notably B. Duhm, *Das Buch Jeremia* (1901), pp. 154ff.

[3] Cf. J. Bright, *Jeremiah*, p. 287.

[4] Cf. S. Herrmann, *Die prophetische Heilserwartungen im Alten Testament*, BWANT 85, Stuttgart 1965, pp. 179ff.

[5] Note the use of the expression 'to make a covenant' and/or 'covenant' in *vv.* 31, 32, 33. For other Deuteronomistic elements see S. Herrmann, *op. cit.*, pp. 181–183.

[6] It occurs in MT xxx 22 where, however, it is probably a gloss (note the change in person). It is not found in the LXX in this verse.

[7] Cf. S. Herrmann, *op. cit.*, pp. 179ff.

covenant ceremony at Shechem (Josh. xxiv). Then again at the coming of kingship Samuel gathers the tribes at Gilgal(?) where a further covenant ceremony takes place (1 Sam. xii),[1] whilst at a later stage still yet another covenant ceremony ends the long period of apostasy under Manasseh and brings about a new beginning under Josiah (2 Kings xxiii). In each instance a covenant ceremony inaugurates a new phase in the relationship between Israel and Yahweh. The relevance of this for the 'new covenant' in Jeremiah xxxi. 31–34 is immediately apparent. In the events of 586 B.C. and the ensuing exile Israel's existence as Yahweh's people had been challenged and questioned as never before. Once again, however, as in the past so also now Yahweh would act to renew the relationship between himself and his people and this renewal, again as in the past, is conceived of in terms of covenant. In this respect the promise of a new covenant in Jeremiah xxxi. 31ff. conforms to the pattern of a series of covenant renewal ceremonies in the Deuteronomistic presentation of Israel's history. Like them it makes its appearance, in this instance as an expectation for the future, at a crucial moment in Israel's history and like them its purpose is to usher in a new phase in the relationship between Yahweh and his people. Similarly, the new covenant like the old involves a response from Israel in terms of observance of the Law, with this major difference, however, that Israel's past failure to obey it is now to be replaced by both the will and the ability to obey which Yahweh will graciously place in her heart:

> I will put my Law within them, and I will write it upon their hearts; and I will be their God, and they shall be my people. And no longer will each man teach his neighbour and each his brother, saying: 'Know Yahweh', for they will all know me, from the least of them to the greatest, says Yahweh; for I will forgive their iniquity, and I will remember their sin no more.
>
> (Jer. xxxi. 33–34)

It is in this respect that the covenant here described is to be new, and in this it undoubtedly represents one of the high points in the entire Old Testament concerning the expectations for Israel's future as Yahweh's people and one which was destined to be of decisive significance for the interpretation of the life and mission of Jesus (cf. esp. Heb. viii. 8–12, x. 16–17). Even in this, however, it points for its origin to the Deuteronomists, for in expressing the promise that Yahweh would graciously enable his people to live according to his will it is essentially paralleled

---

[1] Cf. J. Muilenburg, 'The form and structure of the covenantal formulations', *VT* 9, 1959, pp. 347–365. See, however, the remarks of D. J. McCarthy, *Treaty and Covenant* (1963), pp. 141ff.

by Deuteronomy xxx. 6, which belongs to a passage which also, as we have seen, concerns itself with Israel's future:

> And Yahweh your God will circumcise your heart and the heart of your offspring, so that you will love Yahweh your God with all your heart and with all your soul, that you may live.

Closely related to this passage is Jeremiah xxxii. 36–41, which gives expression to a similar expectation for the future of Israel as Yahweh's people. Once again in both language and style it belongs to the Jeremianic prose tradition. It contains a promise that Yahweh will gather his people from all the lands to which they have been 'scattered' (v. 37), a promise which is formulated in language strikingly similar to Deuteronomy xxx. 1ff.[1] Furthermore, in all essentials it represents a parallel text to Jeremiah xxxi. 31ff. It employs the covenant formula 'they shall be my people and I will be their God' (v. 38); it embodies the promise that Yahweh will make 'an everlasting covenant' with his people (v. 40. Cf. l. 5), that he will give Israel 'one heart and one way' to 'fear' him (v. 39) and that he will place his 'fear' in their 'hearts' so that they will not 'turn away' from him (v. 40). Once again, therefore, we have here a passage which points for its composition to the Deuteronomists and which, like Jeremiah xxxi. 31ff., gives expression to the high water level of their expectations for Israel's future as the people of the covenant.

At this point we may return briefly to Jeremiah xviii. 7–10. Whilst, as we have seen, the framework within which these verses are placed demands that the alternatives of blessing or curse which they set forth be understood as referring to Israel, the question arises whether this exhausts their meaning and significance. That this is not so seems clear from the manner in which the alternatives of being 'plucked up and broken down and destroyed' or 'being built and planted' are addressed not simply to Israel but to 'a nation or a kingdom' (vv. 7, 9). If, however, as seems clear, the expression 'a nation or a kingdom' is understood as designating not only Israel but other peoples, then, remarkable as it may be, we have here what in its beginnings was a conditional promise of salvation announced specifically to Israel now extended to all nations; it has become universal. Thus Yahweh's dominion over the nations is asserted and their relationship to him, as well as their destiny, is determined, as with Israel, by their obedience to his will.[2] The universalism to which this passage points finds clearer expression

---

[1] On this passage see further below pp. 118f.
[2] Cf. S. Herrmann, op. cit., p. 164.

in Jeremiah xii. 14–17[1] (cf. also Jer. ix. 24–25 (EVV 25–26), xxvii. 1–11).

There can scarcely be any doubt that such an extension of this Deuteronomistic conditional promise of salvation represents a late development, possibly reflecting that universalism which finds fullest expression in Deutero-Isaiah. As such, however, it represents the product of theorizing and reflection, for it is not expressed in the Jeremianic prose tradition in eschatological terms and in being applied to the nations other than Yahweh's people Israel it has been deprived of those very conditions which rendered it practicable. That is to say, its realization at this universal level presupposes that the nations, like Israel herself, already know Yahweh's Law.[2]

Those passages in the Jeremianic prose tradition which embody expectations for Israel's future are for the most part dominated by the promise of a return from exile and restoration to the land (xviii. 7–8, xxiv. 4–7, xxix. 10–14, xxxii. 36–37, 43–44) and it is in fact this promise which characterizes the hopes for Israel's future which this prose tradition as a whole sets forth. Thus the 'Book of Consolation' (Jer. xxx–xxxiii) is prefaced with a short statement in prose in which this promise is formulated as a summary interpretation of what follows:

> Thus says Yahweh, the God of Israel: 'Write in a book all the words which I have spoken to you. For behold, days are coming', says Yahweh, 'when I will restore the well-being (ושבתי את־שבות)[3] of my people, Israel and Judah', says Yahweh, 'and I will bring them back (והשבתים)[4] to the land which I gave to their fathers (אל־הארץ אשר נתתי לאבותם)[5] and they shall take possession of it (וירשוה).[6]
>
> (Jer. xxx. 2–3)

In several other short prose passages within the 'Book of Consolation' this same promise is formulated (xxxi. 23–25, 27–30, 38–40, xxxii. 36–37, 43–44, xxxiii. 6ff., 10ff., 12–13). Of these, xxxi. 28[7] is particularly striking (cf. also xxxi. 38–40), for here the terminology of the conditional promise in xviii. 7–10 has been taken up to express a promise for Israel's future restoration:[8]

---

[1] *Ibid.*, pp. 162ff.   [2] *Ibid.*, pp. 163, 164–165.

[3] See further Jer. xxix. 14, xxxi. 23, xxxii. 44, xxxiii. 7, 11, 26. Cf. Deut. xxx. 3.

[4] Cf. Jer. xii. 15, xvi. 15, xxiii. 3, xxiv. 6, xxvii. 22, xxix. 14, xxxii. 37, xxxiv. 22.

[5] Cf. Jer. vii. 7, xvi. 15, xxiv. 10, xxv. 5, xxxv. 15; 1 Kings viii. 34, 40, 48, xiv. 15; 2 Kings xxi. 8.

[6] ירש is a characteristic Deuteronomistic word.

[7] This verse belongs to a short passage in which three apparently quite separate sayings have been placed side by side (xxxi. 27, 28, 29–30). Cf. S. Herrmann, *op. cit.*, pp. 166–167.

[8] For the significance of the use of this terminology throughout the Jeremianic prose tradition see S. Herrmann, *op. cit.*, pp. 162–169 and see further below p. 115.

'And it shall be that as I have watched over them to pluck up (נתש) and break down (נתץ), to overthrow (הרס), to destroy (האביד), and to bring disaster (הרע), so will I watch over them to build (בנה) and to plant (נטע)', says Yahweh.

In the hope and promise which these passages in the Jeremianic prose tradition express for Israel's future restoration from exile as well as in their style and phraseology, therefore, it is plausible to conclude that they owe their composition to the Deuteronomists, who have here further developed and applied the promise for Israel's future after judgement, which we found formulated in several passages in the Deuteronomistic corpus itself.

We have seen, however, that the brief record of the release of Jehoiachin at the end of the Deuteronomistic history (2 Kings xxv. 27ff.) is to be regarded as reflecting to some extent the hopes of the reactivation of the promises to David to which Jehoiachin's release and elevation in exile gave rise. At the same time we have observed that it is only here in this short passage in their history that the Deuteronomists have expressed, and then only in a veiled manner, such a messianic hope. In the light of this we now turn to an examination of some passages in the Jeremianic prose tradition which are concerned with the monarchy and with the role of the promises to David in Israel's future after judgement.

We have already seen that in some of the narratives in the book of Jeremiah (chs. xxvi and xxxvi) the burden of responsibility for Israel's rejection of Yahweh's Word spoken by the prophet Jeremiah is placed upon the shoulders of the king, and it has been argued that in this these narratives display one of the dominant motifs of the Deuteronomistic history according to which Israel's failure to obey the Law and the judgement which this entailed are attributed in like manner to the king. It seems clear, as von Rad has pointed out,[1] that in this the Deuteronomists have given expression to one of the central aspects of the ideology of kingship in the Jerusalem traditions where the total well-being (שלום) of the state is centred on the figure of the reigning Davidic king as Yahweh's Anointed.[2] In the Deuteronomistic theology the success of the monarchy depended in the last analysis not upon the promises to David but upon the faithfulness of each succeeding king to the Law of Yahweh (cf. Deut. xvii. 18ff.; 1 Kings ii. 1-4, ix. 4ff.). We may note here that the manner in which the Deuteronomists have

---

[1] G. von Rad, *Old Testament Theology*, I (1962), pp. 338ff.

[2] Cf. especially A. R. Johnson, *Sacral Kingship in Ancient Israel*², Cardiff 1967, pp. 1ff., 8ff., 12f., 136ff.

rendered the success of the Davidic dynasty conditional upon obedience to the Law is fully reflected in Jeremiah xxii. 1–5, which belongs to the Jeremianic prose tradition. That this passage owes its composition to the Deuteronomists is evidenced by its literary form of a proclamation of Yahweh's Law (v. 3) followed by a promise of blessing for obedience (v. 4) and a threat of judgement in the event of disobedience (v. 5. Cf. also xvii. 19–27). The same motif is expressed in Jeremiah xv. 1–4 which attributes the judgement which Yahweh brought upon his people directly to Manasseh. It can scarcely be doubted that this passage owes its composition to the Deuteronomists for whom also Manasseh, above all the kings of Judah, is singled out as the major cause of Yahweh's judgement upon Judah (cf. 2 Kings xxi. 11ff., xxiii. 26, xxiv. 3).[1]

The passages in the Jeremianic prose tradition which concern themselves with the role of the monarchy or the promises to David in Israel's future after judgement are few. This in itself, we may note, may be taken as reflecting the small part which they play in the promises for the future in the Deuteronomistic literature itself. As we have seen, the promises for the future in the prose in Jeremiah centre upon a return from exile and restoration of the land as well as the establishing of a 'new covenant' in which Yahweh himself is to take the initiative. In this also, as we have seen, the Jeremianic material finds close parallels in the Deuteronomistic corpus.[2]

The passages in the prose in Jeremiah which contain promises for the future centring on the kingship or specifically on the promises to David are xxiii. 1–4 and iii. 15, xxx. 8–9, xxxiii. 14–16, xxxiii. 17–26. Of these, xxiii. 1–4 belongs to a tradition-complex in xxi. 11–xxiii. 8 which centres on kingship and which comprises a number of oracles and sayings, in both verse and prose, which have been brought together in the course of transmission. The individual sayings in xxi. 11–xxii. 30 announce judgement on the Davidic monarchy in general and doom upon some individual kings in particular (Shallum xxii. 10–12, Jehoiakim xxii. 13–17, 18–19, Jehoiachin xxii. 24–30). The prose passage in xxiii. 1–4 takes up the element of judgement but concentrates on promise for the future and as such provides a counter to the sayings of judgement which precede it.[3] It takes the form of a short prose saying in which the terminology of 'shepherd' and 'flock' is

---

[1] Note the expressions: 'and the birds of the air and the beasts of the earth to devour' (Jer. vii. 33, xv. 3, xvi. 4, xix. 7, xxxiv. 30 and in Deut. xxviii. 26); 'and I will make them a horror to all the kingdoms of the earth' (Jer. xv. 4, xxix. 18, xxxiv. 17 and Deut. xxviii. 25).

[2] Cf. above pp. 82ff.

[3] See below pp. 90f. and note 1 on page 91.

employed to designate the king and people and their relationship one to the other. It begins with a condemnation of the 'shepherds who destroy and scatter the flock of my pasture' (*vv.* 1–2. Cf. l. 6) and culminates in a promise that Yahweh will provide his people with 'shepherds' who will care for them (*v.* 4). A further promise that Yahweh will gather the 'remnant' of his 'flock' from the countries to which they have been exiled is contained in *v.* 3. It is possible that this verse represents an insertion or, since it also employs the terminology of 'flock' and 'fold', it may have arisen as a further development of an original unit in *vv.* 1–2, 4. Together with this passage we may include the short isolated saying in iii. 15: 'And I will give you shepherds after my own heart and they shall feed you with knowledge and under-standing'. Both passages, xxiii. 1–4 and its dependent iii. 15, in both style and phraseology belong to the Jeremianic prose tradition and, short though xxiii. 1–4 is, it contains indications of Deuteronomistic composition.[1] In addition the judgement which is announced against the 'shepherds who destroy and scatter my flock' (xxiii. 1–2) together with the promise of 'shepherds' who will 'feed' Israel (iii. 15, xxiii.4) reflects the same ideology of kingship which we have found elsewhere in the Jeremianic prose tradition and which, as we have seen, is entirely in keeping with the Deuteronomistic emphasis upon the solemn obligations and responsibilities of the monarchy in the life of Israel.

In the light of this we may now examine briefly yet another saying in the prose in Jeremiah which centres on the same theme:

'And it shall be in that day', says Yahweh of hosts, 'that I will break the yoke[2] from off their neck[3] and snap off their bonds,[4] and foreigners shall no more hold them in servitude.[5] But they shall serve Yahweh their God and David their king whom I will raise up for them.'   (Jer. xxx. 8–9)

This saying is too short to allow any conclusions concerning authorship on the basis of style and language. There are other indications, however,

---

[1] The use of הִנְנִי with the participle (in this instance שֹׁבֵר) is characteristic of the prose in Jeremiah as also of the Deuteronomistic style. 'The evil of your doings' is frequent in the Jeremianic prose (cf. Jer. iv. 4, xxv. 5, xxvi. 3, xliv. 22. Its occurrence in xxi. 12 is probably a gloss; it occurs in a poetic passage in xxiii. 22), whilst the use of the *hiphil* of נדח (xxiii. 3) is also characteristic of the prose in Jeremiah (cf. Jer. viii. 3, xvi. 15, xxiii. 3, 8, xxvii. 10, xxix. 14, 18, xxxii. 37, it occurs in poetry in xlvi. 28) and is found in Deut. xxx. 1 which, as we have noted, has other points of contact with the material in Jeremiah.

[2] Reading 'yoke' with LXX instead of MT 'his yoke'.

[3] Reading 'their neck' with LXX instead of MT 'thy neck'.

[4] Reading 'their bonds' with LXX instead of MT 'thy bonds'.

[5] For this translation see J. Bright, *Jeremiah*, p. 270. LXX reads 'And they shall no more serve foreigners'.

that it also derives from the Deuteronomists. The promise that Yahweh himself would appoint a king over his people is reminiscent of Deuteronomy xvii. 15. Similarly, the promise that it is this king whom Israel will serve and not foreigners (זרים) may be taken as an echo of the same verse in Deuteronomy xvii which contains the warning that no foreigner (נכרי) is to be king over Israel. More striking, however, is the parallel between the promise formulated in this saying in Jeremiah and that contained in Nathan's words to David in 2 Samuel vii. 8ff.:

> Thus says Yahweh of hosts: 'I took you from the pasture, from tending the sheep, that you should be a prince over my people Israel; and I have been with you wherever you went, and have cut off all your enemies from before you; and I will make for you a great name, like the name of the great ones on the earth. And I will assign a place for my people Israel, and will plant them (ונטעתיו), that they may dwell in their own place, and be disturbed no more; and violent men shall afflict them no more as formerly, and from the time that I appointed judges over my people Israel; and I will give you rest from all your enemies.

In both passages, Jeremiah xxx. 8–9 and 2 Samuel vii. 8ff., the promise is the same: Israel's security among the nations is guaranteed through David whom Yahweh appoints (or will appoint) as king over his people; 'violent men' or 'foreigners' shall no more 'afflict' them or 'hold them in servitude'. On these grounds it is plausible to conclude that in this short prose saying in Jeremiah xxx. 8–9 the Deuteronomists have given expression to the belief that Yahweh would be faithful to and fulfil his promises of old to David.

A further saying which concerns itself specifically with the promises to David is contained in xxxiii. 14–16. This short passage is of particular interest, for it is a prose version of a poetic oracle in Jeremiah xxiii. 5–6. Short though it is, it nevertheless offers clear indications that it belongs to the Jeremianic prose tradition developed by the Deuteronomists. Thus the very fact that it is a prose version of a poetic oracle itself already suggests this, for it conforms to the usual method of the Deuteronomists of taking up traditional material in their possession and reformulating it to a greater or lesser extent in their own prose style. The phrase 'in those days and at that time' in *v.* 15 as against 'in his days' in xxiii. 6 evidences, if only to a small extent, the characteristic repetitive nature of the Jeremianic prose style. Attention may also be drawn to the expression 'to establish the word' (using the *hiphil* of קום) which occurs elsewhere in the prose in Jeremiah in xxviii. 6, xxix. 10 and in Deuteronomy ix. 5; 1 Samuel i. 23, (iii. 2); 1 Kings vi. 12, viii. 20, xii. 15. Furthermore, the promise here expressed that

G

Yahweh will 'establish' or 'perform' his Word reflects strongly the prophecy-fulfilment schema which constitutes one of the most characteristic features of the Deuteronomistic theology.

The question arises of the origin of the oracle in xxiii. 5–6 of which xxxiii. 14–16 is a prose version. Many commentators have attributed it to Jeremiah himself, largely on the grounds that it contains what is believed to be a play on the name Zedekiah (יהוה צדקנו).[1] But this argument in favour of the authenticity of the oracle is not compelling, for the terminology of 'righteousness' (צדקה, צדק) is firmly anchored in the ideology of the Davidic kingship and in the enthronement ritual attached to it (cf. 2 Sam. viii. 15; 1 Kings iii. 6, x. 9; Isa. ix. 6 (EVV 7), xi. 4, 5, xvi. 5, xxxii. 1; Ps. lxxii. 1).[2] Furthermore, throne names of a similar type are assigned to the coming scion of David in Isaiah ix. 5 (EVV 6) which in this respect as in others provides a direct parallel to the saying in Jeremiah xxiii. 5–6.[3] The Jeremianic origin of the oracle cannot therefore simply be adduced from a consideration of the specific terminology employed. Whilst, however, the possibility that the oracle did come from Jeremiah remains, there is one consideration which may indicate that it derived from a source other than him and belongs to a relatively late stage in the development of the Jeremiah tradition. The oracle together with the prose passage which immediately precedes it (xxiii. 1–4) comes at the end of a tradition-complex which not only announces judgement upon the house of David but in one place appears to assert its imminent extinction, for in the saying in xxii. 28–30 any hope for its renewal through Jehoiachin and his line is ruled out. This saying concerning Jehoiachin most probably belongs to an early stage in the formation of the Jeremiah tradition; almost certainly it could not have originated after 561 B.C. when, as we have seen, renewed hopes for the restoration of the Davidic dynasty through Jehoiachin and his line arose. In view of this it seems clear that in the earlier stages of its development the Jeremianic tradition held out no hope for the survival and restoration of the house of David.[4] If this is so

---

[1] So, for example, W. Rudolph, Jeremia[3], pp. 146f.; A. Weiser, *op. cit.*, pp. 204ff.; J. Bright, *Jeremiah*, p. 146.

[2] Cf. S. Herrmann, *op. cit.*, p. 210. For a fuller treatment of the place of 'righteousness' in the ideology of the Davidic kingship see A. R. Johnson, *Sacral Kingship in Ancient Israel*[2], Cardiff 1967, pp. 4ff., 11ff., 136ff.

[3] Cf. S. Herrmann, *op. cit.*, p. 210.

[4] Jer. xxx. 21 contains the promise of a future, native 'governor' and 'ruler' (משל) but it is not clear that he will be of the line of David (cf. W. Rudolph, *op. cit.*, p. 193). There are some grounds for believing that such a promise has its basis in an ancient Judaean tradition (cf. Gen. xlix. 10) which was at a later time related by Micah to the Davidic dynasty (cf. Mic. v. 1) but which in Jer. xxx. 21 has been reasserted with

then the possibility is that the saying in Jeremiah xxiii. 5–6 derived from a source other than Jeremiah himself and found its way into the Jeremiah tradition at a relatively late stage, very probably after the release of Jehoiachin and the expectations to which this gave rise among the exiles after 561 B.C.[1] At the same time it is clear that the promise of a 'righteous branch' contained in this oracle is presupposed by both Haggai and Zechariah (cf. Zech. iii. 8, vi. 12) both of whom in the early post-exilic period regarded it as being on the point of fulfilment in the figure of Zerubbabel. On these grounds it may be argued that the oracle originated in the exilic period, at which time it was also absorbed into the Jeremianic tradition. Subsequently it has been reformulated and placed as the preface to the complex of prose sayings in xxxiii. 17–26 on the indestructibility of the Davidic covenant. That this is so may gain some support from the fact that the material in xxxiii. 14–26 is missing in the LXX, which in this instance may represent an earlier stage in the development of the tradition, the further expansion of which is represented by the MT.

This brings us finally to a brief examination of Jeremiah xxxiii. 17–26. This passage comprises three sayings in prose (*vv.* 17–18, 19–22, 23–26) the first of which is clearly linked to the saying on the 'righteous branch' in *vv.* 14–16. Most commentators have regarded the passage as a whole (i.e. *vv.* 14–26) as late and probably post-exilic, largely on the grounds that it is missing in the LXX and appears to have its background in a situation in which both national and religious zeal had waned and when therefore the emphasis here placed upon the promises to David and the eternal ministry of the Levitical priesthood would have been necessitated.[2] Whilst the view that this passage belongs to a

---

[1] A parallel to such an understanding of Jer. xxiii. 1–6 as having arisen at a later stage in the development of the Jeremianic tradition as a counter to the oracles and sayings of judgement against the Davidic dynasty in xxi. 11–xxii. 30 is to be found in Ezek. xvii where Ezekiel's words of judgement and doom upon Zedekiah in *vv.* 1–21 are countered, as Zimmerli has shown (*Ezechiel*, BKAT 13, pp. 388–390), by *vv.* 22–24 which were added by the prophet's disciples at a later stage in the development of the Ezekiel tradition (cf. also Zimmerli's remarks on Ezek. xxxvii. 24–28, *op. cit.*, pp. 907, 913ff.).

[2] Cf. for example, P. Volz, *op. cit.*, pp. 311f.; W. Rudolph, *op. cit.*, p. 187: A. Weiser, *op. cit.*, p. 314.

---

its original meaning, unrelated to the house of David now (presumably) believed to have been finally terminated (cf. S. Herrmann, *op. cit.*, p. 221 note 22). That the promised ruler was not thought of as one of the house of David might be argued on the grounds that the particular stress on the fact that this ruler would be a native Israelite ('one of themselves . . . from their midst') would hardly have been necessary if a Davidide was intended.

late stage in the development of the Jeremianic prose tradition is very
probably true, it may nevertheless be questioned whether as late a date
for its composition as is suggested by most commentators is warranted.
Like other prose passages in the book which we have examined thus
far, this passage also must be regarded as belonging to the Jeremianic
prose tradition developed by the Deuteronomists. The expression
'David shall never lack (לא־יכרת לדוד) a man to sit on the throne of
the house of Israel' (v. 17) is found elsewhere only in 1 Kings ii. 4,
viii. 25 (=2 Chron. vi. 16), ix. 5 (=2 Chron. vii. 18).[1] Similarly, the
description of the Levites as 'the priests the Levites' (Jer. xxxiii. 18, 21)
is precisely as they are described in the Deuteronomistic literature. The
view noted above that this passage belongs to the post-exilic period is
plausible. On the other hand it is entirely possible that it belongs to a
late stage in the exilic period itself when, after the edict of Cyrus (cf.
Ezra. i. 1–4, vi. 3–5),[2] the possibility of rebuilding the Temple and the
renewal of the sacrificial cult which this would obviously have involved
became a reality and when also the hope of the reactivation of the
promises to David expressed in this passage and then more precisely
formulated in Haggai and Zechariah would have reached their zenith.
The intense manner in which both the covenant with David and the
covenant with the Levites is presented in this passage is just as plausibly
understood against this late exilic background as against that of the
post-exilic period.

We may now summarize our conclusions in this section. We have
seen that the material in the Jeremianic prose tradition which presents
Jeremiah and the prophets as preachers of the Law has both a didactic
and a kerygmatic purpose, for it would have offered to those to whom
it was addressed an explanation of why Israel had undergone Yahweh's
judgement in 586 B.C. and the ensuing exile, whilst at the same time
exhorting them themselves to live in accordance with the requirements
of the Law which their fathers had failed to do. Such an interpretation
of this material immediately raised the question whether the Deuteronomists at whose hands this material took shape could be accredited
with such a kerygma. From an examination of a number of passages in
the Deuteronomistic corpus it was concluded that, contrary to the
views of Noth, the Deuteronomists in their history-work, far from
announcing only a word of judgement were also concerned to proclaim

---

[1] The expression 'sitting/to sit upon the throne of David' is found elsewhere in the
prose in Jer. in xiii. 13, xvii. 25, xxii. 2, 4, 30, xxix. 16, xxxvi. 30. Cf. also Deut. xvii.
18; 1 Kings i *passim*, iii. 6, viii. 20.
[2] For Cyrus's Cylinder see *ANET*[2], p. 316.

to those who had survived the devastation of 586 B.C. the promise that if they 'turned again' to Yahweh he would have compassion upon them so that they could once again realize their existence as his people. At the same time we also saw that the short passage at the end of their history narrating the release of Jehoiachin from prison in exile (2 Kings xxv. 27–30) reflected the hope that Yahweh would be faithful to and fulfil his promises to David. On the basis of these considerations we then turned to an investigation of the promises for Israel's future in the Jeremianic prose tradition where we saw that the hopes thus expressed by the Deuteronomists concerning the restoration of Israel and Yahweh's promises to David have been further and more fully developed. We have also seen that such a development points for its background to the exilic period; and we shall return to a fuller examination of this later.

IV

We now turn to a brief examination of some passages in the prose in Jeremiah which are concerned with the problem of false prophecy. The passages in question are contained in chapters xiv, xxiii, xxvii, xxviii, xxix. Of these, it is widely agreed that chapters xxvii–xxix constitute a separate unit within the Book of Jeremiah.[1] As such, however, they are not to be thought of as having been given their present form and arrangement by an editor but as having already taken shape and been brought together into a unit of tradition in the course of the transmission and development of the original Jeremianic material. Here, as in many other prose passages in the book of Jeremiah, the LXX has a shorter text than the MT; and whilst in some instances this appears to be due to accidental omissions, in others it suggests that the MT represents a more developed form of the tradition than the LXX.

These three chapters have been developed on the basis of two separate events or series of events in the prophet's ministry. Chapters xxvii and xxviii centre on Jeremiah's dramatic presentation with the symbol of the ox-yoke of the inevitable Babylonian conquest and subjection of the minor states of Syria-Palestine including Judah, and the reaction which this symbolic act provoked. Chapter xxix has at its core the letter sent by Jeremiah to those who had been carried into exile in the first deportation in 597 B.C. All three chapters have been

---

[1] Cf. C. H. Cornill, *op. cit.*, pp. 303f.; P. Volz, *op. cit.*, pp. 251ff.; W. Rudolph, *op. cit.*, pp. 172f.; A. Weiser, *op. cit.*, pp. 244ff.

woven together on the basis of the common theme of false prophecy, which, though undoubtedly present to some extent at least in the original material, has been greatly developed by those who transmitted it, for whom this problem appears to have been of particular concern.

In the MT chapter xxvii comprises three units (vv. 1–11, 12–15, 16–22) each of which contains an oracle appealing for submission to the Babylonians and issuing a warning not to be deceived by those (false) prophets who have been forecasting the imminent downfall and collapse of the Babylonian power. The first saying is addressed to certain ambassadors from Edom, Moab, Ammon, Tyre and Sidon who were evidently in Jerusalem for consultations with Zedekiah about what possible concerted action they could take against the forces of Nebuchadnezzar. The second is addressed to Zedekiah himself, whilst the third is addressed to the priests and the people in general. The LXX follows the order of the MT but links the oracle to the priests and people with that to the king by the insertion of 'to you' (*scil.* Zedekiah) at the beginning of *v.* 16.[1]

Apart from a few insertions, Rudolph assigns the material in this chapter to his source A which comprises the original words of Jeremiah.[2] But the majority of commentators reject this. The chapter, even excluding the material omitted by the LXX,[3] forms an excellent example of the verbose and repetitious style which is wholly characteristic of the prose tradition in the book. Thus Duhm assigned almost all of it to a later *Ergänzer*,[4] whilst Mowinckel attributed it to his late Deuteronomistic source C.[5] Volz believed it to have received its present form at the hands of an editor.[6] Weiser assigns it to Baruch[7] as also does Hyatt who, however, finds evidence of some Deuteronomistic editing.[8] Bright classifies it among the prose passages composed by the prophet's disciples.[9]

The LXX has a shorter text of the first unit in this chapter (*vv.* 1–11) than the MT. Apart from a few minor and unimportant variations, the main differences are the omission by the LXX of *vv.* 1 and 7 and part of

---

[1] LXX reads: 'To you and to all this people and to the priests I spoke, saying. . . .' LXX also omits 'very shortly' and at the end adds 'I did not send them'.

[2] Cf. W. Rudolph, *op. cit.*, p. 173.

[3] See below.

[4] B. Duhm, *op. cit.*, p. 217.

[5] S. Mowinckel, *Zur Komposition des Buches Jeremia*, p. 42.

[6] P. Volz, *op. cit.*, pp. 255ff.

[7] A. Weiser, *op. cit.*, p. 245.

[8] J. P. Hyatt, *Jeremiah* (IB 5), pp. 1010ff.

[9] J. Bright, *Jeremiah*, p. 202.

vv. 5 and 8. Of these, however, the omissions in *vv.* 5 and 8 are very probably due to homoeoteleuton.[1] Most commentators follow the LXX in omitting *v.* 1, which is an anachronism in its present form in the MT.[2] *V.* 7 may be a later addition in the MT, though a number of commentators regard it as original.[3]

The essential historicity of the incident recorded need not be doubted. It is difficult, however, to find anything which can be regarded with any confidence as the original oracle or part of it. The introduction in *vv.* 2–4 may be original. *V.* 5 is typical of several other prose passages in the book and contains some Deuteronomistic phraseology.[4] *V.* 6 also belongs to the Jeremianic prose tradition (cf. Jer. xxviii. 14) as also does *v.* 8. *Vv.* 9–10 develop the saying further with a statement concerning false prophets. *V.* 11 appears to be the natural continuation of *v.* 8 from which it has been separated by *vv.* 9–10, which may on this account belong to a later stage in the evolution of the passage as a whole. In spite of all this, however, it is possible that *v.* 8 contains part of the original oracle or saying which is again repeated in *v.* 12, which itself may preserve the original saying: 'Bring your necks under the yoke of the king of Babylon'. But otherwise the material in its present form reveals all the characteristics of the Jeremianic prose tradition.

In the second unit, *vv.* 12–15, the LXX again has a shorter text than the MT reading only 'And to Zedekiah king of Judah I spoke in like manner, saying: "Bring your neck" ' in *v.* 12 and then jumping to 'serve the king of Babylon . . .' in *v.* 14. In this instance the MT text is to be preferred, however, since the last part of *v.* 14 together with *v.* 15 obviously requires the material which immediately precedes it and which the LXX omits. The third and final unit, *vv.* 16–22, is likewise much shorter in the LXX, which reads: 'To you and to all this people and to the priests I spoke, saying: "Thus says Yahweh: 'Do not listen

[1] The scribe's eye may have jumped from the first 'earth' to 'in my power' after the second 'earth' in *v.* 5 in the MT. In *v.* 8 it is possible that the scribe jumped from אשר after וחמםלכה to אשר after ואת in the MT, thus omitting 'which do not serve Nebuchadnezzar the king of Babylon'.

[2] MT reads 'Jehoiakim' instead of Zedekiah. Either we omit the verse (with LXX) or emend the text to read 'Zedekiah' (cf. *v.* 12).

[3] The verse is regarded as secondary by B. Duhm, *op. cit.*, p. 220 and C. H. Cornill, *op. cit.*, pp. 306f. Its authenticity is accepted by P. Volz, *op. cit.*, p. 258; A. Weiser, *op. cit.*, p. 248; J. Bright, *Jeremiah*, p. 200.

[4] For the hymnic element 'It is I who by my great power and my outstretched arm have made the earth, with the men and animals that are on the earth' see Jer. xxxii. 17f., 27, xxxiii. 2f. For 'by my great power and my outstretched arm' see Deut. ix. 29; 2 Kings xvii. 36 and for 'with an outstretched arm' see Deut. iv. 34, v. 15, vii. 19, xi. 2, xxvi. 8; 1 Kings viii. 42. Cf. also Jer. xxxii. 17, 21.

to the words of your prophets who prophesy to you, saying: "The vessels of Yahweh's Temple shall be brought back from Babylon", for it is a lie which they are prophesying to you; I did not send them. If they are prophets, if the word of Yahweh is with them, let them intercede with me.' For thus says Yahweh: 'Even the rest of the furnishings which the king of Babylon did not take when he deported Jehoiachin from Jerusalem shall be taken to Babylon', says Yahweh".' In this instance the LXX represents a different, perhaps earlier form of the tradition than that represented in the MT.

Chapter xxviii is clearly the continuation of xxvii and describes the confrontation between Jeremiah and the prophet Hananiah which arose from the symbolic act involving the ox-yoke. Hananiah rejects Jeremiah's prediction (cf. xxvii. 21–22) that there would be no early return from exile for those carried away in 597 B.C. (vv. 1–4). This is followed by a discourse by Jeremiah on true and false prophets (vv. 5–9). After this Hananiah takes the yoke from Jeremiah's neck and breaks it, announcing at the same time that so also will Yahweh break the yoke of Babylon from the neck of the nations who had become subject to Nebuchadnezzar (vv. 10–11). The final section (vv. 12–17) records that Jeremiah subsequently acquired an iron yoke to replace the wooden one which had been broken by Hananiah, and with this even more stark symbolism again announced that the nations will remain subservient to Babylon: 'An iron yoke have I placed upon the neck of all these nations to serve Nebuchadnezzar king of Babylon' (v. 14). At the same time an oracle of judgement and curse is announced against Hananiah himself (vv. 15–16) and the chapter ends with the record of his subsequent death 'in that same year' (v. 17).

Most commentators attribute the composition of this chapter to Baruch.[1] Once again it seems clear, however, that to understand the purpose for which this narrative was composed in terms of biographical writing is inadequate. Rather, whilst it does preserve the memory of a confrontation between Jeremiah and Hananiah, its primary concern is with the problem of false prophecy. As such it may more plausibly be regarded as having assumed its present form at the hands of the Deuteronomistic traditionists. The style of the chapter is typical of the Jeremianic prose tradition as a whole. We may note also the use of the expression 'to establish the word (of a prophet)' in v. 6 which, as we have seen,[2] occurs elsewhere in the prose in Jeremiah and frequently in

---

[1] Cf. B. Duhm, op. cit., pp. 216f.; W. Rudolph, op. cit., pp. 172ff.; A. Weiser, op. cit., pp. 252f.

[2] See above p. 89.

the Deuteronomistic literature. Furthermore, the criterion formulated in *vv.* 8–9 for discerning the true from the false prophet appears to be based upon Deuteronomy xviii. 21–22.[1] In addition, the grounds on which Hananiah is condemned and cursed are not only that he made the people 'trust in a lie' (*v.* 15) but that he 'spoke rebellion (דבר סרה) against Yahweh' (*v.* 16. Cf. xxix. 32),[2] a phrase which occurs elsewhere only in Deuteronomy xiii. 6 (EVV 5) where it is also the charge brought against false prophets and where likewise, we may observe, the penalty for 'speaking rebellion against Yahweh' is, as in the case of Hananiah, death. Finally, the Deuteronomistic fondness for recording the fulfilment of prophecy is evidenced in the note in *v.* 17 that Hananiah in keeping with the curse pronounced upon him by Jeremiah 'died in that same year' (cf. for example, 2 Kings i. 17, vii. 19–20, viii. 10–15).

On these grounds it seems clear that the Deuteronomists, as in other instances in the prose in Jeremiah, have here been concerned to draw out the implications of an incident in the life of Jeremiah for a problem which was of vital concern for them and for those to whom they addressed themselves. In this instance the problem in question is that of false prophecy and the event in Jeremiah's life which lent itself to the development of this theme was his confrontation with Hananiah. It is no longer possible to ascertain precisely what the content of that confrontation was. It seems clear, however, that it centred on Hananiah's breaking of the ox-yoke as a counter to Jeremiah's symbolic act as well as an oracle of assurance, again as a counter to Jeremiah's oracle of woe, the words of which are probably contained in *v.* 11: 'Thus says Yahweh: "Even so will I break the yoke of the king of Babylon[3] from off the neck of all the nations".' Jeremiah's response to this comprised a re-enactment of his symbolic act, this time with an iron yoke, together with an appropriate oracle of woe the words of which are probably preserved in *v.* 14: 'Thus says Yahweh:[4] "An Iron yoke have I placed upon the neck of all these nations to serve the king of Babylon".'[5]

As in the case of chapters xxvii–xxviii, xxix also centres on the theme of the problem of false prophecy, and here again a particular event in the ministry of Jeremiah, his letter to those carried into exile in 597 B.C.

---

[1] Cf. P. Volz, *op. cit.*, p. 263; W. Rudolph, *op. cit.*, p. 180; A. Weiser, *op. cit.*, p. 255; J. Bright, *Jeremiah*, p. 203.

[2] Both these texts are missing in the LXX.

[3] Omitting 'Nebuchadnezzar' and 'within two years' with LXX.

[4] Omitting 'of hosts the God of Israel' with LXX.

[5] Omitting 'Nebuchadnezzar' with LXX and also the remainder of the verse which is also missing in the LXX.

and the repercussions which this letter evoked, has provided the basis for the development of this theme. Once again the LXX represents a different textual tradition from the MT, the main differences being its omission of most of *v.* 14[1] and *vv.* 16–20, and again this possibly indicates that the LXX preserves an earlier form of the tradition than the MT.[2] As in the case of chapters xxvii and xxviii it is difficult to isolate the original material on which the chapter in its present form has been constructed. Bright considers the original letter to have comprised *vv.* 4–13, 14 as represented in the LXX, 15, 21–23 with an introduction in *vv.* 1, 3.[3] Rudolph and Weiser, both of whom ascribe the chapter to Baruch, take substantially the same view but re-arrange the original material in the order of *vv.* 1, 3 (introduction), 4–7, 10–13 and 14 (LXX), 15, 8–9, 21–23.[4] Volz takes the original letter to have comprised *vv.* 5–9, 12–13 and 14 (LXX), 15, 21–23, thus omitting *vv.* 10–11.[5] Duhm isolated *vv.* 4a, 5–7, 11–13 and 14 (LXX), 15, 21–23 as the original material which he assigned to Baruch.[6] It is questionable, however, whether so much of this material can so confidently be ascribed to the original letter. Leaving aside *vv.* 16–20 which most commentators omit, the letter as it now stands comprises four units: *vv.* 5–7, 8–9, 10–14, 15 + 21–23. Of these, the first (*vv.* 5–7) very probably belonged to the original letter; in both content and language it has all the appearance of being authentic. This authenticity, however, is further substantiated by the unquestionable change in tone which occurs with *vv.* 8–9. Here we have already an expansion of the original material with a warning against being deceived by (false) prophets and diviners (קסמים) with their 'dreams', a warning which reflects strongly that set forth in Deuteronomy xviii. 10–14 (cf. xiii. 2–3 (EVV 1–5)). That these verses derive from the prose traditionists of the book of Jeremiah cannot, in my opinion, seriously be doubted. The same holds true of *vv.* 10–11. Thus we may note that the promise that after 'seventy years'[7] Yahweh would restore his people from exile is found elsewhere in Jeremiah only in the prose passage xxv. 11, 12. Once again we note also the use of the expression 'to establish the word' which is found elsewhere in Jeremiah only in xxviii. 6 and

---

[1] The LXX reads: 'I will manifest myself to you'.
[2] See below.
[3] J. Bright, *Jeremiah*, p. 211.
[4] W. Rudolph, *op. cit.*, pp. 181ff.; A. Weiser, *op. cit.*, pp. 259ff.
[5] P. Volz, *op. cit.*, pp. 264 ff.
[6] B. Duhm, *op. cit.*, pp. 228ff.
[7] For the meaning of this see P. R. Ackroyd, *Exile and Restoration*, p. 240 note 27 where also further bibliography is provided.

xxxiii. 14, both of which are in prose, and frequently in the Deuteronomistic corpus. *Vv.* 13–14 must likewise be regarded as having been
composed by the Deuteronomists. The promise here set forth and the
terminology in which it is formulated are strikingly Deuteronomistic
and are closely paralleled by Deuteronomy iv. 29 and xxx. 1–5:

> You will seek (ובקשתם)[1] me and find (ומצאתם)[2] me; when you seek me
> (תדרשני)[3] with all your heart (בכל-לבבכם),[4] I will let myself be found
> by you, says Yahweh, and I will restore your well-being (ושבתי את-שבותכם)[5]
> and gather (וקבצתי)[6] you from all the nations[7] and from all the places
> where I have driven (הדחתי)[8] you, says Yahweh, and I will bring you back
> to the place from which I sent you into exile.

Vv. 16–20 which are missing in the LXX and may represent a later and
further expansion of the chapter also show strong indications that they
owe their composition to the Deuteronomists.[9] The repetitious nature
of the style is evidenced by the characteristic grouping together of
'sword, famine, and pestilence' (*vv.* 17, 18) and 'a curse, a terror, a
hissing, and a reproach' (*v.* 18). The curse formulated in *v.* 18 'I will
make them a horror to all the kingdoms of the earth' (ונתתים לזועה
לכל ממלכות הארץ) occurs elsewhere only in Jeremiah xv. 4, xxiv. 9,
xxxiv. 17 and Deuteronomy xxviii. 25. Finally *v.* 19 reproduces the
Deuteronomistic *Prophetenaussage.*[10]

Chapter xxix. 15 finds its natural continuation in *vv.* 21–23[11] which
is a further section of Jeremiah's letter to the exiles as presented, in
considerably developed form as has already become clear, in this
chapter. This section contains the curse alleged to have been pronounced by Jeremiah upon two prophets, Ahab and Zedekiah, who
were evidently active among those carried into exile in the deportation
of 597 b.c. and who are here condemned as false prophets. As we have
seen, most commentators regard these verses as an authentic part of the
original letter sent by Jeremiah to the exiles. Once again such a view
must be questioned, however, for the saying appears already to presuppose the execution, not to mention the actual manner of execution,
by the Babylonian authorities of the two prophets in question and the
terrifying effect which this had upon the exiles. In other words, the
saying is *ex eventu.* As such, and in view of its prose form, it is more

---

[1] Cf. Deut. iv. 29.   [2] Cf. Deut. iv. 29.
[3] Cf. Deut. iv. 29.   [4] Cf. Deut. iv. 29.
[5] Cf. Deut. xxx. 3.   [6] Cf. Deut. xxx. 3.
[7] Cf. Deut. xxx. 3.   [8] Cf. Deut. xxx. 1, 4.
[9] These verses reflect chapter xxiv. 8ff.   [10] See above p. 56.
[11] *V.* 20 must be regarded as having been inserted, after the addition of *vv.* 16–19, as
an introduction to *vv.* 21–23.

plausibly regarded as having been composed by the Deuteronomistic traditionists who have here further developed the theme of false prophecy already expressed in *vv.* 8ff. This is further evidenced by the fact that the charge here levelled against the two prophets that 'they spoke a word in my name which I did not command them' (*v.* 23)[1] as well as the penalty which they incurred for having done so appear to be based upon Deuteronomy xviii. 20: 'But the prophet who presumes to speak a word in my name which I did not command him . . . that prophet shall die'.

Jeremiah's letter as developed and presented in this chapter ends at *v.* 23. What follows (*vv.* 24–32) is a description of the repercussions which this letter evoked among some of the exiles. As it now stands the text of this section is confused. It begins with what was evidently intended to be an oracle concerning Shemaiah, yet another prophet among the exiles, but this is interrupted by and not completed after a short *résumé* of the letter which this prophet sent to Jerusalem complaining about Jeremiah's letter to the exiles and demanding that he be silenced (*vv.* 24–28). *V.* 29 then records that this letter was read by Zephaniah the priest to Jeremiah and *vv.* 30–32 record Jeremiah's response to this letter in which he condemns Shemaiah as a false prophet who has made the people 'trust in a lie' and who has 'spoken rebellion against Yahweh'. It seems clear that the essential historicity of the incident recorded cannot be questioned. Once again, however, this section owes its present form to the Deuteronomists: the charges levelled against Shemaiah are couched in the same terminology as that used in the case of Hananiah in xxviii. 15–16 and contain the phrase 'to speak rebellion against Yahweh' which, as we have seen, is dependent upon Deuteronomy xiii. 6 (EVV 5). Similarly, the penalty of death pronounced upon Shemaiah for having spoken such 'rebellion' is, again as in the case of Hananiah, that demanded for false prophets in Deuteronomy xiii. 2–6 (EVV 1–5).

On the basis of our discussion thus far it has emerged that the primary concern of Jeremiah xxvii–xxix is with the problem of false prophecy, and we have seen that the material in these chapters assumed its present form at the hands of the Deuteronomists. Two further passages in the prose in Jeremiah which centre on the same problem are xiv. 11–16 and xxiii. 23–40.

Chapter xiv. 11–16 belongs to a unit of tradition which comprises xiv–xv. 4 and which is composed of four separate and originally unconnected blocks of material in both poetry and prose. The material

---

[1] Omitting 'lying' (שֶׁקֶר) with LXX.

as it is now presented forms two sections, a lament in poetic form in xiv. 1–10 followed by a prose discourse in *vv.* 11–16 and yet another lament in poetic form in xiv. 17–22 followed by a further (predominantly) prose discourse in xv. 1–4. We have already seen that xv. 1–4 in both style and content shows all the signs of having been composed by the Deuteronomists.[1] Its composition as well as the position which it occupies arose directly, however, from the poetic material which immediately precedes it (xiv. 17–22). This material takes the form of a lament and displays the characteristics of the *Gattung* of the lament in the Old Testament.[2] Thus it begins with a description of the plight of the people (*vv.* 17–18) and continues with the plaintive question, very characteristic of the lament form, addressed to Yahweh and asking why he has brought such affliction upon his people (*v.* 19); this is followed by a confession of sin (*v.* 20), an appeal to Yahweh for deliverance (*v.* 21) and finally an expression of confidence and trust in Yahweh (*v.* 22). It is this lament here attributed to Jeremiah which has given rise to the composition of xv. 1–4, which is properly understood only in connection with it. On the one hand it announces that Jeremiah's intercession for the people as expressed in this lament is of no avail; the intercession of even Moses or Samuel could not now avert Yahweh's judgement upon them! By the same token, these verses also constitute Yahweh's response to the lament, a response which in contradistinction to the normally expected oracle of assurance[3] announces woe.

The relationship between xiv. 1–10 and 11–16 is to be understood in a similar manner. Thus again we have a lament (xiv. 1–10) with characteristic features of this literary form: a description of the plight of the people (*vv.* 1–6), a confession of sin (*v.* 7), the plaintive question addressed to Yahweh, in this instance asking why he delays to save (*vv.* 8–9a); there follows an expression of confidence and trust in Yahweh and an appeal to him to deliver his people (*v.* 9b). Once again, however, as in the case of xiv. 17–22, the oracle of assurance which is expected in response to the lament is replaced instead by an oracle of woe (*v.* 10). At this point the prose passage (*vv.* 11–16) begins, and, as in the case of xv. 1–4, is prompted by and is to be understood in connection with the lament which immediately precedes it. *Vv.* 11–12

---

[1] See above p. 87.

[2] For a recent discussion of these laments see H. Graf Reventlow, *Liturgie und prophetische Ich bei Jeremia*, Gütersloh 1963, pp. 154ff. For the form of the lament see S. Mowinckel, *The Psalms in Israel's Worship*, Oxford 1962, vol. I, pp. 195ff.; K. Koch, *The Growth of the Biblical Tradition* (1969), pp. 171ff.

[3] For this see S. Mowinckel, *op. cit.*, vol. I, pp. 217ff.; vol. II, pp. 58ff.; K. Koch, *op. cit.*, pp. 175f.

perform the same function as xv. 1–4: Jeremiah's intercession expressed in the foregoing lament cannot avert the coming judgement of the people; Yahweh 'will consume them by sword, by famine, and by pestilence'.[1] *Vv.* 13–16 arise directly from this oracle of doom: Jeremiah attempts to mitigate Yahweh's wrath by pleading that it is the prophets who must bear the blame since they have deceived the people by their oracles assuring them of peace (*v.* 13). Yahweh's response to this (*vv.* 14–16) condemns these prophets as false—he 'did not send them' (cf. also xxvii. 15, xxviii. 15, xxix. 9, 31)—and both they and the people to whom they prophesy are doomed to be 'consumed by sword and famine' (cf. xliv. 12).

In view of all this, it seems clear that xiv–xv. 4 must be regarded as having assumed its present form at the hands of the Deuteronomists. If this is accepted we may conclude that the prose passage xiv. 11–16 is to be taken together with xxvii–xxix as giving expression to the concern of the Deuteronomists with the problem of false prophecy. We now turn to a brief examination of one final passage in the book of Jeremiah, which is also in prose and which is likewise concerned with this problem, chapter xxiii. 23–40.

This passage belongs to a complex of sayings on the prophets which is partly in prose and partly in poetry (xxiii. 9–40). Whilst *vv.* 23–40 is for the most part composed in prose it embodies snatches of poetry, which indicates that in this instance, the prose traditionists have been working on the basis of older material.[2] The passage comprises two sections. The first (*vv.* 23–32) contains a condemnation of the prophets 'who prophesy lies in my name' (cf. xiv. 14, xx. 6, xxvii. 10, 14, 15, 16, xxix. 9, 21); Yahweh 'did not send them' (cf. xiv. 14, xxvii. 15, xxviii. 15, xxix. 9, 31) nor 'command them' (cf. xiv. 14, xxix. 23). The dreams which they dream are false and not the Word of Yahweh (*v.* 28). Just as this first section condemns as false those who prophesy 'dreams', so also the second section (*vv.* 33–40) condemns those who claim to utter 'the burden of Yahweh', for here also the 'burden of Yahweh' is nothing more than 'every man's own word' (*v.* 36), just as the 'dreams' are 'lying dreams' and not Yahweh's Word. The passage as a whole, therefore, like the others which we have examined (xiv. 11–16, xxvii–xxix), is concerned with the problem of false prophecy, in this instance

---

[1] The grouping together of 'sword, famine, and pestilence' occurs frequently in the prose in Jeremiah. Cf. xxi. 7, 9, xxiv. 10, xxvii. 8, 13, xxix. 17, 18, xxxii. 24, 36, xxxiv. 17, xxxviii. 2, xlii. 17, 22, xliv. 13.

[2] Cf. J. Bright, *Jeremiah*, pp. 147ff. Once again, however, I cannot accept Bright's interpretation of this passage solely in terms of Jeremiah's ministry and teaching. See below pp. 126ff.

with those who claimed to be Yahweh's prophets but whose 'dreams' and oracles were nothing more than the product of their own imagination and not the Word of Yahweh.

How then are we to understand the concern of these prose passages in the book of Jeremiah with this problem? It is clear that it was a problem with which Jeremiah himself was concerned (cf. Jer. ii. 8, v. 13, 31, xxiii. 9–22). But to interpret the prose passages in question solely in terms of his ministry and teaching is, once again, inadequate; their primary purpose, as with other prose passages in the book, is not merely to describe particular instances in the prophet's life and ministry or to preserve the 'gist' or memory of something which he had said. On the contrary, they are properly understood as the product of the traditionists and as such give expression to their solicitude with a problem which was of pressing concern for them and those to whom they addressed themselves. In keeping with their exegetical method and technique evidenced elsewhere in the prose in Jeremiah, these traditionists who, as we have attempted to show, are to be regarded as having belonged to the Deuteronomistic movement, have in this instance made certain incidents and sayings in Jeremiah's ministry the basis for expressing their concern with the problem of false prophecy, with the purpose of providing those to whom they addressed themselves with instruction together with a warning against the dangers which this problem posed for them. The question when and where this problem was an issue in the life of the community and found expression in these particular passages in the book of Jeremiah remains to be considered, and to this we shall turn in our next chapter. Once again, however, by way of anticipation it may be suggested that these passages, like others which we have examined, are readily understood as having taken shape in the exilic period when, in the shadow of the tragic events of 586 B.C., bitter disillusionment with prophecy would have emerged as a dominant factor in the life and thought of those who had experienced those events.

V

Thus far in our investigation we have been concerned for the most part with individual narratives or complexes of narratives and sayings in the prose material in the book of Jeremiah. The standpoint which has been adopted throughout and which some attempt has been made to substantiate is that this material represents the literary expression and deposit of a tradition which developed and took shape at the hands of the Deuteronomists, and which presents an interpretation of Jeremiah's prophetic ministry and preaching on the basis of theological concerns and interests which were of vital importance for them and those to whom they addressed themselves. There now remains to be considered the complex of historical narratives in chapters xxxvii–xlv; and it is to a brief examination of the nature and purpose of this prose material that we must now direct our attention.

As we have seen, these chapters form a continuous, chronologically arranged historical cycle which narrates the events leading up to and arising from the siege of Jerusalem in 586 B.C. and the fate of Jeremiah at that time (xxxvii–xxxviii), a brief account of the fall of Jerusalem, the capture and exile of Zedekiah together with the execution of his sons and the exile of 'the rest of the people' (xxxix. 1–10), the release of Jeremiah from prison and his favourable treatment by the Babylonian authorities (xxxix. 11–14, xl. 1–6)[1], the appointment of Gedaliah as governor of the community which the Babylonians left in Judah (xl. 7–12), the assassination of Gedaliah (xl. 13–xli. 3), the murder of the pilgrims from Shechem, Shiloh and Samaria (xli. 4–9), the rebellion of Ishmael (xli. 10–15), the flight of those who survived Ishmael's rebellion to Egypt against the counsel and under the condemnation of Jeremiah whom they forced to go with them (xli. 16–xliii. 7), a presentation of Jeremiah's ministry in Egypt comprising an oracle of woe against Egypt (xliii. 8–15), an extended prose discourse inveighing against the pagan cults practised by those who fled to Egypt and announcing judgement upon them (xliv), and finally a short prose appendix containing an oracle pronouncing blessing upon Jeremiah's scribe and companion Baruch (xlv).

This material has generally been regarded as having been composed by Baruch as part of his biography of Jeremiah. More recently the view has been widely accepted that the chapters in question are more properly understood as a history of the suffering endured by Jeremiah at the hands of his fellow countrymen during the siege of Jerusalem and after its destruction by the Babylonians in 586 B.C. The most notable presentation of this view, as far as I am aware, has been advanced by H. Kremers who argues that with the exception of certain passages, regarded by him as secondary, these chapters constitute a narrative cycle which as a whole and in its individual parts is to be interpreted as a *Leidensgeschichte* of Jeremiah and Baruch written by Baruch.[2] He

[1] For xxxix. 15–18 see above p. 18 note 2.
[2] H. Kremers, 'Leidensgemeinschaft mit Gott im AT. Eine Untersuchung der "biographischen" Berichte im Jeremiabuch', *EvTh* 13, 1953, pp. 122ff.

assigns the following passages to this *Leidensgeschichte* and regards them as having originally formed a self-contained unit which has been subsequently expanded by other material: xxxvii. 11–16; xxxvii. 17–21; xxxviii. 1–13; xxxviii. 14–28a; xxxviii. 28b, xxxix. 3, 14; xl. 13–xli. 2; xli. 4–9; xli. 10–15; xli. 16–xliii. 6; xlv. Even if, however, it be granted that the material omitted by Kremers is in fact secondary, it is doubtful whether the material which remains does constitute such a *Leidensgeschichte* as he suggests. Thus I find it difficult to accept his view that the central purpose of the narratives of Gedaliah's assassination (xl 13–xli. 2), the murder of the pilgrims from Shechem, Shiloh and Samaria (xli. 4–9) and the rebellion of Ishmael of which these incidents were a part (xli. 10–15) was to describe the physical or mental distress which these events caused the prophet.[1] That he did suffer because of them may be so, but the fact that in none of these narratives is Jeremiah even mentioned renders it very unlikely that their primary concern is with such suffering. It is true that xxxvii–xxxviii do appear to centre on the suffering inflicted upon him during the siege of Jerusalem in 586 B.C. and any exegesis of these chapters must give a prominent place to this. But the cycle as a whole cannot be classified as a *Leidensgeschichte*; its contents are much too varied to warrant such a view.[2]

A more satisfactory assessment of the nature and purpose of the prose tradition-complex in chapters xxxvii–xlv can be achieved only when its relationship with the other prose material in the book of Jeremiah is considered, specifically its relationship with the tradition-complex in chapters xxvi–xxxvi.[3] In addition to chapters xxxvii–xlv, three main tradition-complexes can be discerned in the book of Jeremiah as a whole as follows:

(1) Chapters i–xxv. 1–11 comprising a complex of shorter units of tradition containing oracles of doom against Judah.[4]

(2) Chapters xxv. 12ff., xlvi–li comprising a collection of oracles of doom against foreign nations.[5]

(3) Chapters xxvi–xxxvi. Coming as they do after the collection of oracles of doom against Judah in i–xxv and the fact that they embody

[1] Cf. H. Kremers, *ibid.*, pp. 136f.

[2] Cf. the remarks of M. Kessler, 'Jeremiah 26–45 Reconsidered', *JNES* 27, 1968, p. 87.

[3] For this and what follows see M. Kessler, 'Jeremiah Chapters 25–45 Reconsidered', pp. 82ff. Cf. also P. R. Ackroyd, 'Historians and Prophets', *SEÅ* 33, 1968, pp. 43ff.

[4] For this see C. Rietzschel, *op. cit.*, pp. 122ff.

[5] C. Rietzschel (*ibid.*) presents a detailed study of the evolution and history of this complex.

H

the so-called 'Book of Consolation' in xxx–xxxi + xxxii–xxxiii, chapters xxvi–xxxvi have usually been classified by commentators as comprising *Heilsweissagungen* expressing hope and deliverance for Israel and Judah after judgement.[1] As M. Kessler has pointed out, however, the note of doom which is struck so often in these chapters renders such a classification unacceptable.[2]

This complex is made up of what appear to have been originally separate tradition-units of varying length. We have already seen that chapters xxvii–xxix probably formed a separate unit of tradition which centred on the theme of false prophecy. It can scarcely be doubted that chapters xxx–xxxiii also grew and developed as a separate unit of tradition comprising oracles and sayings of hope and deliverance. It seems clear that the note of hope expressed briefly at the end of chapter xxix has provided the basis for the combination of xxvii–xxix and xxx–xxxiii. Chapter xxxiv centring on the theme of disobedience to the Law was possibly originally a separate unit. The same is probably true of chapter xxxv which is concerned with the same theme. Very probably, however, if these two chapters were originally separate units they were brought together at an early stage. Chapters xxvi and xxxvi which both, as we have seen, centre on the rejection of Yahweh's Word by the king who is the personification of the nation possibly originally belonged together and have been subsequently separated in the formation of the greater complex to which they now belong.

In view of the multiplex nature of the contents of the material in chapters xxvi–xxxvi it is difficult to ascertain the unifying factor which has brought together the separate tradition-units into the complex which they now constitute. Nevertheless, the fact that we have here sayings and oracles which are for the most part presented within the context of historical narratives suggests that the complex as a whole may be regarded as a history of Yahweh's Word proclaimed by Jeremiah—a Word which comprises both judgement and promises of blessing and restoration after judgement—and the rejection of that Word by Judah.[3] Thus the first chapter in the complex, chapter xxvi, describes the rejection of the Word of Yahweh and the vehement opposition which the prophet as spokesman of that Word encountered. In this way it sets the tone for the complex as a whole and was perhaps placed in its present position precisely for this purpose. The same is true also of chapters xxvii–xxviii which centre on the conflict between

---

[1] Cf. for example, W. Rudolph, *op. cit.*, pp. xixff., 168.
[2] Cf. M. Kessler, 'Jeremiah Chapters 26–45 Reconsidered', p. 83.
[3] Cf. M. Kessler, 'Jeremiah Chapters 26–45 Reconsidered', pp. 83f.

Yahweh's Word spoken by Jeremiah and the words of the false prophets as represented and typified by Hananiah. Chapter xxix is occupied with the same theme; once again Yahweh's Word is directly opposed by the words of the false prophets, in this instance prophets who were active among the exiles of 597 B.C. The conflict thus described centres on the question of the restoration of the well-being (שלום) of Judah after the events of 597 B.C. For Hananiah and those whom he represented that restoration was imminent; what had happened in 597 B.C. would quickly be reversed by Yahweh, by whom the power of Babylon would be broken. For Jeremiah, Yahweh's true prophet, what had happened in 597 B.C. was judgement justly imposed upon Judah because of her disobedience, a judgement, furthermore, which was yet to be completed. Hence, for those who had not undergone that judgement and who still remained in the land, the Word was one of inevitable doom (xxvii–xxviii) only after which, in the fullness of time (xxvii. 22), would they experience, together with those who had already undergone judgement and were thus already the object of Yahweh's renewed grace (xxix. 1–14), forgiveness and restoration (xxx–xxxiii). Chapter xxxiv returns to the theme of the rejection of Yahweh's Word, in this instance as formulated in the Law, by those who survived the deportation of 597 B.C. and a further proclamation of the judgement which this evoked. Chapter xxxv is occupied with the same theme. Chapter xxxvi forms the climax to the complex as a whole: the rejection of the Word there described is the ultimate rejection and the judgement which this entailed now becomes absolute; after this the prophet utters no new word until after the destruction of Jerusalem and the deportation in 586 B.C.

This leads to a consideration of the complex in chapters xxxvii–xlv the first unit of which, as we shall see, forms the sequel to and link with the complex in xxvi–xxxvi which immediately precedes it.[1] This further complex comprises four units of material which, with the exception of the final one (chapter xlv), constitute, as we have seen, a short record of the siege and destruction of Jerusalem by the Babylonians in 586 B.C. together with a description of the main events in the life of the community left in Judah after the exile in 586 B.C. and their eventual flight to Egypt.

1. Chapters xxxvii–xl. 6.[2] The narration in chapters xxvi–xxxvi of the rejection of the Word is now followed in these chapters by a

---

[1] Cf. M. Kessler, 'Jeremiah Chapters 26–45 Reconsidered', pp. 84f.
[2] Chapter xl. 1–6 appears to be a second account of Jeremiah's favourable treatment by the Babylonians already recorded in xxxix. 11–14. Cf. M. Kessler, ibid., p. 86.

description of the consequences of that rejection. The faithful prophet who is the spokesman of the Word is himself subjected to violent treatment by those who reject that Word (xxxvii–xxxviii). But both he and the Word of Yahweh which he proclaimed are now vindicated; the Word of judgement upon Judah's disobedience now finds fulfilment and is actualized in the destruction of Jerusalem and the exile of 586 B.C. (xxxix. 1–10),[1] whilst Jeremiah himself is released by the Babylonian victors from the imprisonment imposed upon him by his fellow countrymen (xxxix. 11–14, xl. 1–6).

2. Chapters xl. 7–xliii. 7.[2] This section deals with the period in the land of Judah immediately following the destruction of Jerusalem in 586 B.C. It narrates the appointment of Gedaliah as governor of the community left by the Babylonians (xl. 7–12) and the conspiracy and rebellion of Ishmael by whom Gedaliah was assassinated (xl. 13–xli. 3, xli. 4–15). It reaches its climax, however, in a description of the community's rejection of Yahweh's Word spoken by Jeremiah exhorting them to remain in the land and not to flee, in spite of the murder of Gedaliah and the revolt of Ishmael, to Egypt (xli. 16–xliii. 7). This further act of disobedience is described, as Kessler remarks,[3] in ugly colours and, as we shall see, is reinforced in the third section of this complex.

3. Chapters xliii. 8–xliv. This section describes Jeremiah's ministry among those who fled to Egypt. It begins with an oracle of doom against Egypt; there will be no refuge here for those who have fled from Judah in disobedience to Yahweh's Word, for Egypt also will be destroyed by the Babylonians (xliii. 8–13). Chapter xliv[4] takes the form of a long discourse, abounding in Deuteronomistic words and expressions, which describes the apostasy of the community now living in Egypt. In spite of all that has happened and the catastrophic punishment which Yahweh had inflicted in judgement upon his people, idolatry persists (vv. 1–10). And not only does it persist; it is now openly defended by those in Egypt who engage in it (vv. 15–19). Because of this the 'remnant' which had fled to Egypt are condemned, and condemned in language which is amongst the most bitter and intense in the whole book (vv. 11ff., 24ff.); none of them 'shall escape or survive . . . to return to the land of Judah' (v. 14).

---

[1] Perhaps based upon 2 Kings xxv. 1–12 (=Jer. lii. 4–16).

[2] For this as the second unit in this complex see M. Kessler, 'Jeremiah Chapters 26–45 Reconsidered', p. 85.

[3] M. Kessler, ibid., pp. 85f.

[4] Once again the LXX preserves a shorter text of this chapter than the MT. The differences are for the most part insignificant and suggest that the MT represents a further expansion of an earlier tradition represented by the LXX.

The question now arises of the significance and purpose of these historical narratives in Jeremiah xl. 7–xliv. The view that they constitute a *Leidensgeschichte* or part of a biography of Jeremiah written by Baruch cannot be sustained, for, as we have seen, in a number of them the prophet is not even mentioned. Rather, they are more properly understood quite simply as a history of the fate of the 'remnant' (שארית cf. Jer. xl. 11, 15, xli. 16, xlii. 2, 15, 19, xliii. 5, xliv. 12, 14, 28) left in Judah by the Babylonians after the destruction of Jerusalem in 586 B.C. and the ensuing exile. As such their significance and purpose can be fully understood only when they are considered alongside a number of other passages in the Jeremianic prose tradition, as the following observations seek to show.

We have seen that the primary concern of the complex xxvi–xxxvi taken as a whole is a history of Yahweh's Word proclaimed by Jeremiah and the rejection of that Word by Judah. It emerged from our examination of the material in this complex that the content of Jeremiah's message as there presented was that Judah stood under inevitable judgement and that only after such judgement would she again realize her existence as Yahweh's people. In this connection we saw that in Jeremiah's letter (xxix) those who had undergone judgement and were now in exile in Babylon were already regarded as the object of Yahweh's renewed grace and, as we have also seen, the promises for the future in chapters xxx–xxxiii are directed to them. It became clear from our examination of this letter that it owes its present form to the Deuteronomists. This means that any interpretation of it solely in terms of Jeremiah's ministry in the years after the first deportation in 597 B.C., that is, as providing the 'gist' of the original letter, is inadequate. Once again, as with other prose passages in the book, we must ask the question: what did this prose passage mean for those who composed it and for those to whom it was addressed? The answer to this is that such a passage would have been vital and meaningful for those in exile in Babylon throughout the exilic period, who would have interpreted it as designating them as heirs and future recipients of the blessing and restoration which it promises and who therefore would have regarded themselves as those with whom alone the future of Israel as Yahweh's people lay as against those who had remained in Judah. This view that the future lay with the exiles in Babylon alone was later taken up and fully developed by the Chronicler.[1]

---

[1] For this see most recently P. R. Ackroyd, *Exile and Restoration* ch. xiii. See further below pp. 127ff.

On the basis of this understanding of chapter xxix we may extend our investigation of this theme to Jeremiah xxiv which employs the imagery of the two baskets of figs to describe those who had been carried into exile in 597 B.C., the 'good figs', as against those who remained in Judah, the 'bad figs'. In its present form this passage clearly belongs to the Jeremianic prose tradition the language and style of which are well in evidence throughout.[1] At the same time the striking imagery which it employs indicates that it is based upon an authentic saying of the prophet himself. The fact, however, that it owes its present form to the prose traditionists means once again that any interpretation of it solely in terms of Jeremiah's teaching is inadequate. We have here yet another example of the phenomenon, which we have observed elsewhere in the prose in Jeremiah, in which an oracle or saying originally uttered by the prophet himself has subsequently been developed and applied by those who transmitted it to meet a particular need or provide instruction on a problem which was of concern or relevance to them in the situation in which they lived. Viewed from this point of view the reason why the original prophetic saying concerning the good and bad figs has been subjected to further development and expansion becomes clear, for in drawing a sharp distinction between those who had undergone judgement and were in exile after 597 B.C. and those who had been untouched by that judgement and remained in Judah, it would have continued to be of relevance for those in exile throughout the exilic period and who regarded themselves as the 'good figs' through whom alone renewal would come as against those who remained in Judah. That this is so is evidenced by the inclusion amongst the 'bad figs' of those who fled to Egypt (Jer. xxiv. 8), which very clearly presupposes the situation brought about after 586 B.C. and the murder of Gedaliah and the flight of the Judaean community to Egypt. This means that the composition of chapters xxiv and xxix was motivated primarily by a specifically theological and polemical intention, for they seek to assert the claims of the Babylonian diaspora to be the true remnant of Israel through whom alone renewal and restoration would be wrought by Yahweh as against those who either remained in Judah or lived in Egypt during the exilic period.

This immediately provides us with a key to the understanding of the central purpose of the narratives in Jeremiah xl. 7–xliv. Coming as they do after the description of the destruction of Jerusalem and the

---

[1] Note for example the expressions 'they will be my people and I will be their God' (v. 7), 'I will make them a horror to all the kingdoms of the earth' (v. 9), the use of the *hiphil* of נדח (v. 9. See above p. 88 note 1), 'Sword, famine and pestilence' (v. 10).

ensuing exile to Babylon in 586 B.C. (xxxvii–xxxix), they focus attention on the community which was left in Judah at that time. The question with which they are primarily concerned is whether this community constituted the remnant with whom the future of Israel as Yahweh's people lay. As in the case of chapter xxix but especially chapter xxiv the answer given is uncompromisingly No; the continued disobedience of those who were left in the land, their eventual flight to Egypt and the idolatry which they enthusiastically practised there render this impossible. They are condemned, as we have seen, in language which is amongst the most bitter and vehement in the whole book; apart from a few fugitives, they are quite simply written off without hope or future. Accordingly, as in the case of chapters xxiv and xxix, the material in chapters xl. 7–xliv asserts the view that the future of Israel lay with the Babylonian diaspora and like xxiv but with even greater intensity it polemizes against the Egyptian diaspora during the exilic period.

4. Chapter xlv. This final unit in the complex with which we have been concerned in this section of our study takes the form of an appendix comprising an oracle of blessing upon Baruch. For those who hold that the prose narratives in the book constitute a biography or *Leidensgeschichte* of Jeremiah written by Baruch this short prose passage is of obvious significance. Throughout the foregoing investigation of the prose material in Jeremiah, however, this view has been rejected, and because of this a reappraisal of the significance of chapter xlv becomes necessary.

The fundamental question involved in such a reappraisal is the actual contribution of Baruch to the formation of the Jeremianic tradition. The view advanced in this study regards his contribution to have been considerably less than that which most commentators attribute to him. In spite of this, however, his contribution was nevertheless significant. It seems clear that he was Jeremiah's sole disciple, at least in the active sense of the word, throughout the turbulent years of the prophet's ministry. As such, however, he was not merely a scribe or amanuensis passively recording the oracles and sayings of his master;[1] he appears to have been much more involved than this and to have identified himself actively with the prophet's woeful preaching against Judah which, at least in some instances, placed him in the same

---

[1] Against Mowinckel who in his earlier work on Jeremiah (*Zur Komposition des Buches Jeremia*, Kristiania 1914, p. 30) expressed the view that Baruch was nothing more than a scribe. In his later work (*Prophecy and Tradition*, Oslo 1946, p. 61), however, he rejected his earlier scepticism and accepted the more widely held view that the so-called biographical narratives were composed by Baruch: 'That these narratives originate from Baruch himself is extremely probable, not to say certain'.

peril as his master and incurred for him the same hatred with which Jeremiah himself was opposed (cf. xxxvi. 19, 26; xliii. 3). As Jeremiah's faithful disciple and scribe, Baruch would have been responsible for the recording of his master's sayings and oracles; the scroll which he was instrumental in compiling in 604 B.C. would have remained in his possession and it is obviously probable that he would have recorded and collected other and later sayings of the prophet. At the same time it seems clear that he alone would have possessed the knowledge, at times detailed knowledge, of the particular incidents in the life of Jeremiah which the narratives in the book presuppose and describe. Indeed it is precisely this intimate knowledge of the prophet's life which has been advanced by commentators as the strongest evidence that Baruch actually composed the narratives in question. Such a conclusion does not necessarily follow, however, and as the foregoing investigation of the nature and purpose of these narratives has shown it is in fact highly improbable that he did compose them. It may be assumed, however, that he was the source from whom those who did compose them acquired the detailed knowledge of Jeremiah's life which they presuppose. By the same token, it must also be assumed that the prophet's oracles and sayings were also acquired by the traditionists from Baruch by whom, as we have seen, they were initially recorded and collected. All of this means that Baruch occupied a key position in the formation of the Jeremianic tradition, for it was by him and through him that the prophet's oracles and sayings and the memory of the course of his prophetic ministry were mediated to the traditionists to become the basis for the development and formation of the individual units and complexes of material in the book and eventually the book itself. It is this role played by Baruch as Jeremiah's faithful disciple and scribe and the one through whom the continuation of the tradition was made possible which forms the background to chapter xlv which owes its present form and position at the end of the book of Jeremiah[1] to the traditionists who have here sought to honour Baruch for the role thus played by him as the prophet's disciple and mediator of the tradition.[2]

[1] The arrangement of the material in the LXX, which may be more original than that of the MT, indicates the possibility that the book as originally compiled ended with chapter xlv, the oracles against the foreign nations in xlvi–li having already been placed after xxv (so LXX).

[2] Cf. M. Kessler, 'Jeremiah Chapters 26–45 Reconsidered', pp. 86–87. That the saying is based upon an original oracle of Jeremiah himself is probable. What its original context and meaning was, however, are no longer possible to ascertain with any certainty.

This immediately prompts the question whether there was some direct relationship between Baruch himself and the Deuteronomistic traditionists to whom the book of Jeremiah owes at least substantially its present form. Whilst any attempt to answer this will probably always remain nothing more than speculative, there is nevertheless one possibility which may here be advanced for consideration. As we noted at an earlier stage in our study, a number of recent studies of Deuteronomy have drawn attention to points of contact between this book and Israel's wisdom tradition.[1] If this is accepted it suggests that those who were responsible for Deuteronomy and the Deuteronomistic corpus as a whole contained among their numbers people who belonged to the circles of the Wise. Now we know that Baruch was a scribe and as such may also be regarded as having belonged to the circles of the Wise. If this is so, however, it raises the possibility of a direct relationship between Baruch and the Deuteronomistic circle, more specifically with those of the Wise who belonged to that circle. Whilst, it may be repeated, this is merely a possibility, it nevertheless would offer a plausible explanation of how the oracles and sayings of Jeremiah and the detailed information of his prophetic ministry came into the possession of the Deuteronomistic circle.

VI

In the light of the conclusions arrived at in the foregoing sections of this chapter concerning the nature, purpose and origin of the prose material in Jeremiah and the process whereby the Jeremianic tradition as a whole as presented in the book of Jeremiah grew and developed, some consideration may now briefly be given to the record of the call of the prophet as narrated in chapter i.

Apart from the superscription in *vv.* 1–3 which need not concern us here, the chapter as it now stands comprises four units:

(a) the call and commissioning of Jeremiah as 'a prophet to the nations' (*vv.* 4–10);
(b) the vision of the almond rod (*vv.* 11–12);
(c) the vision of the seething pot (*vv.* 13–16);
(d) a further commissioning of the prophet with a renewed promise of divine protection (*vv.* 17–19).

Of these, (a), (b) and (c) were quite probably originally separate units which have subsequently been linked together in the formation of the

[1] See above p. 47 note 5.

call narrative as it now stands. The original call was probably confined to *vv.* 4–10 although even here, as we shall see, there is probably some secondary material. It is possible also that at least some of the material in section (d) belonged to the original call narrative.

What is of particular interest for our present purposes is that there is evidence that the call narrative in its present form was compiled as a brief anticipatory interpretation of the message of Jeremiah as it is presented in the ensuing chapters of the book and, in addition, that there is also evidence for the possibility that as such this call narrative assumed its present form at the hands of those by whom the Jeremianic tradition was developed and composed, that is, as we have attempted to argue, by the Deuteronomists.

Thus the vision of the almond rod (שָׁקֵד *v.* 11) and the accompanying saying 'I am watching (שֹׁקֵד) over my word to perform it' (*v.* 12) summarizes one of the major themes of the book as a whole, viz. the vindication of Yahweh's Word of judgement and salvation upon his people (cf. xxxi. 28; xliv. 27). Similarly, the vision of the seething pot and the accompanying saying 'out of the north disaster will break forth upon all the inhabitants of the land' (*v.* 14) crystallizes yet another of the main themes in the book, viz. Yahweh's judgement upon Judah at the hands of the Babylonians[1] (cf. Jer. iii. 12, 18, iv. 6, vi. 1, 22, x. 22, xiii. 20, xvi. 15, xxv. 9). We may observe also that *vv.* 15–16 in the same unit contain language which suggests that the original saying, probably contained in *vv.* 13–14, has been expanded by the prose traditionists.[2]

When we turn to an examination of the call vision proper in *vv.* 4–10 here again there is evidence to suggest that it has been given its present form by the traditionists who have developed the prophet's own record of his call in the light of the Jeremianic tradition as a whole. Thus the phrase in *v.* 9a 'I have put my words in your mouth' appears to be directly dependent upon Deuteronomy xviii. 18 where Yahweh speaking of the prophet(s) whom he promises to raise up to succeed

---

[1] Whether or not the 'foe from the north' originally designated the Scythians the book in its present form clearly identifies the foe as the Babylonians. See above pp. 8f.

[2] The construction הִנְנִי with a participle (in this instance קֹרֵא) is characteristic of the prose in Jeremiah; 'all the tribes of the north' occurs elsewhere in Jeremiah only in xxv. 9; 'to burn sacrifice to other gods' occurs elsewhere in Jeremiah only in xix. 4, xliv. 3, 5, 8, 15; the hithpael of שׁחת occurs only in prose passages in Jeremiah (Jer. vii. 2, viii. 2, xiii. 10, xvi. 11, xxii. 9, xxv. 6, xxvi. 2). Compare the phraseology of i. 16 with the prose passages xvi. 11, xix. 4, xxii. 9.

Moses says 'I will put my words in his mouth'. In the light of our examination of the Deuteronomistic conception of the role and function of prophecy in Israel and the manner in which in the prose material in the book of Jeremiah they have portrayed Jeremiah himself as exercising that role and function, it is not unreasonable to see in the use of this phrase in i. 9 an indication that they regarded Jeremiah as 'a prophet like Moses' (cf. Deut. xviii. 15, 18). We may also observe, by way of further support for this suggestion, that another prose passage in the book, and one which is markedly Deuteronomistic, also implies that Jeremiah was regarded as standing in the succession of Moses (and Samuel) (Jer. xv. 1–4).[1] Yet another phrase in the call narrative which may be dependent upon Deuteronomy is 'whatsoever I command you you shall speak' (Jer. i. 7, 17; Deut. xviii. 18).

Perhaps more striking still, however, is the presence in the call vision of Jeremiah of the language of 'plucking up', 'breaking down', 'destroying', 'overthrowing', 'building' and 'planting' (Jer. i. 10), for it is surely not without significance that combinations of these words occur in Jeremiah only in prose and never in poetic passages (cf. Jer. xii. 14–17, xviii. 7–10, xxiv. 5–7, xxxi. 27–28, xxxii. 10, xlv. 4). Furthermore, this terminology wherever it occurs in Jeremiah centres on one of the main themes of the book as a whole, viz. the theme of judgement and salvation after judgement. Accordingly, as with other elements in the call narrative in Jeremiah i, it can plausibly be concluded that the use of this judgement-salvation terminology in v. 10 was intended by those who gave the call narrative its present form as an anticipatory statement of one of the central themes of the Jeremianic tradition as a whole.

[1] See above p. 87.

4

THE HISTORICAL BACKGROUND OF THE JEREMIANIC PROSE TRADITION

IN the foregoing chapters some attempt has been made to show that the prose material in the book of Jeremiah, both the homiletical and the so-called biographical material, represents substantially the deposit and literary expression of a tradition which centres on the prophetic life and ministry of Jeremiah and which was developed by the Deuteronomistic circle. It has been maintained throughout that such a tradition emerged and evolved not as the result of a purely literary activity but within the context of a preaching and teaching activity which addressed itself to the needs of the community in which those responsible for it lived and worked. It has also been argued that the purpose of the circle to which we owe this tradition was not merely to preserve the memory of the words and deeds of Jeremiah, but to present an interpretation of his prophetic ministry and teaching on the basis of theological concerns and interests which were of vital importance for them in the age in which they lived. In order to bring our investigation to a conclusion we now turn to a consideration of the question of when and where this Jeremianic prose tradition originated and was developed as well as the possible *Sitz im Leben* of the preaching and teaching activity which it presupposes.

In the light of the conclusions arrived at in the preceding chapters of our study it follows that in order to determine the historical background of the Jeremianic prose tradition we must also discuss the background of the appearance of the Deuteronomistic history. Accordingly, in what follows we shall preface our discussion of the historical background of the Jeremianic material with a brief discussion of that of the Deuteronomistic history.

I

The question of when the Deuteronomistic corpus made its appearance has been discussed at an earlier stage in our study and we need now only briefly restate the conclusions arrived at there. As we have seen, whilst there is some controversy as to whether this history was compiled in the pre-exilic period and expanded in the exilic period or composed entirely in the exilic period, there can be little doubt that as it now stands it presupposes the fall of Jerusalem in 586 B.C. On the question of the *terminus ad quem* of its composition, the final verses in 2 Kings xxv recording the release of Jehoiachin from prison in exile offer valuable information, for we know that this release can be dated in 561 B.C. In addition, the fact that no indication is given that the second Temple had been or was being rebuilt confirms that 520 B.C. is the latest date. All this suggests that the Deuteronomistic history assumed its final form before 520 B.C. and after 561 B.C. and the probability is that a more precise date would be nearer the latter rather than the former of these two years. There has been some controversy, as we have noted, concerning the *terminus a quo* but it seems clear that the work as a whole presupposes the exilic period and for our present purposes this is all that is necessary.

When we turn to the main purpose of the Deuteronomistic historians, here also the exilic period provides the background against which it can be fully understood. Thus, the preoccupation of the history with recording Israel's increasing disobedience to the Law and her continual rejection of the exhortations and warnings of the prophets sought to explain to those who had suffered the tragedy of 586 B.C. why they stood under Yahweh's judgement. At the same time the word of hope which, as we have seen, finds clear expression in a number of passages is also clearly best understood as belonging to the exilic period when bitter disillusionment and despondency would have cried out loud for such a word.

Whilst, however, the period in which the Deuteronomistic history made its appearance is relatively easy to establish, the place of its origin is very much more difficult to determine. Noth, followed by many recent scholars, believes that the evidence points to Judah itself during the exilic period as the place where the Deuteronomists lived and produced their history.[1] He adduces two main arguments in favour of this view. In the first place it is maintained that the lack of any real interest in an expectation of a return from exile is best understood by regarding those who were responsible for it as having lived not in Babylon, where such an expectation clearly formed the central

---

[1] M. Noth, *Überlieferungsgeschichtliche Studien I* (1943, 1957²), pp. 96f., 107ff.; E. Janssen, *Juda in der Exilszeit* (1956), pp. 17f.; H. W. Wolff, 'Das Kerygma des deuteronomistischen Geschichtswerks', *Gesammelte Studien* (1964), pp. 308–324. For a discussion see also P. R. Ackroyd, *Exile and Restoration* (1968) pp. 65ff.

concern of those who had been deported, but in Judah itself.[1] In the second place, he also argues that a number of the traditions with which the Deuteronomists worked were of a localized nature and had survived the catastrophe of 586 B.C. subsequently to be collected throughout the land and used in the writing of the history.[2] Thus, for example, the Samuel-Saul cycle of tradition (1 Sam. vii. 5–viii. 22, x. 17–27) is believed to have been localized at Mizpah whence the Deuteronomists would have acquired it. Similarly, it is suggested that the material in 1 Kings xii. 32–xiii. 32 (cf. 2 Kings xxiii. 16–18) and 2 Kings xvii. 25–28 was derived by them from Bethel.[3]

To these arguments of Noth, Janssen adds others. He draws attention to the concern of the sermons and speeches in the Deuteronomistic history (and Jeremiah) with Canaanite idolatrous cults and practices and argues that this is best understood against a Judaean background rather than a Babylonian background.[4] He further argues that in Solomon's prayer in 1 Kings viii the Temple is depicted as a house of prayer rather than a place of sacrifice and suggests that this also presupposes a Judaean background, since the ruined Temple would have lent itself for precisely this purpose in the exilic period.[5] Janssen stresses also that the later narratives in Kings place the emphasis on the destruction of Judah and Jerusalem rather than on exile and once again contends that this is in keeping with the situation of people living in Judah after 586 B.C. rather than in Babylon.[6]

In my opinion none of these arguments is convincing. Some of them are very questionable whilst others, far from being arguments in favour of a Judaean background, can just as plausibly (if not more so) be understood as indications of a Babylonian background.

It has been observed that, contrary to Noth's view, a number of passages in the Deuteronomistic history are very much concerned with the hope that Israel having suffered Yahweh's judgement in 721 B.C. and 586 B.C. would once more realize her existence as his people (Deut. iv. 29–31, xxx. 1–6; 1 Kings viii. 46–50).[7] If this is accepted then these passages can very plausibly be understood as having been addressed precisely to those who had been deported, for in each case they are clearly concerned with the punishment of exile (Deut. iv. 25ff., xxx. 1; 1 Kings viii. 46) and with the possibility of Yahweh's forgiveness and grace after judgement. And this remains true even if,

---

[1] M. Noth, op. cit., p. 110 footnote.   [2] Ibid., pp. 96f.
[3] Ibid., p. 97.   [4] E. Janssen, op. cit., p. 17.
[5] Ibid., p. 17.   [6] Ibid., pp. 17–18.
[7] See above pp. 75ff.

as Noth believes, the passages in question had nothing to say about a return from exile. But it seems clear on various grounds that Noth's assertion that the Deuteronomists were unconcerned with such a return home from exile is not correct. Deuteronomy xxx. 1–6 is patently concerned precisely with the possible deliverance from captivity:

> And when all these things come upon you, the blessing and the curse, which I have set before you, and you call them to mind among all the nations where Yahweh your God has driven you, and turn again to Yahweh your God, you and your children . . . then Yahweh your God will restore your well-being and have compassion upon you; and he will gather you again from all the peoples where Yahweh your God has scattered you. If your exiles are in the farthest parts of the heaven, from there Yahweh your God will gather you, and from there he will fetch you; and Yahweh your God will bring you into the land which your fathers possessed, that you may possess it.

H. W. Wolff, whilst accepting Noth's view on this issue has clearly seen the difficulty for that view which arises from this passage.[1] His solution to it is that this passage contains marked parallels in vocabulary with parts of Jeremiah and he interprets this as evidence that its composition has been influenced by the Jeremianic tradition.[2] Two observations may be made on this view. In the first place, even if it is conceded that the Jeremianic tradition has influenced this passage, it nevertheless remains true that it is beyond doubt a Deuteronomistic passage. As such it must be seen as giving expression to something in which the Deuteronomists were interested, whether or not the actual concept behind it originated with them. In the second place, however, and closely associated with this, the very passages in Jeremiah in which Wolff finds the parallels with the Deuteronomistic passage belong for the most part to the Jeremianic prose tradition which, as we have attempted to show, was developed and assumed its present form at the hands of the Deuteronomists. The most plausible interpretation of this is surely that Deuteronomy xxx. 1–10 together with the Jeremianic passages in question assumed their present form precisely because the Deuteronomists were interested in the possibility of a return from captivity.

In view of this the question arises whether the other two passages which embody the Deuteronomistic kerygma (Deut. iv. 29–31; 1 Kings viii. 46–50) are also concerned with the expectation of return from exile. According to Noth 1 Kings viii. 46ff. is strong evidence that

[1] H. W. Wolff, *op. cit.*, pp. 317ff.   [2] *Ibid.*, pp. 318–319.

the Deuteronomists were not concerned with such a return, since here Solomon's request to Yahweh is that Israel would receive compassion at the hands of their captors in exile with no mention of a release from captivity.[1] But this is by no means as clear as Noth suggests. On the contrary, the passage can just as plausibly (if not more so) be interpreted as giving expression to the hope of a return from exile. In the first part of this section in the prayer the possibility of exile as judgement for apostasy is stated (1 Kings viii. 46). In the second part the plea is made that if after such punishment Israel 'turns again' to Yahweh he will both forgive their sins and 'grant them compassion in the sight of those who carried them away captive'. The meaning of this is surely that just as he will forgive Israel's sins so also he will undo the punishment for those sins, that is, bring the captivity to an end. In other words Yahweh's 'compassion' on Israel in this passage is to be understood in the same way as in Deuteronomy xxx. 3 where it means that he will restore her well-being and gather her from exile.

Deuteronomy iv. 29–31 may be interpreted in a similar manner. Here again vv. 25–28 announce the possibility of exile together with a description of its accompanying horrors. Vv. 29–31 then offer the possibility of release from such tribulation; the promise that 'Yahweh will not desert you or destroy you or forget the covenant with your fathers' must surely be interpreted as the promise of a reversal of the curse of exile expressed in vv. 25–28.

If our interpretation of these three passages in the Deuteronomistic history is accepted then it is surely plausible to understand them as presenting a word of hope to those who had been exiled. They would clearly have had more relevance for those who had suffered deportation and exile than for those who had remained in Judah and for whom a promise of return would have had much less significance.

A second consideration in favour of the view that the Deuteronomists lived and worked in exile, and one which arises from what has been stated above, concerns the centrality of the punishment of exile in the Deuteronomistic corpus. We noted above that Janssen argues that the later narratives in Kings place the emphasis on the destruction of Judah and Jerusalem rather than on exile and that this is in keeping with the situation of people who remained in Judah after 586 B.C. Against this, however, it must be argued that the manner in which time after time the threat of being driven out of the land is announced to Israel leaves little room for doubt about the way in which the Deuteronomists conceived of Yahweh's judgement in 721 B.C. and 586 B.C.

[1] Cf. M. Noth, *op. cit.*, p. 108.

(cf. Deut. iv. 25ff., vi. 15, xi. 17, xxviii. 36ff., 63ff., xxix. 28, xxx. 1f.; Josh. xxiii. 13, 15, 16; 1 Sam. xii. 25; etc.). It seems clear that for them the very heart of that judgement was exile and it was exile more than any of the other tragedies of those last desperate years of the Judaean state which motivated the eventual composition of the Deuteronomistic history. In view of this Janssen's argument on the basis of the last chapters in 2 Kings carries little conviction. If this is accepted then once again one is justified in asking whether this marked preoccupation with the curse of exile and deprivation of possession of the land in the Deuteronomistic literature could conceivably have arisen in Judah itself. Once again is it not much more probable that those for whom the exile constituted the real burden of judgement were precisely those who had suffered it?

The other arguments adduced by Noth and Janssen in favour of a Judaean background to the Deuteronomistic history are also very questionable. Thus, whilst it is possible that 1 Kings viii in depicting the Temple as a place of prayer presupposes, as Janssen argues, a Judaean background in the exilic period when the ruined Temple may have been used for this purpose, this chapter can in my opinion just as plausibly be understood as indicating a Babylonian background. In favour of the latter point of view attention may be drawn to the fact that in a number of verses in the chapter prayer is described as being made 'towards' Jerusalem (1 Kings viii. 29, 30, 35, 38, 42, 44) and it is possible that we have here a reflection of the custom, well attested at a later time, of Jews in the diaspora praying 'towards Jerusalem' (cf. Dan. vi. 11 (EVV 10)).[1] To this we may add a further consideration. Throughout the prayer of Solomon prayers are described as being directed to Yahweh as one who 'will hear in heaven' (cf. *vv.* 30, 34, 36, 39, 43, 45, 49). It is clear that this has its basis in the Deuteronomistic 'name-theology' of which this chapter in fact presents the fullest expression.[2] As such it need not necessarily presuppose an exilic

[1] On this and its relationship to the orientation of the Synagogue towards Jerusalem see H. H. Rowley, *Worship in Ancient Israel*, London 1967, pp. 231f. where also further bibliography is provided.

[2] On this 'name-theology' see G. von Rad, *Studies in Deuteronomy* (1953), pp. 37–44 and his *Old Testament Theology*, I (1962), pp. 184f. R. de Vaux, 'Le lieu que Yahvé a choisi pour y établir son nom', *Das Ferne und Nahe Wort* (Festschrift für Leonhard Rost), BZAW 105, Berlin 1967, pp. 219–228, argues that it was the Deuteronomistic historians who first gave expression to this 'name-theology' proper and that it was not, contrary to von Rad's opinion, already present in the original book of Deuteronomy where, de Vaux maintains, the expression 'the place which Yahweh chooses to place his name there' means nothing more than Yahweh's ownership and possession of that place (the temple).

I

situation. Nevertheless, the manner in which Yahweh's dwelling in heaven is so emphasized here (cf. especially *v.* 27) would most certainly have been very meaningful for people who had been deported from Judah; it would have been an assurance that even in exile and far from Yahweh's land their prayers would be heard.[1] For this reason also, therefore, it is plausible to infer that the Deuteronomistic history evolved in Babylon.

As to Janssen's argument that the concern of the Deuteronomists in inveighing against Canaanite idolatrous practices witnesses to a Judaean background, this can be explained by the fact that part of their task, as we have seen, was to describe how Israel after gaining possession of the promised land adopted such practices and in this way incurred Yahweh's judgement. Taken in this sense these sermons and speeches are of little relevance in discussing the question of the background of the history. Finally, Noth's argument concerning the material used by the Deuteronomists as having been collected by them in Judah in the exilic period is not convincing. We simply do not know by what means they came into possession of the sources with which they worked. It may be asked, however, whether for example the Samuel-Saul cycle of stories could not have been in their possession already in the pre-exilic period. There is certainly nothing to suggest that such traditions could only have been acquired by the Deuteronomists after 586 B.C. and still less to suggest that they could only have come into possession of them in the way supposed by Noth.

On these grounds, therefore, the arguments adduced in favour of a Judaean background to the composition of the Deuteronomistic history must be regarded as doubtful and it is clear that using in many instances the same evidence the view that it came into existence in the exile in Babylon is just as plausible.

II

On the basis of these considerations regarding the background of the Deuteronomistic history we now turn to a discussion of the question of the background of the Jeremianic prose tradition which, as we have argued, also developed and took shape at the hands of the Deuteronomistic circle. Once again, as we shall see, the evidence at our disposal does not warrant any assured conclusions on this question. Nevertheless, it does suggest that the balance of probability lies very

---

[1] On this and other aspects of Solomon's prayer see the remarks of P. R. Ackroyd, *Exile and Restoration*, pp. 27–28.

strongly in favour of the view that this Jeremianic prose material took shape and was developed amongst the exiles in Babylon in the exilic period, as the ensuing discussion seeks to demonstrate.

It emerged from our investigation of the nature and purpose of the prose material in Jeremiah that one of its dominant aims was to offer an explanation of the catastrophe which befell Judah in 586 B.C. and that according to the explanation thus provided what had happened was Yahweh's judgement upon Judah's failure to obey the Law and Yahweh's Word mediated to her by Jeremiah and the prophets. As we have seen, the theme expressed here forms one of the dominant features of the Deuteronomistic history and is properly understood as having evolved during the exilic period, when the question with which it is concerned would clearly have been very much to the forefront of the minds of those who lived in the shadow of the destruction of Judah and the ensuing exile. In this respect, therefore, the Jeremianic prose tradition must also be regarded as having emerged during the exilic period.

Another theme which arises directly from this and which likewise points for its origins to the exilic period is the centrality of the Law. It is well known that Judaism emerged from the exilic period as the religion of a book and that the canon of sacred writings which it embodied played an increasingly dominant role in the life of the Jewish people for whom it provided an assurance of their divine election. Henceforth it was the ordering of their life according to the teaching and requirements of this canon of sacred scripture rather than the practice of a particular cult which characterized the religion of the Jews; it was the *Torah* rather than the Temple which constituted the focal point in the life of the people of God in the post-exilic period.

It is quite clear, however, that the primary position thus occupied by the Law in the post-exilic period was no *ad hoc* creation of that period itself; on the contrary, it represents the culmination of a development which probably began in the late pre-exilic period[1] and advanced very considerably after the destruction of the Temple in 586 B.C. when the break-down if not total cessation of the sacrificial cult for those who remained in the land[2] and the impossibility of its continuance for those

---

[1] See below p. 124 note 2.

[2] Scholars are not agreed whether or not the sacrificial cult was maintained at least to some extent in the Temple after 586 B.C. E. Janssen, *op. cit.*, pp. 101f., argues that the Temple site was used during the exilic period for services of lamentation as well as the offering of sacrificial gifts (cf. Jer. xli. 5). Cf. also M. Noth, 'The Jerusalem Catastrophe of 587 B.C. and its Significance for Israel', in *The Laws of the Pentateuch and Other Essays*, London 1966, pp. 263ff. On the other hand D. R. Jones, 'The Cessation of Sacrifice after the Destruction of the Temple in 586 B.C.', *JTS* 14, 1963, pp. 12–31, has argued that sacrificial worship ceased for a period after 586 B.C.

carried into exile created the need for non-cultic forms of religious service. It was precisely in such a situation that the Law began to emerge as the focal point of faith and practice, and there can be little doubt that it was above all the Deuteronomistic circle and the literature which emanated from that circle which was responsible for the birth and initial development of this factor in the life of the people.[1] In the light of this it seems clear that the Jeremianic prose material in which the Law similarly occupies a place of obvious importance is also to be understood as having most probably taken shape and developed in the exilic period.

The question arises where this development which places such emphasis on obedience to the Law took place. It seems clear that it has its basis in the Deuteronomic theology which had already taken shape in the pre-exilic period in Judah; the book of Deuteronomy, whether or not in its original form it was designated the *Torah*,[2] was conceived of as a covenant document which aimed at controlling all essential aspects of Israel's life and the urgent parenetic style which characterizes it is intended throughout to drive home the life or death necessity of obedience to its demands. Nevertheless, the events of 586 B.C. must have greatly enhanced the importance of the Law in the life of the people and, for our present purposes most significant, the crisis which arose for those who had been deported and for whom the erstwhile cultic services of the Temple were now quite impossible can very plausibly be regarded as having provided the most obvious stimulus towards the advancement of the Law to the place of importance which it henceforth acquired. And this finds some substantiation in the fact that the evidence of a later period points to the Babylonian diaspora as those for whom the Law and obedience to the Law was of supreme and vital importance (cf. Ezra vii. 6, 10, x. 3; Neh. viii, ix, x. 28ff., xii. 44, xiii. 3; Zech. vii. 12).

In this connection attention may be drawn to the sermon on the Sabbath in Jeremiah xvii. 19–27 which we have had occasion to discuss at an earlier stage in our investigation of the Jeremianic prose tradition. The question of the origin of the Sabbath in Israel and its

---

[1] Cf. B. Lindars, 'Torah in Deuteronomy', *Words and Meanings*, edit. by P. R. Ackroyd and B. Lindars, Cambridge 1968, pp. 128ff.

[2] The use of the word 'Torah' to designate the book of Deuteronomy occurs in Deut. i. 5, iv. 8, 44, xvii. 18, 19, xxvii. 3, 8, 26, xxviii. 58, 61, xxix. 20, 28 (EVV 21, 29), xxx. 10, xxxi. 9, 11, 12, 24, 26, xxxii. 46 and these passages are generally regarded as later additions by the Deuteronomistic historian to *Urdeuteronomium*. However, some commentators would include iv. 44 as having been the beginning of the original book of Deuteronomy (so, for example, M. Noth, *Überlieferungsgeschichtliche Studien I*, p. 16).

significance and purpose in the pre-exilic period is a familiar problem in Old Testament scholarship and one which thus far has not been satisfactorily resolved.[1] It is clear, however, that in the post-exilic period and onwards it occupied a place of increasing importance in Judaism (cf. esp. Neh. xiii. 15ff.).[2] But once again scholars are virtually unanimous in the opinion that the emphasis thus placed upon observance of the Sabbath in the post-exilic period points for its immediate background to the exilic period in Babylon even though its roots were already firmly established in the pre-exilic period. Such early post-exilic texts as Isaiah lvi. 1–8, lviii. 13f. may be taken as reflecting a new emphasis on observance of the Sabbath which arose in the preceding exilic period. More important still, however, are the references to the Sabbath in the Holiness Code (cf. esp. Lev. xxiii) and in Ezekiel (cf. Ezek. xx. 12f., 16, 20, 21, 24, xxii. 8, 26, xxiii. 38, xliv. 24, xlvi. 1, 3, 4, 12) which are widely regarded as having been composed in the exilic period. Like other aspects of Israel's pre-exilic religious life and institutions, there is thus reason to believe that in the situation brought about by the exile to Babylon the Sabbath acquired a new or at least a renewed significance within the context of the life of those who had been deported. It is precisely because of the place of increasing importance which the Sabbath acquired in post-exilic Judaism that most commentators have regarded the sermon in Jeremiah xvii. 19–27 as having been composed in the post-exilic period. Once again, however, and in view of the preceding discussion, it may be argued that there is no need to look beyond the exilic period itself for the composition of this sermon; like other aspects of the prose material in Jeremiah, it can very plausibly be understood against the background of that period and in Babylon where such a renewed interest in and emphasis upon the Sabbath appears to have arisen.[3]

---

[1] For a discussion see H. J. Kraus, *Worship in Israel* (1966), pp. 76-88.

[2] Cf. H. J. Kraus, *ibid.*, pp. 87f.

[3] The sermon is based to some extent on the law on the Sabbath in the decalogue, for it forbids Israel 'to do' (עשׂה) 'any work' (כל-מלאכה) on the Sabbath (cf. Jer. xvii. 22, 24; cf. Exod. xx. 9, 10; Deut. v. 13, 14) and speaks of 'sanctifying the Sabbath day' (קדש את-יום השׁבת Jer. xvii. 22, 24; cf. Exod. xx. 8, 11; Deut. v. 12). (Does the phrase 'as I commanded your fathers' כאשׁר צויתי את-אבותיכם in Jer. xvii. 22 reflect Deut. v. 12 כאשׁר צוך יהוה אלהיך?) On the other hand the sermon also refers to the carrying of burdens on the Sabbath and of bringing them through the gates of Jerusalem, and in this respect it is strikingly reminiscent of Neh. xiii. 15ff. where the same terminology is employed. This need not imply that the latter is dependent upon the former, though such a view is possible. On the contrary, it is possible that both passages reflect a well established though otherwise unattested apodictic law forbidding the carrying of burdens on the Sabbath in Jerusalem. Cf. further S. Herrmann, *Die prophetischen Heilserwartungen im Alten Testament*, BWANT 85 (1965), pp. 173ff.

Yet another theme with which we saw the Jeremianic prose traditionists to have been concerned was the problem of false prophecy. It is
well known that the post-exilic period witnessed the eventual disappearance of the prophetic function in Israel.[1] Once again, however, the
conditions which led to the decline and cessation of prophecy did not
emerge in the post-exilic period itself but were initially brought about
by the destruction of Judah in 586 B.C. and the resulting exile. It is
true that already in the pre-exilic period the danger of false prophets
constituted a very real problem for Israel (cf. for example Deut. xiii.
1–5 (EVV 2–6); Hos. ix. 8; Mic. iii. 5–6; Zeph. iii. 4) and Deuteronomy
xviii. 20–22 evidences an attempt on the part of the Deuteronomic
authors to deal with it.[2] The fact, however, that in spite of the assur-
ances of 'peace' on the part of the official prophets, the tragic events of
586 B.C. befell Judah, must have led to deep disillusionment with
prophecy and would have given rise to an increasing suspicion of and
opposition to the prophetic office, all of which would have contributed
very significantly to the decline and eventual disappearance of it in
post-exilic Judaism; prophecy now met with a crisis which it never
succeeded in overcoming. Such disillusionment is already poignantly
expressed in Lamentations ii. 14, which is generally regarded as
deriving from the period immediately after 586 B.C. in Judah itself:[3]

> Your prophets have observed for you
>   false and deceptive visions;
> they did not expose your iniquity
>   to restore your well-being,
> but have observed for you oracles
>   false and misleading.

But the polemic already contained here is developed at more length and
with much greater intensity in Ezekiel xiii where the false prophets are
condemned with a vehemence unsurpassed in the rest of the Old
Testament.[4] Such a condemnation must be taken as evidence that
feeling against the prophets was even more intense in the community
in exile than in the homeland and, as Johnson has argued, it was
probably such a strong reaction against prophecy in Babylon that
led ultimately to its decline and disappearance which eventually found
permanent expression in the work of the P school and in the Chronicler's

---

[1] On this see further A. R. Johnson, *The Cultic Prophet in Ancient Israel*[2] (1962),
pp. 66ff.

[2] On this see further E. W. Nicholson, *Deuteronomy and Tradition* (1967), p. 68.

[3] For a different translation of this text and a possible connection between it and
Ezek. xiii see A. R. Johnson, *op. cit.*, p. 67.

[4] On this see W. Zimmerli, *Ezechiel*, BKAT 13, 1956ff., pp. 281ff.

work.[1] In view of these considerations the material in the Jeremianic prose tradition centring on the same problem may also most plausibly be regarded as having been developed in the exilic period. Furthermore, if this material assumed its present form at the hands of the Deuteronomists then it may be taken as reflecting their continued and indeed increased concern with a problem for which their Deuteronomic predecessors had already attempted to legislate at an earlier time (Deut. xviii. 20–22). Finally, in view of the very substantial amount of material in the prose in Jeremiah which deals with the problem of false prophecy and in view also of the fact that one of the passages in this material is addressed precisely to those who were in exile in Babylon (Jer. xxix) the balance of probability lies strongly in favour of the view that this material took shape and was composed in Babylon rather than in Judah during the exilic period.

Perhaps the strongest argument in favour of the view that the Jeremianic prose tradition evolved in Babylon during the exilic period arises from the material within it which displays what can only be understood as an attitude of censure towards the community which remained in Judah during that period; and it is to a consideration of this material that we may now turn.

The destruction of Jerusalem in 586 B.C. was the great watershed in the history of Israel, and the religion which emerged from the ensuing exilic period and was further developed in the post-exilic period was distinctively different in many important respects from that of the pre-exilic period.[2] The emphasis upon the Law and the related development of a canon of sacred scripture as well as the importance attached to the observance of the Sabbath, the significance of the rite of circumcision, the institution of the synagogue, and other characteristic features of Judaism assumed at least their normative form in the exilic period, even though in many instances they had their roots already in the pre-exilic period. What is of signal importance is the fact that the bulk of the evidence in the Old Testament points unmistakably to the exiles in Babylon as those among whom these distinctive features and institutions of Judaism emerged, eventually to be brought back to Judah itself and there established over the years largely through the leadership of such individuals as Sheshbazzar, Zerubbabel, Nehemiah and Ezra. Thus according to the Chronicler's history, which comprises the books of Chronicles, Ezra and Nehemiah, the continuity of the

[1] Cf. A. R. Johnson, *op. cit.*, pp. 69ff.
[2] On the significance of 586 B.C. see the article of Noth referred to above on p. 123 note 2.

Israelite-Jewish religion was maintained by those in exile in Babylon, and in this respect the substantial historicity of the Chronicler's record can scarcely be doubted. In this same history, however, this continuity is explained on the grounds that not only were those in exile the true remnant of Israel but that they were the only remnant, for according to the standpoint here expressed the catastrophe of 586 B.C. was believed to have resulted in either the destruction or exile of the people as a whole so that the land was left empty and desolate for seventy years to 'enjoy its sabbaths' (2 Chron. xxxvi. 17–21).

Such a view is quite clearly not in accord with the historical realities of the situation which resulted from the destruction of Judah in 586 B.C., for there is an abundance of evidence to show that not only was not all the population either killed or exiled but that, on the contrary, a very considerable community remained in the land after 586 B.C. Furthermore, there is not inconsiderable evidence to suggest that this community engaged in a great deal of activity, religious, literary and otherwise.[1] In view of this the Chronicler's description of the situation in Judah after 586 B.C. must be regarded as having been based not upon historical fact but upon an assessment of those who remained in the land as having been totally rejected by God and accordingly of no historical consequence.

The question arises of the origins of such an interpretation of the situation in Judah during the exilic period.[2] The answer which immediately springs to mind is that it had its basis in the deep division between the Jews and the Samaritans which was very much a live issue in the third century B.C. when the Chronicler's history made its appearance. The influence of this division can certainly be detected in a number of places in this history.[3] Nevertheless, it may plausibly be suggested that the Chronicler's assessment has its roots not in the Samaritan-Jew division but in the antagonism which arose between those who returned from exile in Babylon and those who had remained in Judah during the exilic period,[4] an antagonism which in turn points unmistakably for its beginnings, as we shall see, to the exilic period itself and the attitude of the community deported to Babylon towards

---

[1] On the exilic period in Judah see E. Janssen, *Juda in der Exilszeit*, already referred to frequently in the course of the foregoing study, and the relevant sections in P. R. Ackroyd, *Exile and Restoration*.

[2] I am indebted for much of what follows to an unpublished paper by my colleague Dr. Ronald Clements entitled 'The Babylonian Exile as Judgement and Renewal'. I am grateful to Dr. Clements for placing this paper at my disposal.

[3] Cf. for example, E. Janssen, *op. cit.*, p. 121; W. Rudolph, 'Problems of the Book of Chronicles', *VT* 4, 1954, p. 404.

[4] Cf. Ezra. iv. 1–5; Neh. ii. 19ff.; iv. 1ff.; vi. 1ff.

the community left in Judah which emerged at that time. That is to say, the exile created a division in the old population of Judah which deepened during the exilic period and was further intensified in the period after the return and ultimately found expression in the Chronicler's history and theology.

The negative attitude of those in exile towards those who remained in the land was theologically motivated; it was based upon the belief that the true remnant of Israel through which renewal and restoration would eventually be wrought by Yahweh were those who had been carried into exile.

Such a belief finds clear expression in the preaching of Deutero-Isaiah, whose ministry belonged to the last years of the exile in Babylon.[1] For him the exilic community was the personification of Zion and Jerusalem (Isa. lii. 2); they are 'all the remnant of the house of Israel' (xlvi. 3), 'Israel/Jacob my servant' (Isa. xli. 8–9, xliv. 1–2, 21, xlv. 4, xlviii. 20, xlix 3) and 'my glory' (xlvi. 13). By contrast the land from which they had been carried away lies desolate and waste (Isa. xliii. 28, xliv. 28, xlix. 8, 19, li. 3, lii. 9). Though 'robbed and plundered' and 'hidden in prisons' (Isa. xlii. 22), Israel's redemption from exile is at hand and she is called forth from Babylon to return 'to raise up the tribes of Jacob and to restore the preserved of Israel' (xlix. 6), that is, those of the old tribes who had remained in Judah and who could be expected to rally to the summons given from Babylon. In and through the redemption of the true Israel in exile those in the land would thus themselves experience renewal.

But this attitude towards those who remained in Judah which underlies the preaching of Deutero-Isaiah is openly declared in the sharpest possible terms in Ezekiel xxxiii. 23–29 which in this respect constitutes a *locus classicus* for the understanding of this attitude.[2] Evidently the Judaean community were claiming that they constituted the remnant of Israel through which national renewal would eventually come and they found assurance for such a claim in the Abrahamic traditions:

> The word of Yahweh came to me: 'Son of man, the inhabitants of these waste places in the land of Israel keep saying: "Abraham was only one man,

[1] This view has recently been contested by J. D. Smart, *History and Theology in Second Isaiah*, Philadelphia 1965, who argues for a Palestinian background for the prophet's preaching. The vast majority of scholars accept, however, that Isa. xl–lv presupposes Babylon in the exilic period. Cf. the remarks of P. R. Ackroyd, *Exile and Restoration*, pp. 120, 128ff.

[2] For the view that this passage does refer to those left in Judah after 586 B.C. see W. Zimmerli, *op. cit.*, p. 818.

yet he got possession of the land; but we are many; the land is surely given us to possess".'

(Ezek. xxxiii. 23–24)

Ezekiel is bidden to denounce such an assertion and pronounce judgement upon those responsible for it:

> Say this to them: 'Thus says the Lord Yahweh: "As I live, surely those who are in the waste places shall fall by the sword; and him that is in the open field I will give to the beasts for food:[1] and those who are in strongholds and in caves shall die by pestilence. And I will make the land a desolation and a waste; and her proud might shall come to an end; and the mountains of Israel shall be so desolate that none will pass through".'

(Ezek. xxxiii. 27–28)

The basis of such an attitude towards those who remained in the land after 586 B.C. is not to be found in any contrast in terms of morality drawn between them and those who had been exiled. It is true that in this passage Ezekiel enumerates the sins of the Judaean community (Ezek. xxxiii. 25f.). But this must not be regarded as implying that the exilic community had manifested a spirit of repentance; for Ezekiel such repentance would be brought about in the future by Yahweh himself (cf. Ezek. xi. 19f., xxxvi. 25ff., xxxvii. 23). The real difference between the two communities was not in this but in the fact that the exilic community was seen to have experienced judgement and as such to be now open to Yahweh's renewed grace on the basis of which a new beginning could be made. In this Ezekiel reflects the belief already expressed in the pre-exilic prophetic tradition according to which it was only through judgement that Israel could be saved. It is this assessment of the exilic community as constituting the true remnant of Israel here expressed by Ezekiel and implied in the work of Deutero-Isaiah which was further and fully developed in the post-exilic period to find ultimate expression in the work of the Chronicler.

The importance of all this for our present purposes is that precisely the same attitude towards those who remained in the land as well as the belief that those in exile in Babylon constituted the true remnant of Israel is found fully expressed in the Jeremianic prose tradition which, as we have argued, also emerged in the exilic period. Our examination of the tradition-complex in Jeremiah xxvi–xxxvi revealed that the content of Jeremiah's message as there presented was that Judah stood under inevitable judgement and that only after such judgement would she again realize her existence as Yahweh's people. We saw that in Jeremiah's letter to the exiles as developed by the prose

[1] Cf. BH³, *in loc.*

traditionists in chapter xxix those who had undergone judgement and were now in exile in Babylon were already regarded as the object of Yahweh's renewed grace and that the promises for the future in chapters xxx–xxxiii were directed to them. We saw also that chapter xxiv assumed its present form at the hands of the prose traditionists who, working on the basis of an original saying of Jeremiah himself, have developed the same theme: the 'good figs' are those in Babylon who represented the true remnant of Israel as against the 'bad figs' who are those who remained in the land or fled to Egypt after 586 B.C. Finally, it emerged that the central theme of the narrative-complex in Jeremiah xl. 7–xliv. was the same. Coming as it does after the record of the destruction of Jerusalem and Judah in 586 B.C. and the ensuing exile to Babylon (Jer. xxxvii–xxxix), it focuses attention on the community which was left in Judah at that time. The question with which it is primarily concerned is whether this community constituted the remnant with whom the future of Israel as Yahweh's people lay and the answer given is uncompromisingly No. On the contrary, these people are condemned in language which is amongst the most vehement in the whole book. Hence by a process of elimination, so to speak, this narrative-complex also points to the Babylonian exiles as those among whom the true remnant of Israel was to be found.

In thus asserting the claims of the Babylonian diaspora to be the true remnant of Israel this very substantial amount of material in the Jeremianic prose tradition is fully representative of what we have already found in Ezekiel and Deutero-Isaiah. Accordingly, if we are correct in seeing this material in Jeremiah as having taken shape and been composed in the exilic period there is every reason to believe that in representing the claims of the Babylonian diaspora its most obvious place of origin was in a circle which lived amongst the Babylonian exiles rather than in Judah itself.

This in turn means that we must regard the Deuteronomistic circle to whom we have attributed this material in the book of Jeremiah as having worked in Babylon rather than in Judah during the exilic period. Moreover, and by way of further support for this view, it is possible to find in the Deuteronomistic literature itself some evidence, even if in less clearly defined terms, of an attitude towards those who remained in the land after 586 B.C. which is similar to that which is characteristic of the Jeremianic prose tradition, Ezekiel and Deutero-Isaiah. In the description of the final destruction of Jerusalem in 586 B.C. 2 Kings xxv narrates that the Babylonian victors left only 'some of the poor of the land (מִדַּלַּת הָאָרֶץ) to be vinedressers and ploughmen' (*v.* 12) whilst '*Judah* was taken into exile from its land' (*v.* 21). It is possible that such a description of those who were left in the land was intended to stress the impression which the destruction of the state made rather than to give an accurate description of it.[1] Yet in view of what we concluded above it is equally possible and certainly plausible to regard the use of the expression 'the poor of the land' in 2 Kings xxv as having its basis in the view that those who were deported were the true remnant of Israel whilst those who remained in the land were of little or no significance.[2] And this seems to be confirmed by what immediately follows in the text, for the narrative proceeds to narrate the brief history of the community left under the rulership of Gedaliah, the assassination of the latter and the flight of that community to Egypt (*vv.* 22–26). Thus what hope may have remained for a new beginning in the land itself now also disappears just as in Jeremiah xl. 7–xliv the community left in the land is written off as the possible bearers of the hope for the future. And significantly enough it is precisely at this point that our attention is directed to the release of Jehoiachin (*vv.* 27–30) and, by the same token, to the Babylonian exile—the land lies destroyed (2 Kings xxv. 1–21), the community, such as it was, left in the land is without hope (*vv.* 22–26) and the real hope for the future lies with the Babylonian diaspora (*vv.* 27–30).[3]

At this point some consideration must be given to Jeremiah lii which

---

[1] Cf. E. Janssen, *op. cit.*, pp. 18, 32f.; P. R. Ackroyd, *Exile and Restoration*, pp. 29f.

[2] E. Janssen, *op. cit.*, pp. 49ff. finds a polemical element in the use of the expression 'the poor of the land' by the Deuteronomists who, it is argued, represented the views of the 'people of the land' (עם־הארץ) here regarded as the established land-owning population. Such an interpretation of the meaning of the expression 'the people of the land' is, however, very questionable (cf. E. W. Nicholson, 'The Meaning of the Expression עם הארץ in the Old Testament', *JSS* 10, 1965, pp. 59–66) and this renders equally doubtful Janssen's suggestion concerning the significance of the use of 'the poor of the land' (cf. also the remarks of P. R. Ackroyd, *Exile and Restoration*, p. 66 and the references provided there). On the basis of the later belief that the poor were the true heirs of Israel (e.g. Matt. v. 3; Luke vi. 20, 24) Ackroyd himself tentatively advances the suggestion that the expression 'the poor of the land' in 2 Kings xxv may possibly indicate that since Judah had been condemned and its leaders who had failed were now in exile, a new community would emerge from the poor who remained in the land (*ibid.*, p. 66 note 17). [There appears to be some ambiguity in Ackroyd's view, however, for in another place (*ibid.*, p. 30) he states that 'to those among whom the Deuteronomic movement was found, the *dallat ha'ares* were not impressive—in general—for their piety and religious understanding'. If this is so, is it likely that the Deuteronomists would have regarded them as those through whom a new beginning would be made?]

[3] Cf. E. Zenger, 'Die deuteronomistische Interpretation der Rehabilitierung Jojachins', *BZ* 12, 1968, pp. 28ff.; P. R. Ackroyd, 'Historians and Prophets', *SEÅ* 33, 1968, pp. 41–42.

forms, though with significant differences, a parallel account of 2 Kings xxiv. 18–xxv.[1] The most significant difference between the two narratives is the omission in Jeremiah lii of any reference to Gedaliah and the community left in Judah under his rulership and the presence instead of a summary of the numbers of people exiled and the stages of the deportations (including the deportation in 597 B.C. and adding a third deportation not recorded in 2 Kings). In view of this, Ackroyd has argued persuasively that the narrative in Jeremiah lii takes up an even more negative attitude than does 2 Kings xxv towards the situation in Judah:

> 'The implication of *v.* 27 with its reference to the captivity of Judah (so in 2 Kings) is made explicit by the detailing of the numbers deported in each stage of the events. Thus nothing was left to Judah which could have any real significance for the future. The completion of the narrative with the release of Jehoiachin then serves the same purpose as in 2 Kings; the king is released and this is a token of the working of divine grace.'[2]

Here again, therefore, we have evidence that for those responsible for the development of the Jeremianic prose tradition the future of Israel as Yahweh's people lay not in Judah itself during the exile but with the exiles in Babylon and, once again, it seems clear that such a standpoint is best understood as having been taken up by people who were in fact in exile in Babylon.

A further indication that the Jeremianic prose tradition presupposes the exilic period in Babylon arises from our consideration of the nature of the promises for the future of Israel expressed in that material. We have seen that the majority of passages in question centre on the promise of a return to the land for those who have been deported (xviii. 7–10, xxiv. 4–7, xxix. 10–14, xxx. 2–3, xxxi. 23–25, 27–30, xxxii. 36–41, 42–44, xxxiii. 6–9, 10–11, 12–13). It seems clear that promises for the future which appear in material composed in the exilic period and which so emphasize the hope of a return to and repossession of the land are properly understood when they are seen as having been addressed precisely to a community which had in fact been removed from the land and was now in exile. Such promises would obviously have been much more relevant for people in exile than for those who remained in Judah in the exilic period.

On these grounds, therefore, there are impressive arguments in favour of the view that the Jeremianic prose tradition developed and assumed at least substantially its present form in the exilic period in Babylon rather than in Judah.

---

[1] For what follows see P. R. Ackroyd, 'Historians and Prophets', pp. 42–43.
[2] *Ibid.*, p. 43.

III

Throughout the foregoing study it has been maintained that the Jeremianic prose material took shape not at the hands of individual 'authors' and 'editors' but within the context of a preaching and teaching activity which arose in response to the needs of a community and was addressed directly to that community. By this is meant that not only the material which can be attributed directly to Jeremiah himself but also that which can be regarded as secondary was in both its origin and at every stage of its development addressed to an audience. Thus the original oracles and sayings of Jeremiah, having been delivered in the particular historical situation in which he ministered, were subsequently transmitted and grouped together in accordance with the didactic and kerygmatic purposes of the traditionists. At the same time they were in many instances adapted and developed by the traditionists who also, as we have seen, made certain events and instances in the life and times of Jeremiah the basis for furthering their teaching and preaching interests. In this way there emerged separate tradition-units which were then eventually united, again in accordance with the purposes of the traditionists, into larger tradition-complexes. The result is that the book of Jeremiah in its present form was, at least substantially, the immediate result, so to speak, of the combination of a number of larger tradition-complexes.[1]

If such a view of the origin and development of the Jeremianic tradition is accepted then the preaching and teaching activity which it presupposes would have been carried out in a particular *Sitz im Leben* and the question immediately arises what that *Sitz im Leben* was. In view of the conclusions arrived at above that the Jeremianic prose tradition took shape and developed in the exilic period in Babylon, the suggestion which immediately springs to mind in considering this question is that the preaching and teaching activity which the Jeremianic tradition presupposes was carried on in the synagogue.[2] This does not necessitate the view that the synagogue during the exilic period was anything approaching the institution which was later fully developed in Judaism. But it is widely agreed that the origins of the synagogue are to be traced to the exilic period in Babylon when those who had been deported would have found occasions to come together for prayer and

---

[1] For a brief discussion see above pp. 105ff.

[2] A connection between some material in Jeremiah and the synagogue was long ago suggested by P. Volz, *Jeremia*, p. 300 and subsequently by W. Rudolph, *Jeremia*, p. xvi. Cf. more recently, E. A. Leslie, *Jeremiah*, New York and Nashville 1954, pp. 281, 283, 293; C. Rietzschel, *Das Problem der Urrolle*, pp. 21f.

meditation and to receive instruction.[1] Such gatherings not only would have contributed very significantly to the preservation of Israel's religion but also would have provided the opportunity for the further development of that religion and its orientation to meet the present needs of the people. For our present purposes it is entirely plausible to suggest that it was within the context of these gatherings that the Jeremianic tradition took shape and was developed. By this means the words of Jeremiah and his life as Yahweh's faithful prophet were given a contemporary relevance and those who had undergone judgement and found themselves scattered among the nations and far from the land of their fathers were assured that the Lord who had justly punished them for their sins was even now preparing to give them a future and a hope.

> I will let myself be found by you, says Yahweh, and I will restore your well-being and gather you from all the nations and from all the places where I have driven you, says Yahweh, and I will bring you back to the place from which I sent you into exile.
>
> (Jer. xxix. 14)

[1] For a recent presentation of this view with extensive bibliography see H. H. Rowley, *Worship in Ancient Israel*, London 1967, pp. 213–245, esp. pp. 224ff.

5

CONCLUSION

THE investigation of the growth and formation of the Jeremiah tradition, that is, the process whereby the book of Jeremiah took shape and assumed its present form, raises a multiplicity of problems. Broadly speaking two main stages in the evolution of the material in the book may be discerned: (1) the oracles and sayings of Jeremiah himself spoken during his prophetic ministry from his call in 626 B.C. to his exile to Egypt after the murder of Gedaliah, and (2) the subsequent transmission of these sayings and oracles in the exilic period during which they were utilized and in many instances expanded or developed to meet the changing circumstances in the life of the exilic community; the composition of narratives and stories intended to present the theological significance of incidents and events in the life and times of Jeremiah; and the addition of other material. The book of Jeremiah had thus probably assumed substantially its present form by the end of the exilic period.[1]

There is every reason to believe that already during Jeremiah's lifetime his oracles and sayings were committed to writing, for Jeremiah xxxvi records that in 605/4 B.C. a scroll of his early oracles and sayings was compiled by his disciple Baruch who, we may assume, would subsequently have expanded it with other and later sayings of his master. Numerous attempts have been made to isolate the scroll of 605/4 B.C. from the present book of Jeremiah. But there has been wide variation in the proposals advanced by commentators and it is very unlikely that we shall ever be able to determine precisely the contents of that scroll. The most we can say is that the contents of the *Urrolle* are very probably to be found for the most part within chapters i–xxv of the present book.[2]

---

[1] Allowance must be made for the probability that some of the material in the book was added at later periods. C. Rietzschel, *Das Problem der Urrolle* (1966) finds some very late material in the oracles against foreign nations (Jer. xlvi–li).

[2] It is highly doubtful whether we can point to any one particular section of chapters i–xxv as the *Urrolle*. Rietzschel (*op. cit.*, pp. 127ff.) argues that the *Urrolle* is to be found within chapters i–vi of which it formed the basis. But I find it impossible, for example, to doubt that the Temple sermon, the original form of which underlies

The foregoing study has been concerned with the second stage in the formation of the Jeremiah tradition. Even here, however, no attempt has been made to deal with the development of this stage as a whole but only with the problem of the provenance, composition and purpose of the prose material, which constitutes the most characteristic aspect of this stage and provides the key to understanding the process whereby and the situation in which the tradition as formed by the preaching of Jeremiah (stage 1) was further developed and given substantially its final form (stage 2). Little has been said of the poetic material in the book or of its relevance and significance for those who developed the second stage of the Jeremiah tradition.

Throughout our investigation of this prose material in the book of Jeremiah it has constantly been insisted that it is not to be thought of as having been developed within the context of a purely or predominantly literary activity on the part of individual authors and editors working privately, so to speak. It has been emphasized that just as the tradition came into existence as the result and deposit of Jeremiah's preaching to his contemporaries so also its further development was carried out by people who addressed themselves to a listening audience, more specifically, to gatherings of those in exile for worship and instruction, gatherings which probably constituted the beginnings of what eventually developed into the institution of the synagogue. As we have seen, what these people sought to do was to present to the community in which they lived and worked an interpretation of the prophetic life and ministry of Yahweh's prophet Jeremiah and to draw out, expand or otherwise develop for their own situation and time the significance of his oracles and sayings. They were not, it must be stressed, merely concerned with recording (or providing the gist of) Jeremiah's words spoken in times past; they were primarily engaged in *kerygma* and *didache*.

In bringing this study to a conclusion, however, it must be made clear that the interpretation of individual prose discourses and sermons in the book of Jeremiah in terms of a period and situation later than that in which Jeremiah himself ministered is not to be taken as precluding an understanding of many of them in terms of his own preaching. Thus, for example, whilst in its present form the Temple sermon in chapter vii. 1–15 comes from those who later developed the Jeremiah tradition, there can be little doubt that it is based on an authentic saying of the

chapter vii, was not contained in the scroll compiled in 605/4 B.C. In addition, it is not impossible that the *Urrolle* contained some oracles of hope for the future such as are found in the so-called 'Book of Consolation' in chapters xxx–xxxi.

K

prophet himself in which he inveighed against those who believed that
the mere presence of the Temple in Jerusalem was a guarantee against
Yahweh's judgement upon their evil doings. Or again, the saying
prompted by the two baskets of figs in chapter xxiv must be understood
as having had its original context in the period immediately after the
first deportation in 597 B.C. and then, as we have seen, later developed
to apply to the situation of the exiles in Babylon. Or yet again, the
sermon on the release of slaves in chapter xxxiv. 8–22 though in its
present form the work of the Deuteronomists points for its basis to
Jeremiah's attack on the treachery of Zedekiah and the Judaean
nobility on the occasion described. Likewise, without getting involved
in the vexed question of Jeremiah's attitude to the Deuteronomic
reform carried out by Josiah, it is by no means impossible that the
sermon in chapter xi 1–13 on 'the words of this covenant' is based on
the genuine tradition of something Jeremiah had said in support of that
reform and the demands of the book of the Law which played a vital
part in it. In other instances the original Jeremianic basis of subsequently developed prose discourses and sermons is more obvious. An
example of this is found in chapter xviii where *vv.* 1–6, 11a have all the
appearance of having been the original material which has subsequently been expanded by the addition of *vv.* 7–10, 11b–12. Similarly,
in chapter xix, *vv.* 1–2, 10–12 probably represent the original saying of
Jeremiah which has been further developed by the addition of *vv.* 3–9,
13, 14–15.

This does not mean that every prose sermon or discourse in the book
can be understood in a similar manner; some appear to be the *ad hoc*
creations of the Deuteronomists who developed the Jeremiah tradition.[1]
This much is clear, however, that wherever possible the exegete should
attempt to relate these prose discourses and sermons to the ministry and
preaching of Jeremiah himself and then, equally important, show how
they have subsequently been developed or adapted to meet the needs
of the later period and situation in which they were given their present
form.

[1] In particular, I consider it probable that the 'new covenant' passage in Jer. xxxi.
31ff. is entirely the work of the Deuteronomists (see above pp. 82ff.).

LIST OF ABBREVIATIONS

AcOr	*Acta Orientalia*
ANET[2]	*Ancient Near Eastern Texts relating to the Old Testament* (2nd edit., J. B. Pritchard, Princeton 1955)
ASTI	*Annual of the Swedish Theological Institute*
ATD	Das Alte Testament Deutsch
BH[3]	Biblia Hebraica (3 Aufl., Stuttgart)
BJRL	*Bulletin of the John Rylands Library*
BKAT	Biblischer Kommentar: Altes Testament
BWANT	Beiträge zur Wissenschaft vom Alten und Neuen Testament
BZ	*Biblische Zeitschrift*
BZAW	Beihefte zur Zeitschrift für die alttestamentliche Wissenschaft
CBQ	*Catholic Biblical Quarterly*
EvTh	*Evangelische Theologie*
ExpT	*The Expository Times*
FRLANT	Forschungen zur Religion und Literatur des Alten und Neuen Testaments
HTR	*Harvard Theological Review*
IB	Interpreter's Bible
ICC	International Critical Commentary
IEJ	*Israel Exploration Journal*
JBL	*Journal of Biblical Literature*
JBR	*Journal of Bible and Religion*
JNES	*Journal of Near Eastern Studies*
JSS	*Journal of Semitic Studies*
JTS	*Journal of Theological Studies*
LXX	The Septuagint
MT	The Massoretic Text
OTS	*Oudtestamentische Studiën*
RHPhR	*Revue d'Histoire et de Philosophie Religieuses*
SEÅ	*Svensk Exegetisk Årsbok*
SVT	*Supplements to Vetus Testamentum*
TGUOS	*Transactions of the Glasgow University Oriental Society*
ThZ	*Theologische Zeitschrift*
TLZ	*Theologische Literaturzeitung*
TTZ	*Trierer Theologische Zeitschrift*
VT	*Vetus Testamentum*
WMANT	Wissenschaftliche Monographien zum Alten und Neuen Testament
ZAW	*Zeitschrift für die alttestamentliche Wissenschaft*
ZTK	*Zeitschrift für Theologie und Kirche*

BIBLIOGRAPHY

ACKROYD, P. R., 'The Vitality of the Word of God in the Old Testament', *ASTI* 1, 1962, pp. 7–23.

'Historians and Prophets', *SEÅ* 33, 1968, pp. 18–54.

Exile and Restoration, London 1968.

ANDERSON, G. W., 'Some Aspects of the Uppsala School of Old Testament Study', *HTR* 43, 1950, pp. 239–256.

AUGUSTIN, F., 'Baruch und das Buch Jeremia', *ZAW* 67, 1955, pp. 50–56.

BENTZEN, A., *Introduction to the Old Testament*, 2nd edition, Copenhagen 1952.

BEYERLIN, W., *Herkunft und Geschichte der ältesten Sinaitraditionen*, Tübingen 1961. References in this book to English trans. by S. Rudman, *Origins and History of the Oldest Sinaitic Traditions*, Oxford 1965.

BIRKELAND, H., *Zum hebräischen Traditionswesen*, Oslo 1938.

BOECKER, H. J., *Redeformen des Rechtslebens im Alten Testament*, WMANT 14, Neukirchen 1964.

BRIGHT, J., 'The Date of the Prose Sermons of Jeremiah', *JBL* 70, 1951, pp. 15–35.

A History of Israel, Philadelphia 1959, London 1960.

Jeremiah, Anchor Bible, New York 1965.

BRUEGGEMANN, W., 'The Kerygma of the Deuteronomistic Historian', *Interpretation* 22, 1968, pp. 387–402.

BURNEY, C. F., *Notes on the Hebrew Text of the Books of Kings*, Oxford 1903.

CARPENTER, J. E., *The Composition of the Hexateuch*, London 1902 (with G. Harford).

CHEYNE, T. K., *Jeremiah, His Life and Times*, London 1888.

CLEMENTS, R. E., 'The Babylonian Exile as Judgement and Renewal' (unpublished).

COLENSO, J. W., *The Pentateuch and Book of Joshua Critically Examined*, Part VII, London 1879.

CORNILL, C. H., *Das Buch Jeremia*, Leipzig 1905.

CROSS, F. M., 'The Contribution of the Qumran Discoveries to the Study of the Biblical Text', *IEJ* 16, 1966, pp. 81–95.

DRIVER, S. R., *Deuteronomy*, ICC, 3rd edition, Edinburgh 1902.

DUHM, B., *Das Buch Jeremia*, Tübingen and Leipzig 1901.

EISSFELDT, O., *Einleitung in das Alte Testament*, 3rd edition, Tübingen 1964. References in this book to English trans. by P. R. Ackroyd, *The Old Testament: An Introduction*, Oxford 1965.

ENGNELL, I., *Gamla Testamentet I*, Stockholm 1945.

'Methodological Aspects of Old Testament Study', *SVT* 7, Leiden 1960.

'Jeremias bok', *Svenskt Bibliskt Uppslagsverk*, 2nd edition, Stockholm 1962, cols. 1098–1106.

ERBT, W., *Jeremia und seine Zeit*, Göttingen 1902.

FOHRER, G., 'Jeremias Tempelwort (Jeremia 7. 1–15)', *ThZ* 5, 1949, pp. 401–417 reprinted in his *Studien zur Alttestamentliche Prophetie*, BZAW 99, Berlin 1967, pp. 190–203.

Einleitung in das Alte Testament, Heidelberg 1965 (10th completely revised edition of E. Sellin, *Einleitung in das Alte Testament*, first published 1910).

References in this book to English trans. by D. Green, *Introduction to the Old Testament*, New York and Nashville 1968.

FRANKENA, R., 'The Vassal-Treaties of Esarhaddon and the Dating of Deuteronomy', *OTS* 14, 1965, pp. 122–154.

GEHMAN, H. S., See under Montgomery, J. A.

GERSTENBERGER, E., *Wesen und Herkunft des 'Apodiktischen Rechts'*, WMANT 20, Neukirchen 1965.

GORDON, T. C., 'A New Date for Jeremiah', *ExpT* 44, 1932/33, pp. 562–565.

GRAY, J., *I and II Kings*, London 1964.

GROSS, H., 'Gab es in Israel ein prophetisches Amt?', *TTZ* 73, 1964, pp. 336–349.

GUILLAUME, A., 'The Root אוֹן in Hebrew', *JTS* 34, 1933, pp. 62–64.

GUNNEWEG, A. H. J., *Mündliche und schriftliche Tradition der vorexilischen Prophetenbücher*, FRLANT 73, Göttingen 1959.

HAHN, H., *The Old Testament in Modern Research*, Philadelphia 1954, London 1956.

HARFORD, G., See under CARPENTER, J. E.

HERRMANN, S., *Die prophetische Heilserwartungen im Alten Testament*, BWANT 85, Stuttgart 1965.

HOLLADAY, W. L., 'Prototype and Copies: a new approach to the poetry-prose problem in the Book of Jeremiah', *JBL* 79, 1960, pp. 351–367.

HÖLSCHER, G., *Die Profeten*, Leipzig 1914.

'Komposition und Ursprung des Deuteronomiums', *ZAW* 40, 1922, pp. 161–255.

'Das Buch der Könige: seine Quellen und seine Redaktion', *Eucharisterion. Festschrift für Gunkel*, FRLANT 18, 1923, pp. 158–213.

HORST, F., 'Die Anfänge des Propheten Jeremia', *ZAW* 41, 1923, pp. 94–153.

HYATT, J. P., 'The Deuteronomic Edition of Jeremiah', *Vanderbilt Studies in the Humanities*, I, Nashville 1951, pp. 71–95.

The Book of Jeremiah, IB 5, New York 1956.

'The Beginning of Jeremiah's Prophecy', *ZAW* 78, 1966, pp. 204–214.

JANSSEN, E., *Juda in der Exilszeit*, FRLANT 69, Göttingen 1956.

JOHNSON, A. R., *The Cultic Prophet in Ancient Israel*, 2nd edition, Cardiff 1962.

Sacral Kingship in Ancient Israel, 2nd edition, Cardiff 1967.

JOHNSTONE, W., 'The Setting of Jeremiah's Prophetic Activity', *TGUOS* xxi, 1965/66, pp. 47–55.

JONES, D. R., 'The Traditio of the Oracles of Isaiah of Jerusalem', *ZAW* 67, 1955, pp. 226–246.

'The Cessation of Sacrifice after the Destruction of the Temple in 586 B.C.', *JTS* 14, 1963, pp. 12–31.

KAISER, O., *Einführung in die exegetischen Methoden*, München 1964.

KAUFMANN, Y., *The Religion of Israel*, English trans. by M. Greenberg, London 1961.

KENNETT, R. H., 'The Date of Deuteronomy', *JTS* 7, 1906, pp. 481–500.

KESSLER, M., 'Form-Critical Suggestions on Jer. 36', *CBQ* 28, 1966, pp. 389ff.

'Jeremiah Chapters 26–45 Reconsidered', *JNES* 27, 1968, pp. 81–88.

KOCH, K., *Was ist Formgeschichte? Neue Wege der Bibelexegese*, 2nd edition Neukirchen 1967. References in this book to English trans. by S. M. Cupitt, *The Growth of the Biblical Tradition*, London 1969.

KÖHLER, L., *Der hebräische Mensch*, Tübingen 1953. References in this book to English trans. by P. R. Ackroyd, *Hebrew Man*, London 1956.

KRAUS, H.-J., *Die prophetische Verkündigung des Rechts in Israel*, Zollikon 1957. *Gottesdienst in Israel*, 2nd edition, München 1962. References in this book to English trans. by G. Buswell, *Worship in Israel*, Oxford 1966.

KREMERS, H., 'Leidensgemeinschaft mit Gott im AT. Eine Untersuchung der "biographischen" Berichte im Jeremiabuch', *EvTh* 13, 1953, pp. 122ff.

LESLIE, E. A., *Jeremiah*, New York 1954.

LINDARS, B., 'Torah in Deuteronomy', *Words and Meanings*, Essays presented to D. Winton Thomas, ed. P. R. Ackroyd and B. Lindars, Cambridge 1968, pp. 117–136.

LINDBLOM, J., *Prophecy in Ancient Israel*, Oxford 1962.

LOERSCH, S., *Das Deuteronomium und seine Deutungen*, Stuttgart 1967.

LONG, B. O., *The Problem of Etiological Narrative in the Old Testament*, BZAW 108, Berlin 1968.

MALFROY, J., 'Sagesse et Loi dans le Deutéronome', *VT* 15, 1965, pp. 49–65.

MARTI, K., *Das Buch Jesaja*, Tübingen 1900.

MAY, H. G., 'Towards an Objective Approach to the Book of Jeremiah: The Biographer', *JBL* 61, 1942, pp. 139–155. 'Jeremiah's Biographer', *JBR* 10, 1942, pp. 195–201.

McCARTHY, D. J., *Treaty and Covenant*, Analecta Biblica 21, Rome 1963. 'II Samuel 7 and the Structure of the Deuteronomistic History', *JBL* 84, 1965, pp. 131–138.

McKANE, W., *Prophets and Wise Men*, London 1965.

McKAY, J. W., *Josiah's Reformation: Its Antecedents, Nature and Significance*, Ph.D. dissertation (unpublished), Cambridge 1969.

McKENZIE, J. L., 'Reflections on Wisdom', *JBL* 86, 1967, pp. 1–9.

MILLER, J. W., *Das Verhältnis Jeremias und Hesekiels sprachlich und theologisch untersucht*, Assen 1955.

MONTGOMERY, J. A., *Kings* ICC, Edinburgh 1951, (with H. S. Gehman).

MORAN, W. L., 'The Ancient Near Eastern Background of the Love of God in Deuteronomy', *CBQ* 25, 1963, pp. 77–87. 'A Note on the Treaty Terminology of the Sefire Stelas', *JNES* 22, 1963, pp. 173–176.

MOWINCKEL, S., *Zur Komposition des Buches Jeremia*, Kristiania 1914. *Prophecy and Tradition*, Oslo 1946. *Offersang og Sangoffer*, Oslo 1951. References in this book to English trans. by D. R. Ap-Thomas, *The Psalms in Israel's Worship*, I and II, Oxford 1962. *Studien zu dem Buche Ezra-Nehemia*, II, Oslo 1964.

MUILENBERG, J., 'The "Office" of Prophet in Ancient Israel', *The Bible in Modern Scholarship*, ed. J. P. Hyatt, London 1966, pp. 74–97. 'The form and structure of the covenantal formulations', *VT* 9, 1959, pp. 347–365.

NEWMAN, M. L., *The People of the Covenant*, New York and Nashville 1962.

NICHOLSON, E. W., 'The Meaning of the Expression עַם הָאָרֶץ in the Old Testament', *JSS* 10, 1965, pp. 59–66. *Deuteronomy and Tradition*, Oxford 1967.

NIELSEN, E., *Oral Tradition*, London 1954.

Noth, M., *Überlieferungsgeschichtliche Studien I*, Halle 1943, 2nd unaltered edition Tübingen 1957.

'La castastrophe de Jerusalem en l'an 587 avant Jesus-Christ et sa signification pour Isräel', *RHPhR* 33, 1953, pp. 81–110 = 'Die Katastrophe von Jerusalem im Jahre 587 v. Chr. und ihre Bedeutung für Israel', *Gesammelte Studien zum Alten Testament*, 2nd edition, München 1960, pp. 346–371. References in this book to English trans. by D. R. Ap-Thomas, 'The Jerusalem Catastrophe of 587 b.c. and its Significance for Israel', *The Laws in the Pentateuch and Other Essays*, Edinburgh 1966, pp. 260–280.

Amt und Berufung im Alten Testament, Bonner Akademische Reden 19, Bonn 1958. References in this book to English trans. by D. R. Ap-Thomas, 'Office and Vocation in the Old Testament', *The Laws in the Pentateuch and Other Essays*, Edinburgh 1966, pp. 229–249.

'Zur Geschichtsauffassung des Deuteronomisten', *Proceedings of the XXII Congress of Orientalists, Istanbul, 1951*, II, Leiden 1957, pp. 558–566.

Das zweite Buch Mose, Exodus, ATD 5, Göttingen 1959. References in this book to *Exodus*, English trans. by J. S. Bowden, London 1962.

Die Geschichte Israels, 3rd edition, Göttingen 1956. References in this book to *The History of Israel*, revised English trans. by P. R. Ackroyd, London 1960.

Nyberg, H. S., *Studien zum Hoseabuch*, Uppsala 1935.

Oesterley, W. O. E., *Introduction to the Books of the Old Testament*, London 1934, (with T. H. Robinson).

Pfeiffer, R. H., *Introduction to the Old Testament*, London 1948.

von Rad, G., 'Die falschen Propheten', *ZAW* 51, 1933, pp. 109ff.

Deuteronomiumstudien, 2nd edition, Göttingen 1948. References in this book to English trans. by D. Stalker, *Studies in Deuteronomy*, London 1953.

Theologie des Alten Testaments, I, München 1957. References in this book to English trans. by D. Stalker, *Old Testament Theology*, I, London 1962.

Theologie des Alten Testaments, II, München 1960. References in this book to English trans. by D. Stalker, *Old Testament Theology*, II, London 1965.

Das fünfte Buch Mose, Deuteronomium, ATD 8, Göttingen 1964. References in this book to English trans. by D. M. Barton, *Deuteronomy*, London 1966.

Reventlow, H. Graf, 'Prophetenamt und Mittleramt', *ZTK* 58, 1961, pp. 269–284.

Liturgie und prophetische Ich bei Jeremia, Gütersloh 1963.

Rietzschel, C., *Das Problem der Urrolle*, Gütersloh 1966.

Ringgren, H., 'Literarkritik, Formgeschichte, Überlieferungsgeschichte', *TLZ* 91, 1966, pp. 641–650.

Robinson, T. H., 'Baruch's Scroll', *ZAW* 42, 1924, pp. 209–221.

Introduction to the Books of the Old Testament, London 1934 (with W. O. E. Oesterley).

Rost, L., *Überlieferung von der Thronnachfolge Davids*, BWANT III: 6, Stuttgart 1926.

Rowley, H. H., 'The Early Prophecies of Jeremiah in their Setting', *BJRL* 45, 1962–63, pp. 198–234 reprinted in *Men of God*, London 1963, pp. 133–168.

Worship in Ancient Israel, London 1967.

Rudolph, W., 'Problems of the Book of Chronicles', *VT* 4, 1954, pp. 401–409.

Jeremia, 3rd edition, Tübingen 1968.

Schofield, J. N., 'The Significance of the Prophets for the Dating of Deuteronomy', *Studies in History and Religion*, ed. E. A. Payne, London 1942.

Skinner, J., *Prophecy and Religion: Studies in the Life of Jeremiah*, Cambridge 1922.

Smart, J. D., *History and Theology in Second Isaiah*, Philadelphia 1965.

Smith, W. Robertson, *The Religion of the Semites*, 3rd edition by S. A. Cook, London 1927.

Soggin, J. A., 'Kultätiologische Sagen und Katechese im Hexateuch', *VT* 10, 1960, pp. 341–347.

Steck, O. H., *Israel und das gewaltsame Geschick der Propheten*, WMANT 23, Neukirchen 1967.

Talmon, S., 'Double Readings in the Massoretic Text', *Textus* 1, 1960, pp. 144–184.

Teeple, H. M., *The Mosaic Eschatological Prophet*, *JBL* monograph series, no. 10, 1957.

Thomas, D. W., 'A Note on the Hebrew root נחם', *ExpT* 44, 1933, pp. 191–192.

Timm, H., 'Die Ladeerzählung (1 Sam. 4–6; 2 Sam. 6) und das Kerygma des deuteronomistischen Geschichtswerks', *EvTh* 26, 1966, pp. 509–526.

de Vaux, R., 'Le lieu que Yahvé a choisi pour y établir son nom', *Das Ferne und Nahe Wort* (Festschrift für Leonhard Rost), BZAW 105, Berlin 1967, pp. 219–228.

Volz, P., *Der Prophet Jeremia*, Leipzig and Erlangen 1922.

Weinfeld, M., 'The Dependence of Deuteronomy upon Wisdom' (Hebrew), *Yehezkel Kaufmann Jubilee Volume*, ed. M. Haran, Jerusalem 1960, pp. 108–189.

'The Source of the Idea of Reward in Deuteronomy' (Hebew with an English summary), *Tarbiz* 30, 1960, pp. 8–15.

'The Origins of Humanism in Deuteronomy', *JBL* 80, 1961, pp. 241–247.

'Traces of Assyrian Treaty Formulae in Deuteronomy', *Biblica* 46, 1965, pp. 417–427.

'Deuteronomy: the Present State of the Enquiry', *JBL* 86, 1967, pp. 249–262.

Weiser, A., *Einleitung in das Alte Testament*, 4th edition, Göttingen 1957. References in this book to English trans. by D. M. Barton, *Introduction to the Old Testament*, London 1961.

Das Buch des Propheten Jeremia, ATD 20–21, Göttingen 1952, 1955.

Wellhausen, J., *Prolegomena zur Geschichte Israels*, Berlin 1883. References in this book to *Prolegomena to the History of Israel*, English trans. by J. S. Black and A. Menzies, Edinburgh 1885.

Whitley, C. F., 'The Date of Jeremiah's Call', *VT* 14, 1964, pp. 467–483.

Widengren, G., *Literary and Psychological Aspects of the Hebrew Prophets*, Uppsala Universitets Årsskrift, no. 10, 1948.

'Oral Tradition and Written Literature among the Hebrews in the Light of Arabic Evidence, with Special Regard to Prose Narratives', *AcOr* 23, 1959, pp. 201–262.

Wolff, H. W., 'Das Kerygma des deuteronomistischen Geschichtswerks', *ZAW* 73, 1961, pp. 171–186 reprinted in *Gesammelte Studien zum Alten Testament*, München 1964, pp. 308–324.

Zenger, E., 'Die deuteronomistische Interpretation der Rehabilitierung Jojachins', *BZ* 12, 1968, pp. 16–30.

Zimmerli, W., *Ezechiel*, BKAT 13, Neukirchen 1956ff.

INDEX OF BIBLICAL REFERENCES

INDEX OF AUTHORS

GENERAL INDEX